LITERATURE, LANGUAGE, AND THE CLASSROOM

This book is a festschrift dedicated to Promodini Varma, a meticulous scholar, teacher, and administrator of extraordinary rigour, grit, and perception. It presents reflections on researching and teaching English literatures and languages in India. It concerns itself broadly with literary modernism and English language teaching and classroom pedagogy, some of the core concerns of the literary fraternity today. The volume examines how the literary and cultural manifestations of modernity have pervasively informed not just much of our disciplinary framework but many of the key issues—decolonisation, globalisation, development—our society grapples with.

With essays on William Butler Yeats and Arthur Conan Doyle, E.M. Forster, D.H. Lawrence, and Rudyard Kipling, the volume presents fresh insights on familiar canonical ground. It discusses ELT and classroom pedagogy and provides grounded appraisals of teaching and translating for multilingual classroom audiences given the demands of employability and the hierarchical dynamics of educational institutions. An interview on feminist pedagogy and theatre and an essay on urban nostalgia and redevelopment act as pertinent outliers, reflecting the ongoing transition to more multisited and interdisciplinary research and praxis.

An engaging read on some of the most pressing concerns in the field, this book will be of great interest to scholars and researchers of literature and literary criticism, English language studies, and education.

Sonali Jain is Associate Professor (English) in Bharati College, University of Delhi. Her doctoral work at Jawaharlal Nehru University centred on Vijay Tendulkar and the semiotics of cinema. She was Translator-in-Residence at the University of East Anglia, UK, in 2008 and has translated Tendulkar's play *Baby* into English. She has also edited Strindberg's *Miss Julie*. Her areas of interest include psychoanalytic theory, film studies, and translation. She is trained in psychodynamic psychotherapy and is a painter: her works of art have been exhibited in a number of group shows.

Anubhav Pradhan is Assistant Professor in the Department of Liberal Arts, IIT Bhilai. His research straddles urban history, heritage, planning, and writing as well as colonial cultural contact and the intersections of empire and modernity. He is Deputy Editor of *South Asia Research*; editor of *Articulating Urbanity: Writing the South Asian City* (forthcoming, 2022) and co-editor of *Kipling and Yeats at 150: Retrospectives/Perspectives* (2019). He has taught at Ambedkar University Delhi, South Asian University, Jamia Millia Islamia, and the University of Delhi and has served Primus Books, Delhi as their Senior Marketing Editor. He has also been associated as a researcher with the Centre for the Study of Developing Societies and the Indian Institute for Human Settlements. He reviews frequently for national and international journals and has presented his work in a wide range of conferences all over the world.

LITERATURE, LANGUAGE, AND THE CLASSROOM

Essays for Promodini Varma

Edited by Sonali Jain and Anubhav Pradhan

LONDON AND NEW YORK

First published 2022
by Routledge
2 Park Square, Milton Park, Abingdon, Oxon OX14 4RN

and by Routledge
605 Third Avenue, New York, NY 10158

Routledge is an imprint of the Taylor & Francis Group, an informa business

© 2022 selection and editorial matter, Sonali Jain and Anubhav Pradhan; individual chapters, the contributors

The right of Sonali Jain and Anubhav Pradhan to be identified as the authors of the editorial material, and of the authors for their individual chapters, has been asserted in accordance with sections 77 and 78 of the Copyright, Designs and Patents Act 1988.

All rights reserved. No part of this book may be reprinted or reproduced or utilised in any form or by any electronic, mechanical, or other means, now known or hereafter invented, including photocopying and recording, or in any information storage or retrieval system, without permission in writing from the publishers.

Trademark notice: Product or corporate names may be trademarks or registered trademarks, and are used only for identification and explanation without intent to infringe.

British Library Cataloguing-in-Publication Data
A catalogue record for this book is available from the British Library

Library of Congress Cataloging-in-Publication Data
A catalog record for this book has been requested

ISBN: 978-0-367-47964-0 (hbk)
ISBN: 978-0-367-50391-8 (pbk)
ISBN: 978-1-003-04977-7 (ebk)

DOI: 10.4324/9781003049777

Typeset in Sabon
by Apex CoVantage, LLC

CONTENTS

Notes on contributors   vii

Introduction: towards a framing of parts   1
ANUBHAV PRADHAN

1 William Butler Yeats and Arthur Conan Doyle: links, affinities, and the occult   12
R.W. DESAI

2 Ibsen's ghost in Forster's *The Longest Journey*   29
SUMANYU SATPATHY

3 Redefining British masculinity in *Captains Courageous*   43
CHETAN

4 Reading poetry through translation: a brief note on a Hindi translation of Shakespeare's sonnets   53
RAJIVA VERMA

5 Teaching gender and sexuality in translated literature   64
RUTH VANITA

6 Radical unlearnedness in proletarian schooling: dilemmas of discipline and teaching in D.H. Lawrence's *Education of the People* and *Fantasia of the Unconscious*   74
DIVYA SAKSENA

7 Holding environments: an enquiry into institutional minds   85
SONALI JAIN

CONTENTS

8 The challenges of *skilling* the undergraduate English language learner for the glocal market 98
ANJANA NEIRA DEV AND SAMEER CHOPRA

9 Evidence-based decision-making in our teaching: why is it important and how do we do it? 110
RAMA MATHEW

10 Developments in teaching college English at the University of Delhi 121
MUKTI SANYAL

11 Theatre, feminism, and society: notes from a practitioner 134
ANURADHA MARWAH IN CONVERSATION WITH ANUBHAV PRADHAN AND SONALI JAIN

12 Nostalgic possibilities: planning and heritage in Shahjahanabad 147
ANUBHAV PRADHAN

Index 162

NOTES ON CONTRIBUTORS

R.W. Desai, retired Professor of English, University of Delhi, and editor of *Hamlet Studies* (1979–2003), is the author of *Shakespearean Latencies* (2002) and *Yeats's Shakespeare* (1971). He has also written a novel on gender difference, *Frailty, Thy Name is (W) O Man* (1993), and a collection of short stories, *Of War and War's Alarms and 21 Other Stories* (2005). Recently, he and his wife Jyoti made a University Grants Commission–sponsored film of six key scenes from *Hamlet* and then a similar Delhi University–sponsored film on Marlowe's *Doctor Faustus*, each scene being followed by a panel discussion.

Sumanyu Satpathy is currently Professor of Eminence at KR Mangalam University. A former Professor and Head of the Department of English, University of Delhi, he was also Fellow at the Indian Institute of Advanced Study, Shimla. As Visiting Professor, he has taught at University of Granada, Frankfurt University, and Exeter University, among several others. His areas of specialization include Modernism, Queer Theory, and Odisha Studies. Among his most recent publications are *Will to Argue: Studies in Late Colonial and Postcolonial Controversies* (2017) and *Southern Postcolonialisms: The Global South and the 'New' Literary Representations* (2009).

Chetan is Assistant Professor of English at Bharati College, University of Delhi. He has submitted his PhD thesis on Rudyard Kipling at the Department of English, University of Delhi, and was awarded an MPhil in 2013 with the submission of a thesis titled "The Past and The Present in the Fiction of Umberto Eco". His book *Umberto Eco: Rethinking History and Fiction* was published in 2014. He has also published some academic essays in national and international journals. His research interests are Nineteenth Century British Writing on India, Victorian Literature, Crime and Detective Fiction, and Postmodern Popular Fiction.

Rajiva Verma studied in the universities of Delhi and Warwick and taught in the former for several decades. After retiring from the Department of English, he became an advisor in the University's Institute of Lifelong Learning and oversaw the production of online lessons for undergraduate students. He is the author of *Myth, Ritual, and Shakespeare* (1990) and of many articles on Shakespeare in journals and books, including studies of Shakespeare in Hindi translation and in Hindi film adaptations. He is a founding member and a former President of the Shakespeare Society of India.

Ruth Vanita taught at Delhi University and is now Professor at the University of Montana. She volunteered as founding co-editor of *Manushi* for 13 years. The author of many books, including *Dancing with the Nation: Courtesans in Bombay Cinema* (2018), *Gender, Sex and the City: Urdu Rekhti Poetry in India 1780–1870* (2012), *Love's Rite: Same-Sex Marriage in India* (2005), and *Sappho and the Virgin Mary: Same-Sex Love and the English Literary Imagination* (1996), she has published over 70 scholarly articles and translated several works from Hindi and Urdu. Her first novel, *Memory of Light*, was published by Penguin in 2020.

Divya Saksena received her first three degrees from the University of Delhi, where she also worked as Lecturer of English at Gargi College. She earned her PhD from the George Washington University, USA and taught at Middle Tennessee State University for several years as Associate Professor before moving to Canada to live and work. Relocating to India in 2016, she has been involved in curriculum development and instructional design projects as well as gender and women's studies, with publications in these areas. Currently, her research interests are focused on theories of education, learning evaluation methodology, autobiography, and gender.

Anjana Neira Dev is Associate Professor of English at Gargi College, University of Delhi. She is profoundly interested in the dynamics of the undergraduate classroom. Her areas of research interest include Comparative Education; Pedagogy in Tertiary Education; Assessment and Evaluation; Indian Writing in English: Poetry and Fiction; English for Special Purposes: Academic Writing, Creative Writing, Technical Writing and Business Communication; Detective and Crime Fiction; and Teaching English in the Indian Classroom. She has published extensively in these areas and enjoys sharing ideas in focus groups with like-minded people.

Sameer Chopra is Assistant Professor of English at Gargi College, University of Delhi. Currently enrolled as a PhD scholar at the Department of English, University of Delhi, he takes special interest in queer literary and visual cultures of South Asia, European Modernism, and ELT. He owes his abiding engagement with the pedagogies of English language and literature to the rigorous training he underwent as a BEd student at the Central Institute of Education, University of Delhi.

Rama Mathew is an ELT consultant and retired as Professor of Education from the University of Delhi, where she was also Dean of the Faculty of

Education. She taught at the EFL University (Hyderabad) for several years. She has been involved in many teacher development and assessment projects, including the English in Action project in Bangladesh. Currently, she is supporting teachers in Sierra Leone to carry out classroom-based research. Her research interests include language assessment, teaching English to young learners, continuing professional development of teachers, multilingual education, and making English accessible to learners online.

Mukti Sanyal retired as Officiating Principal, Bharati College, University of Delhi. Over the last 40 years, she has been doing community service in the field of ELT, conducting lectures and workshops all over the country. Her activism helped it become a part of the English Honours curriculum in Indian universities. Recipient of the Best Lecturer award from the Government of Delhi and a Charles Wallace Trust fellowship, she has co-authored well-received course books like *Fluency in English I & II*, *English at the Workplace I & II, Language, Literature and Creativity*, and *The Individual and Society*.

Anuradha Marwah, Associate Professor in the Department of English, Zakir Husain Delhi College, is the author of three novels—*The Higher Education of Geetika Mehendiratta* (1992), *Idol Love* (1999), and *Dirty Picture* (2007)—and five plays that have had several public performances. Her play *Ismat's Love Stories* was shortlisted for the Hindu Playwright Award 2016. She has recently directed *Medea* (Hindustani), which was selected for India's first community-curated theatre festival at Shadipur. She is a recipient of the Charles Wallace Writer's Residency (2001) and the Fulbright-Nehru Academic and Professional Excellence fellowship to the University of Minnesota–Twin Cities (2017).

INTRODUCTION

Towards a framing of parts

Anubhav Pradhan

Why this book?

This book was born in the most unlikely of places and in the most unlikely of ways. As I sat contemplating a murky future by Krabi's stormy marina in the monsoon of 2017, I couldn't help looking back with considerable fondness at the years gone by. I was in Thailand for a big Asian Studies conference, yes, but I had also been without a job for months and was due not to return home to Delhi but to Bangalore for a fellowship of somewhat uncertain fame. I was enrolled for a PhD but had been out of academics for almost two whole years: a marketing job with a publisher had given little scope to interact and form connections with scholars from my home turf of English literary studies. With tempests brewing as much on the torrid horizon as in my troubled heart, the only solace lay in looking back: I *had been* a lecturer not too long ago, I *had been* part of a promising department, I *had worked* under a very competent and inspiring boss. Teaching is what I'd always thought I'd end up doing, what I'd geared myself to do through years of reading and research. I had been fortunate in having had an excellent start, in having the opportunity to do such work as few others my age usually get to do, and could not but feel grateful to the one person who had made much of it possible: Promodini Varma.

Promodini, or PV as many of us know her, is familiar to most of us as the long-standing Principal of Bharati College in the University of Delhi. PV was close to superannuation at the end of a long and eventful career when I joined Bharati as a lecturer on ad hoc basis in 2013. An alumna of Miranda House, she was among the first batch of lecturers with whom the college was established as an off-campus women's college in 1971. Having had the privilege of ready acquaintance with the University of Reading's Beckett Collection, one of the largest and most comprehensive such repositories in the world, her doctoral thesis was something of a pioneering intervention for the Indian academe at the time. She has extensive, almost unrivalled, experience of editing, academic and otherwise, and has successfully dabbled in translation as well. Nonetheless, for somebody whose primary body of work lies so deeply in the annals of high modernism, PV is known to us more for her contributions to ESL and ELT than the play of being in Beckett's later plays. Unlike many others of her generational pedigree, PV is one of those rare academic doyens who found satisfaction not just in literature but also in language. As an administrator with a keen eye for research, she has been at the heart of the curricula reform and pedagogical transformations which have changed the way English is studied and taught in Indian colleges. Her textbooks have been found indispensable by universities across the country and have helped generations of college students grapple with and come to terms with English as a language.

It was under PV's tutelage and encouragement that I found my footing as a very eager, very green, young lecturer fresh out of master's. Catering to many first-generation women learners, the English Department at Bharati was one of the first in the university to balance the teaching of literature with language in an evidence-based manner—something unknown in many of the supposedly better campus colleges. This hierarchy, artificial and inflated, has become one of the key paradoxes of our profession. English departments thrive in all kinds of institutions in India, primarily because—crudely put—we still suffer from an enduring inferiority complex which sees education incomplete without a certain kind of mastery over spoken and written English. Yet most English lecturers design to touch ELT: very few of us actually enjoy the challenge of an ELT classroom, which is usually heterogeneous and varied in terms of its proficiencies. Teaching English language is, for the most, a grudging burden, routinely allotted by an unwritten but pervasive protocol to only the most inexperienced junior faculties. All departments at all levels acknowledge its need, but few actually bother to dwell on it or research into it. The typical English department in India is excessively oriented towards our many canons, established and emergent, and hardly any doctoral work is conducted in this domain. It is to PV's credit that she gave Bharati the astute, visionary leadership which transformed its English department into one of the most receptive, responsive cohorts in Delhi.

But this book is not meant to be a paean to PV. It is, yes, a token of the deep gratitude which many others and I owe her, but it is not simply a statement of this fact. Those of us who have come together for this book do so not as much to celebrate her scholarship and her contributions to teaching and research over five decades as to put on record our respect for her as a person: honest, just, and fair in equal measure. It is easy, in academics, to find erudite scholars, to acquire that veneer of smooth sophistication which, more often than not, cloaks the petty insecurities and malice that come from dwelling too long and sure in an ivory tower. There is also no dearth of researchers, of keen and incisive commentators who can penetrate to the depths of a contention and propose radical new ways of seeing the order of things. Yet it is rare to come across an academic who marries a flair for research and teaching with administration, who excels as much in the solitary realm of scholarship as in the public, performative sphere of classroom teaching as in the perilous bog of management—but who still remains true to the values she espouses in and through her work. Our collective endeavour in this book is to acknowledge and honour these qualities as we perceive them in PV's impactful life and work, not just as an inventive teacher, a penetrating scholar, a capable administrator, or a steadfast friend, but a happy and uncommon mixture of all of these.

Whither academia?

Much has been said and written about the crisis in English literary studies in general and English literary studies in India in particular, so I will not attempt to give a review of the intergenerational hand-wringing and heartache which have brought us where we are today. Perhaps the trope of crisis in itself has been used to the point of abuse, and now that many of us have made successful and thriving careers out of it, we can finally contemplate making our peace with it. If postcolonialism was the poster boy of the 1990s and the 2000s, then the previous decade has seen a sustained dismantling of the IWE canon into various subsets organised around gender, caste, and bodily experience respectively. Liberalism, beaten but not out, continues to be the operational principle of our discipline. The typical undergraduate syllabus now spans across its regional, national, and transcontinental iterations to foreground, by and large, representational politics of racial, gender, and religious minorities. Classroom pedagogy and research trends all indicate movement in this direction, with deep and heavy contextualisation complemented by careful interrogation of textual norms and mores becoming standard practice. All of this has been accompanied by a spurt in translation, a movement which may be seen as not as much a return to as a reinvention—even appropriation—of the vernacular. From being the esoteric preserve of a handful of departments, comparative literature and translation have gained considerable ground to shatter disciplinary boundaries and infuse new vigour in the practice of our profession.

Nonetheless, most of us know full well that English continues to be a popularly sought undergraduate degree in this country not because literature appeals to the masses but because many of our students come with the mistaken belief that their three years in college will improve their language proficiency. Educational reforms over the past decade or so have resulted in growing alignment of our curricula and pedagogy with perceived global norms through contentious and hasty implementation of the semester system and the choice-based credit system. In this new academic environment, the student is being posited as a consumer while teachers are getting repackaged as service providers. Skilling and training students for the market have replaced the earlier ideal of educating them for life, but in most cases colleges simply lack the infrastructure and resources and teachers lack the interest and vision to actually invest in their pupils' needs. The proliferation of canonical radicalism is also occurring increasingly in silos, in departmental subcommittees which are convivial battlefields to claim pieces of curricular turf: even the recent resurgence of interest in liberal education seems predicated upon a careful calculus of progressively prohibitive access to differential qualities of education. In the midst of all this, English departments have taken recourse to becoming selectively entrepreneurial. A host of ability and skill enhancement courses, compulsory and otherwise, have been introduced at the undergraduate level, with administrative diktats to hand-hold students through seminars, workshops, and placements.

These and other experiments, many of which are here to stay, have drastically changed the academe to make it hyperactive with a nervous, tense energy. The days when a professor's bibliography could be a tome or two of sustained work of over decades are the stuff of collective nostalgia. Publication is now an imperative, as are organising and attending conferences and workshops. Teachers' recruitments and promotions have been linked to research in emulation of the American model: lecturers are expected to quantify their outputs in terms of publications and presentations at every stage of their career. The aim, ostensibly, is to incentivise research and encourage better exposure to market trends and demands, all to improve institutional rankings which, in turn, are hoped to improve the entire collegiate system. As the Indian experience shows, though, such a paradigm shift in policy undertaken without building an enabling environment conducive to research and free thinking results only in greater degrees of inequity and predation. Faced with regular capitulation of senior staff to constant administrative pressure, our much-vaunted liberalism often appears to be nothing more than a detailed charade put on for the benefit of gullible students: we hardly ever practise with each other what we preach with such gusto in our writings and our classrooms. Workload has increased, as has our overall research output, but an unprecedented number of young lecturers across disciplines have extremely fragile, contractual tenure with little benefits and no access to grants and funds nominally available to tenured colleagues.

As an entire generation of practising and aspiring lecturers and researchers come to terms with a new normal of bitter scarcity and callous apathy, what can we expect from teaching and studying literature today? It is likely that our research output will continue to increase and be quantified according to more complex metrics of weightage. Compulsive conferencing will give us more opportunities to duly showcase our merit to regulatory bodies and peers on social media, while proliferation of theses and textbooks without the rigour of the traditional checks and balances will continue to lower the quality of our scholarship. Some of us persist with agitation and criticism, with the heavy—often hopeless—task of challenging systems with big and small acts of solidarity and fellowship, but on the whole we seem likely to keep on championing liberal values and agendas in our classrooms but not supporting them in our professional lives and engagements. A book such as this, in honour of a person such as PV, is perhaps only a token of the nostalgic idealism which can be put out. A varied selection of scholarship flitting from the heart of British literary modernity to radical, institutional feminism to practising and teaching translation to teaching and skilling students, this book presents a series of interventions geared to nuance our understanding of the two foundational pillars of our discipline—both literature and language—in equal measure. By celebrating PV in this manner, we hope with the futility of such stubborn hopes that the qualities she has been known to embody and espouse will be emulated by more of us in the future.

Navigating this book

Long in the making, this book went through as many as eight iterations of what it would look like before we finally settled down to the 12 essays we present to you. We toyed, for some time, with the idea of having distinct sections to indicate PV's primary research interests but in the end preferred keeping the arrangement dynamic and open to conversation—as all good scholarship must be. We begin with a keenly perceptive essay by R.W. Desai on the possible points of contact between Arthur Conan Doyle and William Butler Yeats, two of the most popular and well-read authors of British literary modernity. Closely reading their later work in conjunction with their shared interest in the occult and in spiritualism, Desai detects strains of mutual appreciation and influence marking their attitude to clairvoyance and its revelatory role in communicating clues of hidden truths to society. While his attempts to link Doyle's and Yeats's reformist tendencies to their ready receptivity to the supernatural may need more substantiation, his essay on the whole provocatively explores those subterranean currents of modernity which we, as teachers, often shy from delving into in our classrooms. I take Desai's essay as a good example of the glaring gap between what we research and what we end up teaching, and the pressing need for a more penetrating pedagogy to transform our working engagement with our discipline.

From Doyle's and Yeats's prophetic spirits of days gone by and days yet to come, we move next to Ibsen's long shadow on succeeding generations of modernists. Sumanyu Satpathy's essay dwells upon E.M. Forster's layered response to the prevailing Ibsenism of his time in *The Longest Journey* (1907), his second novel. Satpathy argues that Forster's conflation of physical deformity and sexual non-conformity in the novel may be seen as a measured reworking of Ibsen's irresistible biological determinism, at play so amply in his iconic play *Ghosts* (1882). Suggesting that Forster is no simple Ibsenite and that his warily discreet treatment of homosociality in the novel qualifies as an affirmation of the heart and mind over the body, Satpathy's conjunctional reading of Forester and Ibsen allows for a neat decoding of modernity's constant struggle with and repurposing of the Victorian baggage it grew up with. Additionally, reading Satpathy after Desai also proves to be a rewarding exercise: from the occult and mysticism to Darwinian naturalism, the two essays capture well that exultant, even reckless, spirit of introspective experimentation which came to characterise British literary modernity. Ghosts, after all, are of many kinds, taking many forms and shapes, and we owe it to ourselves to look deep and fathom the daemons which constitute our core.

Our third essay takes us from this reflective mode of canonical high modernism to the bluster and excitement of popular juvenile fiction. Chetan's essay on British masculinity in Rudyard Kipling's *Captains Courageous* (1897) links the novel's transformative motif to the reformative zeal prevalent in fin de siècle popular culture. This, he argues, presaged a kind of imperialism critically different from its high Victorian counterpart: Harvey Cheyne's metamorphosis is of the life-affirming kind, through which he learns the value of camaraderie and solidarity and comes to appreciate the true nature and purpose of his privilege. Premised on conquest of not simply foreign lands but also one's own follies in pursuit of a higher, common good, this theory of imperialism—as it were—puts its emphasis on relentless improvement of one's character and inner being through the baptism of hard, manual labour. While such a thesis is now fairly familiar, it is also one which is easy to simplistically misread as an apologia for the "White Man's Burden". To do so, however, would be to fall victim to that excess of critical fury which sustained doses of postcolonial academics tends to generate. In teaching as in research, it is important to retain that degree of nuance which helps us understand that which we cannot condone.

This note of nuance and understanding allows us to make a providential segue into this book's next thematic interest, translation. Rajiva Verma's delightful essay on Rajendra Dwivedi's *Shakespeare ke Sonnet* (1958) makes the insightful recommendation that we move from reading and teaching poetry *in* translation to *through* translation instead. Observing that English departments across India are already teaching a considerable variety of texts translated from Indian languages, Verma urges us to strategically acknowledge our bilingualism and put it to good use in classrooms given the uneven language proficiencies usually at play. Picking up Shakespeare, that holiest of all our canonical cows, to illustrate the feasibility of such a pedagogical reform, he offers an informed and intuitive reading of Dwivedi's landmark experiment with Shakespeare: the erudition of the attempt, shortcomings of the arcane and formal register, and the lessons we may learn from this and similar works of translation of the canon into Indian languages. Readers may find Verma's piece to be a refreshing departure from the stuffy, cut-and-paste theoretical overtures which often pass for criticism in our conferences and anthologies. His wry jab at the worsening neglect of the British literary canon is also likely to resonate with those of us—marginalised as we

INTRODUCTION

now are—who yearn for a balance between decolonisation of the mind and appreciation of our discipline's foundational canon.

We follow this provocative essay by an equally thoughtful piece on teaching in translation by Ruth Vanita. Foregrounding gender and sexuality as the prisms through which she has designed her pedagogy on translation, Vanita gives an insider's overview of the way Indian-language texts are generally taught in the American academia. Her four-pronged typology is useful and merits reproduction here: Indian literature courses where students have some measure of familiarity with the language but study texts in translation; world literature courses where students are unacquainted with the languages, Indian and otherwise; courses where students study Indian-language texts in translation along with those originally in English; and Indian literature courses where students only study translated texts and do not know the source languages. Through her own long experience of teaching all such courses in American universities, Vanita highlights the successes and challenges of dealing with Indian literature in translation: while it is more fruitful to teach Indian texts alone in translation or those Indian texts which are originally in English, it is always problematic teaching translated texts along with English ones. She rightly points out to the inevitable loss of *rasa* and the attendant unfavourable comparison with English texts in the latter case, given particularly the untranslatability of many Indian-language words and concepts. One of her minor asides, on the proliferation of that decontextualised kind of teaching and research which peddles ideological positions without working towards a deep familiarity with creative traditions and forms, might also provoke readers to think about how English departments in India are appropriating translation without thorough, systematic engagement with questions of language, literariness, and form.

Such questions, however, are neither new nor specific to our present context in any way. As Divya Saksena shows in our next essay, the tussle to find balance between the vocational and the abstract in teaching young minds has been one of the foundational questions of modernity as we have known it. Closely reading D.H. Lawrence's commentaries, novels, and letters in light of his attempt to find that elusive star equilibrium between teacher and student, Saksena suggests that we look also at the darker, more challenging aspects of the human soul in order to frame a more innate and intuitive pedagogy. This kind of teaching entails a radical unlearnedness for the educator, a letting go of those ingrained social biases which still make disciplining and pre-mediation second nature for so many of us in our work. Love and a questing, secular faith are the hallmarks of this theory of education, building upon efficacy and failure as creative, regenerative faculties hidden in each and every one of us. While much of this may seem extremely woozy to practical partisans of scientific method, Saksena is quick to point out that although Lawrence himself tended to romanticise at various points in his career, he was nonetheless certain about the centrality of the individual in the teaching-learning process—it is a learning well worth remembering and putting into practice.

Thinking of teaching as practice, it is necessary to also think critically of institutions as the deeply contested sites wherein much of the relentless drama of academics unfolds. My co-editor Sonali's essay on the inner theatre of faculty and staff in all women's institutions in India offers a rare comment on the psychological processes which constitute and inform the leadership, work culture, and interpersonal attitudes in such colleges. Presenting an overview of multiple behavioural types which may be seen in constant interaction with each other, Sonali's useful decoding of patriarchal models of control and discipline voluntarily put in place in women's colleges may help us understand that abiding paradox of why and how a considerable majority of women faculty members in colleges—women's as well as co-educational—are vehemently opposed to feminist politics and research or only pay lip service to them in their lectures and seminars but hardly ever practise what they zealously preach. One of her key assertions, however, is that institutions still function—more or less—as holding environments which facilitate their staff's and students' growth by motivating them to self-explore in a safe and reliable setting. This is an important role to keep in mind when thinking of how colleges and universities should function: education is as much about skilling as it is about coming to terms with and addressing the mental health issues all of us experience to varying degrees.

It is difficult to deny, though, that skilling is one of the key imperatives of our times. Anjana Neira Dev and Sameer Chopra take this pressing concern head-on in our next essay, where they discuss the challenges of skilling undergraduate students in what they provocatively term as the glocal market. Dev and Chopra emphasise that teachers have to act as facilitators if we are to successfully equip our students with the requisite English communication skills to confidently navigate the demands of the job market. Observing that our pedagogy has, for the most, been geared towards acquainting students with English largely in terms of its grammar and not preparing them to use it in everyday contexts of work and leisure, they recommend that learning be made collaborative so that knowledge can be co-constructed in classrooms. They underline the complications presented by large class sizes and heterogeneity in executing Communicative Language Teaching in Indian classrooms, clarifying that these are structural and not situational in nature, but simultaneously suggest some handy, practical measures which can be adopted by lecturers at their own individual level to overcome these problems. In some ways, it will also be instructive to read Dev and Chopra in conjunction with Saksena: some interesting confluences may be detected in their shared belief in teachers' efficacy and role of overcoming barriers—institutional and otherwise—in pursuit of transformative pedagogical ideals.

Such transformative agendas, however, have to be as evidence-based as they can be. This is what Rama Mathew underscores in her enjoyable essay on responsive pedagogies for classroom teaching. Mathew's contention that evidence in the context of education is not simply and necessarily just tangible and retainable is an important one. Ephemeral evidence, which can be oral and experiential in the primary sense, is also a significant component of the teaching-learning process, which we must take into account at all times. Asserting that classrooms are complex places which cannot be simplified into any straightforward process or protocol, Mathew reminds us that classrooms are sites of collective interaction and that summative examinations have repeatedly failed in improving students' abilities and actually testing proficiencies. She suggests that we should, as teachers, aim to become educational connoisseurs if we are to do justice to our students: we should not only look beyond and work to curtail the heaps of data which appeal so viscerally to technocratic administrators, but also develop and refine our own instincts on the layered dynamics at play in classrooms between and among teachers and students. Coming from her long and rich experience of sustained research on education and ELT, Mathew's essay is an important signpost for all of us as we assess not only where we are and how we got there but also where we ought to go and how in the future.

Speaking of assessments, it will be pertinent now to turn to Mukti Sanyal as she charts the fascinating journey which college English has taken over the past four decades in the University of Delhi (DU). Sanyal's essay is especially important for this book for being a participant's perspective on the radical transformations which slowly occurred over time in collegiate ELT in DU, presenting a rare and relatively unknown insider's account of how the field has changed over the past few decades. This is a story which sheds light on PV's career as well, interwoven as it is with the three waves of teachers' activism and pedagogical reforms which Sanyal identifies in the late 1980s, in 2005, and in 2008 respectively. While it may seem obvious to many lecturers of my own generation that ELT must necessarily be integral to any kind of collegiate English, this acknowledgement and its resultant institutionalisation came slowly—and grudgingly—to university professors and administrators. Residues of the once-pervasive bias against ELT in DU and its colleges are still experienced by young lecturers every now and then in interviews and appointment panels though, where those with experience of teaching only communication and proficiency courses are treated at a palpable disadvantage to others with experience of the literature syllabus.

On this familiar note of our continuing inability to practise what we publicly preach, let us now move to the joys and challenges of practice—something which many of us, as English lecturers, are unfamiliar with. In our broad, freewheeling conversation with Anuradha Marwah, we try to find out what it means to juggle multiple hats as not only a college lecturer involved with the nuts and bolts of teaching, assessment, and administration but also a leftist, feminist, and independent theatre practitioner in an institutional and social environment which is increasingly inimical to most forms of radicalism. Marwah's experience as one of the mainstays of pandies' theatre group puts her among those rare English lecturers who have managed to go beyond the safe and comfortable confines of their colleges into the glorious, unpredictable messiness of the world at large—the proscenium, the street corner, and the *basti*. Holding that writing is both liberative and performative for her, Marwah asserts that cultural practitioners in the realm of the performative arts have a fundamental social responsibility to speak truth to power. On the basis of her experience of grassroots theatre activism, she underscores theatre's healing, recuperative role in situations of conflict and tension. This role, she suggests, can be strengthened by more systematic and rigorous engagement with drama in our undergraduate syllabus across disciplines.

But having discussed our disciplinary framework for so long now, it is fitting perhaps that we end this book with an outlier which dabbles as much in literature as in urban planning and heritage management. My essay for this volume, on the curious intersection of nostalgia and planning for Delhi's Shahjahanabad, may not have merited inclusion in this book except for PV's own interest in and work on the heritage of Delhi. I discovered this very close to her retirement in 2015, when she shared a slim volume she had authored in the late 1980s on the monuments of Delhi and regaled me with stories of scampering up and down all kinds of derelict ruins to get the right shots for her book. I was, then, only beginning my career as an urbanist, having just finished a cumbersome MPhil dissertation and juggling imperial gothic and racial anxieties on one hand and sustainable housing and slum rehabilitation on the other. Nostalgia was one of many ideas floating around in the deep recesses of my mind, and I resolved upon reading PV's book to dedicate to her the first essay I would write on the matter whensoever in the near or distant future. Readers—and colleagues—may find this a different kind of scholarship to engage with, not fully perhaps to their taste but not wholly irrelevant, I hope, to their experiences of their lives and cities.

Parting notes

Endings can often be more difficult than beginnings. There is pressure, always, to strike some deep, critical note which would impress itself and stay in readers' minds for a long time to come. Let me try, instead, to end this long introductory ramble by putting on record the debt of gratitude which Sonali and I hold to all those who have been part of this book's journey. We approached two dozen academics over three years for this book, most of whom readily agreed but had to eventually pull out due to administrative and other commitments. We are grateful for their goodwill to this project, as also to our present final set of contributors for steadfastly staying with us. We were particularly fortunate to get Desai and Verma on board, not only for being old colleagues of PV but for being of that generation which taught and mentored her in many ways. Satpathy, Saksena, Vanita, and Mathew are all contemporaries who have worked with her and have a rich experience of writing, research, and public engagement, much of which is palpable in their contributions to this volume. Dev, Marwah, and Chetan are all younger colleagues who have each benefitted at different points in their careers with her support and example. This book would not have been complete without Sanyal, who has been her close and active ally in the ELT revolution with which she is so justly associated. We are thankful, also, to John Pilling of the University of Reading, who was unable to write a fresh piece for this volume but nonetheless sent these warm words of appreciation for PV:

> I remember Promodini fondly across the years—too many of them for comfort, alas—and would wish to participate in any celebration of her life and work, if not with an essay, nonetheless with affection. When she returned home in the early 1980s she gave me a folder of Indian paintings which I had framed and which are still hanging in the front hall of my house. They have stayed with me through a number of changes of residence. She was a diligent scholar and a most pleasant person.

It is this, more than anything else, which is the true touchstone of success in a scholar's life: not just the publications and presentations and awards and positions held, but the willingness of so many colleagues and friends to take out time and commit with rigour in honour and celebration of her as a person. Working on this book to create something worthwhile and memorable has been an enriching and rewarding experience for each one of us, and we hope it will prove enjoyable and instructive in equal measure to you as well.

1
WILLIAM BUTLER YEATS AND ARTHUR CONAN DOYLE
Links, affinities, and the occult[1]

R.W. Desai

Points of contact

What degree of awareness did these authors have of each other, both of Irish descent and involved in the study of the occult and spiritualism? Both achieved international fame: Yeats (1865–1939) for his memorable poems and plays, winning the Nobel Prize in 1923; Doyle (1859–1930) for creating Sherlock Holmes and his faithful companion Dr Watson, culminating in the publication of his superb detective novel *The Hound of the Baskervilles* (1901). Doyle's public recognition of Yeats's stature as poet-prophet occurs in *The Land of Mist* (1926) and *The Edge of the Unknown* (1930). Reciprocally, Yeats's appreciation of Doyle's views on the occult appears in his spiritualist play *The Words Upon the Window-Pane* (1930). This chapter also records instances of circumstantial evidence suggesting their mutual recognition of each other's work. Apart from being great writers, they were social reformers of a high order. Doyle devoted three years of his life to securing the acquittal of two men wrongly sentenced.[2] For Yeats, the disastrous consequences of unfettered individual freedom in sex and marriage, which threatened to destabilise society, is the theme of his play *Purgatory* (1938) written five months before his death.

In the year of Doyle's death, 1930, each mentions the other by name, but going back four decades there is considerable circumstantial evidence to suggest a meeting of minds: both were members of The Society for Psychical Research, which, Doyle says, he had "joined in 1893 or 1894 and must now be [in 1930] one of the oldest members" (*Edge* 104), while Yeats was an associate member from 1913 to 1928 (Brown 192); both were members, along with Dickens, of The Ghost Club (see the history by Murdie on the official website); both were well versed in Sir William Crookes' researches (*Edge* 137), and Yeats recalled that "somebody years ago, at, I think, a meeting of the Society . . . suggested that we transfer thought at some moment when we cease to think of it". It is likely that this person was Doyle, since a tragic incident that he records from his correspondence with an English lady tallies with Yeats's explanation of the "Dreaming Back" process of the dead whereby the "unconsciousness" of the living is "inhabit[ed]" by what the dead are experiencing (*Vision* 1937, 226–27). In Yeats's consolatory, poignant, yet cheerful little poem "Shepherd and Goatherd" that he evidently felt might help Lady Gregory to come to terms with the death of her 37-year-old son Robert, whose combat plane was shot down on 23 January 1918 on the Italian front, his spirit re-lives his life in reverse: "jaunting, journeying/ To his own dayspring,/He unpacks the loaded pern/Of all 'twas pain or joy to learn,/Of all that he had made,/The outrageous war shall fade".

Doyle's account, similarly, "takes us back into the black days of the war" in a letter he received from the English lady mentioned above whose brother was killed at the front. "At that hour", Doyle records:

> the lady went through his whole experience, visualized the battlefield, heard the guns [and] had every reason at the time to think that her brother was at the depot and not in the firing-line. It was after the Armistice that official news was given of his death.
>
> (*Edge* 58)

This remarkable thought-transference, if narrated by Doyle at the meeting, could well have been remembered by Yeats many years later, the death of the lady's brother having taken place in the same context of war as that of Major Robert Gregory.

Affinities

Hitherto, the relationship between the two authors lacked a focus: while an interest in spiritualism is present in their early writings, they developed a concentrated absorption in the occult in 1916/17 through the instrumentality of their wives, Lady Jean Conan Doyle and Mrs Georgie Yeats (nee Hyde-Lees), respectively. They were greatly activated in this pursuit on account of the death by pneumonia of Doyle's son Captain Kingsley Conan Doyle while on active military service, and in the case of Yeats by the death of Major Robert Gregory—noted earlier—as a result of which Yeats wrote two of what many readers regard as among his most deeply moving poems, "An Irish Airman Foresees His Death" and "In Memory of Major Robert Gregory". Within the next ten years both authors wrote extensively on their experiments in spiritualism: Doyle's *The New Revelation* (1918), *The Land of Mist* (1926), *The History of Spiritualism* (1926), and *The Edge of the Unknown* (1930) contain his most detailed treatment of the subject, while during these decades appeared Yeats's *Per Amica Silentia Lunae* (1917) and *A Vision: An Explanation of Life Founded Upon the Writings of Giraldus and Upon Certain Doctrines Attributed to Kusta Ben Luka* (1925), which was re-published with revisions and additions in 1937. *A Vision* (1925) concludes with the marvellously evocative poem "All Souls' Night", which he wrote during "moments of exaltation" (*Critical Edition* xii), the opening stanza of which I quote:

> Midnight has come, and the great Christ Church bell,
> And many a lesser bell, sound through the room;
> And it is All Souls' Night
> And two long glasses brimmed with muscatel
> Bubble upon the table. A ghost may come;
> For it is a ghost's right,
> His element is so fine
> Being sharpened by his death,
> To drink from the wine-breath
> While our gross palates drink from the whole wine.

Further affinities between the two authors may be seen in Doyle's 'Preface to *The Edge of the Unknown*:

> We who believe in the psychic revelation, and who appreciate that a perception of these things is of the utmost importance, certainly have hurled ourselves against the obstinacy of our time. Possibly we have allowed some of our lives to be gnawed away in what, for the moment, seemed a vain and thankless quest. Only the future can show whether the sacrifice was worth it.
>
> (Doyle 4)

Somewhat similar to Doyle's anticipation of the hostile criticism his book would invite is the comment of one of Yeats's oldest friends, George Russell, editor of *The Irish Statesman*, whose opinion on Yeats's *A Vision* (1925) was sought by Yeats's sister Elizabeth, a publisher, who feared that her brother's "wits were astray". Russell replied:

> My opinion is that *anything* Willie writes will be of interest now or later on, and a book like this, which does not excite me or you, may be, possibly will be, studied later on when the psychology of the poet is considered by critics and biographers . . . Some will dislike it or think it fantastic nonsense, others will study it closely.
>
> (Hone 406)

Another noteworthy similarity between the two authors is that they kept separate and distinct in their most memorable creative writing their oppositional commitments. In the case of Doyle, no one will dispute that for the general public Sherlock Holmes is his most unforgettable fictional character—even more memorable than Hamlet or Falstaff—but Doyle refrains from introducing the supernatural in any of the mysteries that he solves. In "A Scandal in Bohemia", Dr Watson observes that Holmes is "the most perfect reasoning and observing machine that the world has seen" (I 209), and John Dickson Carr, his biographer, notes that "Doyle went out of his way to make Holmes deny all belief in the supernatural" (330). In *The Hound of the Baskervilles* Holmes admits the possibility of "forces outside the ordinary laws of nature" but adds, "we are bound to exhaust all other hypotheses before falling back upon this one" (II 24–25). Even as late as "The Adventure of the Sussex Vampire", published just three years before Doyle's death, Holmes summarily dismisses the belief in "walking corpses who can only be held in their grave by stakes driven through their hearts" with an emphatic "Rubbish Watson, rubbish!", adding, "the world is big enough for us. No ghosts need apply" (II 55). Likewise, Yeats was told by his ghostly "Instructors" (as he termed them) that they did not want him "to spend what remained of life explaining and piecing together those scattered sentences . . . We have come to give you metaphors for poetry", they famously declared (*Vision* 1937, 8), advice that Yeats heeded and kept the supernatural out of his greatest poems like "Among School Children", "Leda and the Swan", or "Sailing to Byzantium", among others too well known to need listing. In his elegy on Yeats, Auden saw the astonishing poetry behind the vast and complicated paraphernalia of the occult in *A Vision* (1925 and 1937) as his cheeky yet complimentary apostrophe shows: "You were silly like us: your gift survived it all" ("In Memory" 65). Thus did both Doyle and Yeats have two distinct sides of their creative identities and kept them apart consistently.

Yeats's *The Words Upon the Window-Pane* (1930)

While all of the above circumstantial evidence is suggestive of an interaction between the two authors, what follows is the mutual direct mention of the other in the context of the extra-sensual and the occult. In failing health during the last decade of his life, Yeats was now an avid reader of crime fiction: he wrote to Lady Gregory on 7 April 1930, "When I am not reading detective stories I am reading Swift" (Wade 773; see also 743, 762, 772). During this phase he wrote two of his most powerful plays, *The Words Upon the Window-Pane* and *Purgatory*, both being permeated by the occult, murder, and the afterlife. The former was first performed at the Abbey Theatre in Dublin on 17 November 1930, the year of Doyle's death on 7 July, and contains—as far as I know—Yeats's first and only mention of Doyle by name (line 28). The play dramatises Jonathan Swift's involvement with two women, Stella and Vanessa. It opens with preparations for a séance to be held in an eighteenth-century house which "belonged to friends of Jonathan Swift, or rather of Stella", and "somebody cut some lines from a poem of hers upon the window-pane—tradition says Stella herself". Dr Trench, the President of the Society, explains this to John Corbet, a Cambridge doctoral student doing research on Swift. Corbet is apologetic in his response, hoping that the medium Mrs Henderson "will not mind my skepticism. I have looked into Myers' *Human Personality* and a wild book by Conan Doyle, but am unconvinced". Most probably this "wild book" is Doyle's *The Land of Mist* (1926) and, as we shall see later, it describes the happenings during a séance which would, understandably, have interested Corbet. Yeats's play re-enacts the purgatorial dreaming-back process of Swift's relationship with the two women, neither of whom he married for fear of transmitting his incipient insanity (or perhaps syphilis) to his progeny. During the séance Mrs Henderson, speaking in the stentorian voice of Swift, reprimands Vanessa for trying to displace Stella through her sexuality: "How dare you write to her? How dare you ask if we were married? How dare you question her?" The crucial question the play raises is whether the spirit of Swift is genuine or a fraud.

After the séance is over Corbet gives Mrs Henderson a one-pound note, more than any of the others have paid her, and says:

> This is my contribution to prove that I am satisfied . . . When I say I am satisfied I do not mean that I am convinced it was the work of spirits. I prefer to think that you created it all, that you are an accomplished actress and scholar. In my essay for my Cambridge doctorate, I examine all the explanations of Swift's celibacy offered by his biographers and prove that the explanation you selected was the only plausible one.

MRS. HENDERSON: Who are you talking of, sir?
JOHN CORBET: Swift, of course.
MRS. HENDERSON: Swift? I do not know anybody called Swift.
JOHN CORBET: Jonathan Swift, whose spirit seemed to be present to-night.
MRS. HENDERSON: What? That dirty old man?
JOHN CORBET: He was neither old nor dirty when Stella and Vanessa loved him.
MRS. HENDERSON: I saw him very clearly just as I woke up. His clothes were dirty, his face covered with boils. Some disease had made one of his eyes swell up, it stood up from his face like a hen's egg.
JOHN CORBET: He looked like that in his old age. Stella had been dead a long time. His brain had gone, his friends had deserted him. The man appointed to take care of him beat him to keep him quiet.
DR. TRENCH: [at doorway] Come along, Corbet. Mrs. Henderson is tired out.

Presumably, John Corbet leaves unconvinced, but the audience is at least half convinced after hearing Mrs Henderson's accurate description of Swift in the last days of his life. Perhaps a less accomplished playwright would have had the curtains close after Corbet obeyed Dr Trench's summons, but Yeats is on Doyle's side and will not allow Corbet's attack on *The Land of Mist* by calling it "a wild book by Conan Doyle" to pass unchallenged. Accordingly, the play does not end after Corbet and the others exit, leaving Mrs Henderson alone onstage:

MRS. HENDERSON: *counts the money, finds her purse, which is in a vase on the mantelpiece, and puts the money in it.*
MRS. HENDERSON: How tired I am! I'd be the better of a cup of tea. *[She finds the teapot and puts kettle on fire, and then as she crouches down by the hearth suddenly lifts up her hands and counts her fingers, speaking in Swift's voice]*. Five great Ministers that were my friends are gone; ten great Ministers that were my friends are gone. I have not fingers enough to count the great Ministers that were my friends and that are gone. *[She wakes with a start and speaks in her own voice]*. Where did I put that tea-caddy? Ah! there it is. And there should be a cup and saucer. *[She finds the saucer]*. But where's the cup? *[She moves aimlessly about the stage and then, letting the saucer fall and break, speaks in Swift's voice]* Perish the day on which I was born!

THE END

The crux of the play, it seems to me, is not the rivalry between Stella and Vanessa (as some Yeats scholars have assumed) but, fundamentally, John Corbet's erroneous dismissal of Mrs Henderson as a fraud and, yet more fundamentally, his summary dismissal of the entire notion of spiritualism as being "wild". It is not mere coincidence that this derogatory description of Doyle's book by Corbet is Yeats's defence of the book by echoing Doyle's own dismissal of his so-called wild belief: "When I add", Doyle writes, "that I am a Doctor of Medicine, specially trained in observation, and that as a public man of affairs I have never shown myself to be wild or unreasonable" ("The Psychic Question" 15), a statement that adds a further link in the Doyle–Yeats chain of mutual influence between the two authors.

Mrs Henderson's soliloquy, then, is a dramatic tour de force that demolishes the sceptical view through her utterances in the voice of Swift, the last an incredibly powerful one echoing Job 3:3 with which the play ends. In fact, Yeats's 14-page Note following the play makes precisely this point by granting that "almost always truth and lies are mixed together" by the medium but then goes on to ask how we can account for the medium's "knowledge of events . . . and names beyond the medium's knowledge or ours?" as is suggested in Mrs Henderson's utterances when alone onstage (968). As Richard Ellmann observes, "The medium in Yeats's play *The Words Upon the Window-Pane* is suspected of being a fraud but in the end is shown to have incontrovertible clairvoyant power" (*Eminent* 111). In his own experience Yeats tells us elsewhere that Mrs Yeats's "automatic writing" was derived from "the communicators" having dictated "a system of symbolism strange to my wife and to myself", for "I had proof they were not dependent on her memory or mine" (*Vision* 1937, 9, 20).

Doyle's *The Land of Mist* (1926)

As noted, Yeats's play and Doyle's *The Land of Mist* are so closely linked in various ways that it might not be wrong for us to feel that the play was modelled on chapter 2 of the book. Here Professor Challenger's daughter Enid and her colleague Edward Malone, both being journalists for the *Daily Gazette* "writing joint articles upon the religious denominations of London", visit the Spiritualist Church to attend a séance. Verbal echoes in this chapter like "Mr. Hardy Williams, our energetic secretary", in Doyle and "Miss Mackenna, our energetic secretary", in Yeats are indicative of Yeats having read Doyle; but more importantly and inversely Doyle's "Is it the Second Coming?" echoing—as we shall see—the title of Yeats's magnificent poem "The Second Coming". More than mere verbal echoes, the links are thematic as well: the séance is interrupted midway by the sudden appearance of Mr Miromar, a "tall, pale-faced bearded man . . . who [holds] up his hand with a quietly impressive gesture" and delivers a "message" to the gathering, the essence being a warning against the coming chaos that Europe and the rest of the world face because:

> things have now reached a climax. The very idea of progress has been made material. It is progress to go swiftly, to send swift messages, to build new machinery. All this is a diversion of real ambition. There is only one real progress—spiritual progress.

He goes on to outline the political turmoil into which the world has descended after the Great War of 1914–1918:

> The nations heaped up fresh loads of sin, and sin must be ever atoned for. Russia became a cesspool. Germany was unrepentant of her terrible materialism which had been the prime cause of the war. Spain and Italy were sunk in alternate atheism and superstition. France had no religious ideal. Britain was confused and distracted. . . . America had abused her glorious opportunities.

WILLIAM BUTLER YEATS AND ARTHUR CONAN DOYLE

A voice from the back asks:

> "Is this the end of the world, mister?" "No", said the stranger, curtly. "Is it the Second Coming?" asked another. "Yes".
>
> (*Land* 310–26)

Yeats's poem had been six years in the public domain when Doyle's *The Land of Mist* was published. The poem's opening lines anticipate the chaos that Doyle describes—"Turning and turning in the widening gyre/The falcon cannot hear the falconer; /Things fall apart, the centre cannot hold;/ Mere anarchy is loosed upon the world"—and, as Terence Brown remarks, have become a "prophetic anticipation of the monstrous unfolding of twentieth century world history" (271). The poem was first published in *The Dial* in November 1920 (Jeffares 238). Three years later Yeats was awarded the Nobel Prize for Literature, which, as Hone records, accorded him "a mark of universal recognition" and "people wrote to Yeats from all over the world" (355, 357). Surely Doyle's recognition of Yeats's international fame is acknowledged in this chapter of *The Land of Mist* published three years later in 1926. Yeats's rough beast slouching towards Bethlehem to be born and Doyle's warning of impending destruction came to fruition 13 years later on 1 September 1939 with the outbreak of the World War. Reversing the calendar 25 years to the brink of the Great War, we find Holmes telling Dr Watson at the conclusion of "His Last Bow" after the capture of the German Von Bork, an agent of the Kaiser, that "There's an east wind coming, Watson." "I think not, Holmes. It is very warm." Holmes replies:

> Good old Watson! You are the one fixed point in a changing age. There's an east wind coming all the same, such a wind as never blew on England yet. It will be cold and bitter, Watson, and a good many of us may wither before its blast. But it's God's own wind none the less, and a cleaner, better, stronger land will lie in the sunshine when the storm has cleared.
>
> (II 457)

Perhaps Holmes' prognostication lodged deeply in Yeats's creative consciousness when he wrote "The Second Coming" two years later in January 1919 (Ellmann, *Identity* 290). Stallworthy points out that in early drafts of the poem he had written "The Germans to Russia to the place", which he then deleted and substituted with "The Germans are now to Russia come", both of which he discarded in the final version. Stallworthy adds:

> By the end of July 1917 the Russian front had crumbled in face of the enemy. In October of that year the Bolsheviks brought off their

revolution, and at the Treaty of Brest-Litovsk, on 3 March 1918, Lenin had surrendered to the Germans.

(18)

Interestingly, Harold Bloom thinks that Yeats should have retained his earlier title of the poem, "The Second Birth", but in his lengthy criticism (317–19) he overlooks the fact that Matt. 24:27 describes "the *coming* of the Son of Man" which is corroborated by Heb. 9:28, "shall he appear the *second* time without sin unto salvation" (my italics). Thus, Yeats's title "The Second Coming" subsumes his earlier tentative title "The Second Birth" and has Biblical authority besides being portentous, prophetic, and inexorable. In chapter 2 of Doyle's *The History of Spiritualism* (1926), the Second Coming is mentioned twice, its advent, Doyle states, being referred to by the spiritualist Edward Irving (1792–1831), who saw it as an ameliorative presence *following* "the days of wrath". This representation is quite unlike Mr Miromar's depiction of the chaotic events *preceding* the Second Coming, these being in accord with Yeats's rough beast, which is menacing rather than benign. If, then, Doyle's Mr Miromar is explicitly thinking of Yeats's poem, we may go further and examine his sister poem "A Prayer For My Daughter" written immediately after "The Second Coming" during the period 26 February–June 1919 (Ellmann, *Identity* 290), expressing a father's concern for his month-old daughter, fearing the hazards she may face when "the future years had come,/Dancing to a frenzied drum" and, as Stallworthy perceptively notes, "not for nothing did Yeats have them printed next to each other" (24). In a different context Yeats had observed that in the Irish poet Brian Merriman's lines on Bastardy, "the bastard's speech in *Lear* is floating through his mind" (*Explorations* 285); likewise, is the "east wind coming" that Holmes predicts to Dr Watson no less than four times within just seven lines "floating through" Yeats's mind in "A Prayer for My Daughter"? Remarkably, the "wind" features in various forms in five of the poem's ten stanzas: in stanza 1, "roof-levelling wind"; in stanza 2, "the sea wind scream upon the tower"; in stanza 7, "battery of the wind"; in stanza 8, "angry wind"; in stanza 9, "every windy quarter how". And, as in Holmes' last words to Watson, after the "cold and bitter" east wind, a "cleaner, better, stronger land will lie in the sunshine when the storm has cleared" seems to have resonances in the concluding lines of the poem: "And may her bridegroom bring her to a house/Where all's accustomed, ceremonious".

But to return to the séance at the Spiritualist Church which continues in lively fashion with "the solemn and comic" alternating, and while the two journalists remain interested but unconvinced, Edward Malone, like Yeats's sceptical John Corbet, whispers to Enid, "It is all clever quackery and bluff." Meanwhile, Mrs Debbs, the clairvoyant, has spotted them and announces, "We have friends here to-night, and it may interest them to come in contact with the spirit people." "She is very pale, very thin, with an aquiline face and eyes shining brightly from behind her gold-rimmed glasses." Master narrator that Doyle is, he prepares the reader for the climax with exquisite craftsmanship. Mrs Debbs declares:

> There is a presence building up behind the gentleman with a moustache—the gentleman who sits next to the young lady. Yes, sir, behind you. He is a man of middle size, rather inclined to shortness. He is old, over sixty, with white hair, curved nose and a white, small beard of the variety that is called goatee. He is no relation, I gather, but a friend. Does that suggest anyone to you, sir?
>   Malone shook his head with some contempt. "It would nearly fit any old man", he whispered to Enid. "We will try to get a little closer. He has deep lines on his face; I should say he was an irritable man in his lifetime. He was quick and nervous in his ways. Does that help you?" Again Malone shook his head. "Rot! Perfect rot", he muttered. "Well, he seems very anxious, so we must do what we can for him. He holds up a book. It is a learned book. He opens it and I see diagrams in it. Perhaps he wrote it—or perhaps he taught from it. Yes, he nods. He taught from it. He was a teacher". Malone remained unresponsive. "I don't know that I can help him any more. Ah! there is one thing. He has a mole over his right eyebrow". Malone started as if he had been stung. "One mole?" he cried. The spectacles flashed round again. "Two moles—one large, one small". "My God!" gasped Malone. "It's Professor Summerlee".

In both Doyle's narrative and Yeats's play sudden recognition displaces scepticism, making them partners in promoting a cause.

Partners

Conan Doyle's final work *The Edge of the Unknown* was published in July 1930, the year of his death. As in Yeats's *The Words Upon the Window-Pane*, Doyle reciprocally here for the first and only time mentions Yeats by name. Chapter 6 entitled "The Alleged Posthumous Writings of Known Authors: Oscar Wilde, Jack London, Lord Northcliffe, Dickens, Conrad, Jerome" has an arresting reference to Yeats by Oscar Wilde's spirit in the form of clairvoyant writing. "From time to time", Doyle tells us, "communications have come through mediums which are alleged to emanate from men who have been famous in literature". The communication from Oscar Wilde is as follows: "I knew Yeats well—a fantastical mind, but so full of inflated joy in himself that his little cruse of poetry was erupted only with infinite pains over the span of many years" (89). Doyle's comment on this snide judgement is outright rejection: "His [Wilde's] literary criticism was acid and unjust, but witty." Evidently, Doyle knew Yeats's poetry, hence his disagreement with Wilde's barb. In his Preface to *The Casebook of Sherlock Holmes*, Doyle points out that writing the stories has not "prevented me from exploring and finding my limitations in such varied branches of literature as history, poetry, historical novels, psychic research, and the drama" (II 462). His little-known poem "Victrix", "How was it then with England?", which he humorously and modestly describes as marking "my highest point, perhaps, on the foothills of Parnassus" (*Edge* 68), is not a trivial foray into poetic composition but is memorable, haunting, and reminiscent of Kipling's "Recessional", "God of our fathers, known of old". Besides, it is worth remembering that Doyle was the author of four volumes of poetry yet, unfortunately, was hardly recognised as a poet on account of his fame as the creator of Sherlock Holmes.

Given the circumstantial evidence that we have, there can be little doubt that Yeats had read Doyle's *The Edge of the Unknown*, published posthumously in 1930, and so knew of the dead Wilde's spirit having harshly criticised him and his poetry, and of Doyle's disagreement with the attack, prompting Yeats to retaliate against Wilde in his "Introduction" to *The Oxford Book of Modern Verse 1892–1935*, which he edited and published in 1936. Yeats writes: "Wilde, a man of action, a born dramatist, finding himself overshadowed by old famous men he could not attack, for he was of their time and shared its admirations, tricked and clowned to draw attention to himself" (vii). Comparing the two assessments—Wilde's of Yeats and Yeats's of Wilde—we may well find amusing a striking point of similarity: is not Wilde's critique of Yeats ("full of inflated joy in himself") being mimicked by Yeats in his counter-attack ("tricked and clowned to draw attention to himself") by echoing the pronoun "himself" as indicative of Wilde's inflated ego? Doyle of course had died six years earlier, but it is happily ironical that in the last year of Doyle's life the two authors came together in their works, though (perhaps) never meeting each other in person. If Doyle's rejection of Wilde's hostile criticism of Yeats and his poetry is his salute to, and defence of, Yeats, then, reciprocally, Yeats had earlier saluted the spirit of the departed Doyle in *The Words Upon the Window-Pane* by demonstrating that Doyle's "wild book" was not so wild, after all.

Resonances

In conclusion, my attempt will be to bring together similar aspects of the two authors' approach to the occult in their last works, Doyle's *The Edge of the Unknown* published a month before his death on 7 July 1930 and Yeats's disturbing play *Purgatory* performed on 10 August 1938 at the Abbey Theatre in Dublin five months before his death on 28 January 1939.

As I have pointed out elsewhere, "influence study is complex and often dubious" (xx), thus leaving its acceptance to the discretion of the reader. Given the shared interest of the two authors, a certain degree of overlapping in their writing might be expected. After the enactment of *Purgatory*, Yeats's final publication was his 38-page pamphlet *On the Boiler* in which he included *Purgatory* as the epilogue, concerning which he wrote, "I have put there my own conviction about this world and the next" (Wade 913). The central character is an Old Man whose mother, the descendant of a great Anglo-Irish Protestant family, had fallen in love with "a groom in a training stable;/Looked at him and married him./Her mother never spoke to her again,/And she did right", the Old Man vehemently tells his 16-year-old son, whom he describes as "a bastard that a pedlar got/Upon a tinker's daughter in a ditch".

The "big old house" in which the Old Man was born 66 years ago is now a ruin—"My father burned down the house when drunk", he tells his son, and that as a boy of 16 himself, he stabbed him to death and left the body to be consumed by the flames. Now, 50 years later, the Old Man has brought his 16-year-old son to see the ruin: "Stand there and look,/Because there is somebody in that house".

BOY: There's nobody here.
OLD MAN: There's somebody there . . . Listen to the hoofbeats! Listen! listen!
BOY: I cannot hear a sound.
OLD MAN: Beat! Beat!

> This night is the anniversary
> Of my mother's wedding night,
> Or of the night wherein I was begotten.
> My father is riding from the public house
> A whiskey bottle under his arm.
>   (*A window is lit showing a young girl*)
>
> Do not let him touch you! It is not true
> That drunken men cannot beget.
> She must live
>
> Through everything in exact detail.
> Driven to it by remorse.

The opening sentence of Doyle's second chapter in *The Edge of the Unknown* is:

> There is nothing more wonderful, more incredible, and at the same time, as it seems to me, more certain, than that past events may leave

a record upon our surroundings which is capable of making itself
felt, heard, or seen for a long time afterwards.

(43)

In *Purgatory* the *Boy*'s response is one of contemptuous dismissal:

BOY: What are you saying? Out with it!
    (*Old Man points to window*)
BOY: My God! The window is lit up
    And somebody stands there, although
    The floorboards are all burnt away.

In the same second chapter Doyle gives several instances of ghost visitations which consist of "an endless repetition of the tragedy which they once enacted" (49). Similarly, in *Purgatory* the two characters involved are complicit in the sexual act, their miscegenation compelling the endless repetition of the tragedy. The shocking conclusion follows in which the Old Man stabs his son to death while muttering:

My father and my son on the same jack-knife!
That finishes—there—there—there—
        (*He stabs again and again.
        The window grows dark*)

. . . .

I finished all that consequence.
I killed that lad because had he grown up,
He would have struck a woman's fancy
Begot, and passed pollution on.
I am a wretched foul old man

And therefore harmless. When I have stuck

This old jack-knife into a sod
And pulled it out all bright again,
And picked up all the money that he dropped
I'll to a distant place, and there
Tell my old jokes among new men,
        (*He cleans the knife and begins
        to pick up money*)

Hoof beats! Dear God
How quickly it returns—beat—beat—

Doyle's chapter gives two instances of a re-enactment of a violent and bloody conflict:

> In a light resembling that of the moon [the watchers] were aware of two elderly men engaged in a terrific struggle. One got the other down and killed him, bundling the body through the door into the cave beyond. He then buried the knife with which the deed was done.
>
> (50)

The second instance describes an elderly father who kills his son for having an affair with his considerably younger second wife:

> The result was a struggle in which the son was killed by the father. It is not to be wondered at that so horrible an event should leave a great psychic disturbance behind it, and the lodge was found to be a storm-centre of the unknown forces.
>
> (52)

Doyle's comment on the two incidents is:

> One can certainly imagine that in so fratricidal a strife there would be a peculiar intensity of emotion on the part of both the actors, which would leave a marked record if anything could do so. That the record was indeed very marked is shown by the fact that the sight was not reserved for people with psychic qualities . . . but that everyone . . . saw the apparition even after the lapse of so many years.
>
> (51)

While Yeats's two plays and Doyle's *The Land of Mist* establish the authenticity of the mediums' disclosures, both authors look beyond this goal and address important societal issues: the powerful social message of *Purgatory* is the disastrous consequence of unfettered individual freedom in sex and marriage. Eugenic purification is the predominant subject of Yeats's *On the Boiler* to which the play is an appendage, and Yeats quotes from Burton's *Anatomy of Melancholy*, "An husbandman will sow none but the best and choicest seed upon his land; he will not rear a bull or an horse except he be right shapen in all parts, or permit him to cover a mare, except he be well assured of his breed" (215), and comments, "And how careful then should we be in begetting our children!" (*On the Boiler* 418–19).

Equally concerned as to the damage done to society by unsolved crimes and the miscarriage of justice is Doyle in *The Edge of the Unknown*, where, in chapter 14 entitled "A New Light on Old Crimes", he records several cases of horrendous crimes that baffled the police until the perpetrators were revealed and brought to book through the intervention of a clairvoyant. (Today, the narco-analysis test, more popularly known as the lie-detector test, is regarded by the law as a help towards arriving at the truth, while DNA profiling uniquely identifies the individual by just a drop of blood, saliva, or semen). Ninety years ago, Doyle had pointed out that "many innocent people have suffered death and yet have experienced no super-normal help which might have saved them" (190–91). In the chapter's conclusion he suggests the antidote for such "painful cases where innocent men have gone to the scaffold" in these words:

> It should be possible at every great police-centre to have the call upon the best clairvoyant or other medium that can be got, and to use them freely, for what they are worth. None are infallible. They have their off-days and their failures. No man should ever be convicted upon their evidence. But when it comes to suggesting clues and links, then it might be invaluable.
>
> (192)

As is clear from this statement, far from being gullible or credulous, Doyle's suggestion is unexceptionable: "clues and links" may well lead the investigators to find the truth, which, indeed, was the case in several examples that he gives of irrefutable evidence being uncovered, like the bones, body parts, or even the corpse, and the murderer then being identified. Both Doyle and Yeats are deeply concerned about malpractices in society and offer remedies. Their writings should be viewed as not only great aesthetic creations but also attempts to grapple with contingent reality, whether in crime detection or in eugenics. We may question their methodologies for reform, but we cannot doubt their laudable motives.[3]

Notes

1 When Anubhav invited me to contribute to this Festschrift I was happy to accept, not only because Promodini had been given the Distinguished Teacher Award by the University of Delhi in 2009, but also because she and her co-editor Anubhav mentioned in their Introduction to *Kipling and Yeats at 150* (New York: Routledge, 2019) that the "psychic elements" in the two authors could well have been an additional field for investigation. Since these elements are intensely present in Yeats and Doyle, my essay is an attempt to fulfil this insightful expectation.
2 The books in Yeats's personal library do not include any of Doyle's works, but as Wayne Chapman and Edward O'Shea point out, many books were given away or lost in transit when the Yeats family changed residence from time to time. Likewise, the catalogue of Doyle's library and bookshop does not include any work by Yeats. See Google: <www.library thing.com//catalog/ACDoyleLibrary&collection=1&deepsearch=>

3 Despite his numerous engagements and extensive travels Doyle devoted three years of his life to securing the acquittal of George Edalji, a Parsee solicitor in Birmingham, from the charge of horse-maiming, and of clearing Oscar Slater, who had spent 16 years in jail, from the charge of a murder he had not committed. See Carr, chs. xv, xvii, and xix.

Works cited

Auden, W.H. "In Memory of W.B. Yeats." *Collected Shorter Poems 1930–1944*. London: Faber & Faber, 1953.
Bloom, Harold. *Yeats*. New York: Oxford UP, 1970.
Brown, Terence. *The Life of W.B. Yeats: A Critical Biography*. Oxford: Blackwell, 1999.
Burton, Robert. *The Anatomy of Melancholy*. 1621. Ed. Holbrook Jackson. Rpt. New York: Vintage, 1977.
Carr, John Dickson. *The Life of Sir Arthur Conan Doyle*. New York: Harper and Brothers, 1949.
Chapman, Wayne. *The W.B. and George Yeats Library: A Short-title Catalog*. Clemson: Clemson UP, 2011.
Desai, R.W. *Yeats's Shakespeare*. Evanston and Chicago: Northwestern UP, 1971.
Doyle, Arthur Conan. *The Edge of the Unknown*. 1930. Rpt. New York: Berkeley Medallion Books, 1968.
———. *The History of Spiritualism*. London: Cassell & Co., 1926.
———. "The Land of Mist." *The Professor Challenger Stories*. London: John Murray, 1952.
———. "The Psychic Question as I See It." *The Case for and Against Psychical Belief*. Ed. Carl Murchison. Worcester, MA: Clark UP, 1927.
———. *Sherlock Holmes: The Complete Novels and Stories*. 2 vols. Ed. Loren Estleman. Toronto: Bantam Books, 1986. (All references to the Sherlock Holmes stories are from this edition).
Ellmann, Richard. *Eminent Domain: Yeats Among Wilde, Joyce, Pound, Eliot and Auden*. New York: OUP, 1967.
———. *The Identity of Yeats*. New York: Oxford UP, 1964.
Hone, Joseph. *W.B. Yeats, 1865–1939*. 1943. Rpt. London: Macmillan, 1965.
Jeffares, A. Norman. *A Commentary on the Collected Poems of W.B. Yeats*. Stanford: Stanford UP, 1968.
Kelly, John, ed. *The Collected Letters of W.B. Yeats 1865–1895*. Vol. I. Oxford: Clarendon, 1986.
Murdie, Alan. "A Very Brief History of the Ghost Club." <www.ghostclub.org.uk/history.html>. Accessed 7 November 2019.
O'Shea, Edward. *A Descriptive Catalogue of W.B. Yeats's Library*. Shrewsbury: Garland Press, 1985.
Stallworthy, Jon. *Between the Lines: W.B. Yeats's Poetry in the Making*. Oxford: Clarendon, 1963.
Wade, Allan, ed. *The Letters of W.B. Yeats*. London: Rupert Hart-Davis, 1954.
Yeats, W.B. *Autobiographies*. London: Macmillan, 1955.
———. *A Critical Edition of Yeats's A Vision (1925)*. Ed. George Mills Harper and Walter Kelly Hood. London: Macmillan, 1978.

———. *Explorations*. Ed. Mrs. W.B. Yeats. New York: Macmillan, 1962.

———. ed. "Introduction." *The Oxford Book of Modern Verse 1892–1935*. 1936. Rpt. New York: Oxford UP, 1966.

———. *Mythologies*. New York: Macmillan, 1959.

———. "Purgatory." *On the Boiler*. Dublin: The Cuala Press, April 1938.

———. "The Second Coming." *The Collected Poems of W.B. Yeats*. London: Macmillan, 1950.

———. *Uncollected Prose by W.B. Yeats: First Reviews and Articles 1886–1896*. 2 vols. Ed. John P. Frayne. London: Macmillan, 1970.

———. *A Vision: An Explanation of Life Founded Upon the Writings if Giraldus and Upon Certain Doctrines Attributed to Kusta Ben Luka*. By William Butler Yeats. London: Privately printed for subscribers only by T. Werner Laurie, Ltd., 1925.

———. "The Words upon the Window-Pane." *The Collected Plays of W.B. Yeats*. London: Macmillan, 1952.

2
IBSEN'S GHOST IN FORSTER'S *THE LONGEST JOURNEY*

Sumanyu Satpathy

E.M. Forster's quasi-Bildungsroman, *The Longest Journey* (1907), is replete with allusions—from title onward—to a host of authors such as Aristophanes, Shakespeare, Bacon, Milton, Shelley, Keats, Meredith, Henry James, and also to *The Book of Genesis*, Darwin, and, above all, Ibsen. Of these, the last-mentioned author's is by far the most pervasive presence (even ahead of the titular one of Shelley's) in the novel. For long neglected as one of Forster's less successful works,[1] *The Longest Journey*—as I wish to show through an enquiry of how it is engaged in a serious dialogue with the playwright, particularly with his *Ghosts*—is nevertheless a demanding and problematic text.

In Forster's long reading list for 1899, one can find Ibsen's *Pillars of Society* and *John Gabriel Borkman* (Furbank 70). That he had ingested more Ibsen than this by the time he actually got down to writing *The Longest Journey* becomes evident from the novel itself. The iconoclastic playwright, along with Zola and Flaubert, stood for the *avant-garde* in literature and had caught the imagination of young intellectuals all over Europe:[2] how Joyce came under his spell is well-known.[3] Forster may have consciously avoided Flaubert's influence,[4] but the naturalism of Zola's or Ibsen's kind seems to have left a deep impression on him. What use does he make of Ibsen in his *The Longest Journey*, which is replete with allusions to *Ghosts*? How does the play operate as an intertext and affect our understanding of the novel? And where does that leave Forster in the history of modernist fiction? These are questions that the present essay attempts to answer.

Stumbling steps

Among the more obvious borrowings from *Ghosts* is the idea of Rickie inheriting his father's deformity. In Ibsen's play, "[Jacob Engstrand's] left leg is somewhat deformed, and he wears a boot with a built-up wooden sole" (Ibsen 197). Apart from this literal lameness of Engstrand, Mr Alving's moral turpitude is also described as the "stumbling steps" (Ibsen 220). Thus, in Ibsen, lameness functions as a trope for moral failings in a character. In attributing a similar deformity to Rickie, and also to his father, who has obvious moral flaws besides, Forster clearly invites us to draw a parallel between the two texts. The parallelism is sustained through the whole length of his novel and does not leave us until close to the end. The allusions are neither incidental nor coincidental. There are significant overtures to as well as departures from the *Ghosts* motif.

For example, soon after ascribing the inheritance of the lame foot from father to son, the narrator reverses the order of inheritance and describes Mr Elliott thus:

> In appearance he resembled his son, being weakly and lame, with hollow little cheeks, a broad white band of forehead, and stiff impoverished hair. His voice, which he did not transmit, was very suave, with a fine command of cynical intonation. Nor did he transmit his eyes.
>
> (Forster 27)

Going a step further, he spares Rickie any further humiliation by divesting him of certain other hereditary features: "The peculiar features [of Mr Elliot's eyes] . . . the unkindness of them, the cowardice, the fear in them, were to trouble the world no longer" (Forster 27). Similarly, Rickie is not as heartless as his father. When his mother asks the young Rickie where his left hand is, he says, "The side my bad foot is"—such is the devastating effect of paternal subjugation. Unpleasant to her ears, she corrects him and clarifies that she meant him to say, "The side my heart is" (Forster 29). Besides bringing out the contrast between the loving mother and the cynical father, Forster succeeds in pointing out the degree of conformity to which Rickie had submitted himself at this stage of his life. Hints at biological determinism that Ibsen, drawing upon Darwin and Mendel, had helped popularise throughout Europe are given in such authorial asides as "God alone knows how far we are in the grip of our bodies" (Forster 31), cleverly leaving out the mind, the spirit, and the heart/soul. This latter fact injects some irony into Rickie's naive acquiescence soon after: "I shall be as wax in your hands mama" (Forster 32). Though, when at Cambridge, he was to outgrow many of the received prejudices, he grows up believing in what he has been told (his deformity and conformity are coexistent until much later in the novel). As Gerald reports, "He says he can't marry, owing to his foot . . . His grandfather was crooked, his father too, and he's as bad. He thinks that it's hereditary, and may get worse next generation" (Forster 55). Again, when Rickie turns up at her place with Agnes, Mrs Failing says:

I feel twenty-seven years younger. Rickie you are so like your father. I feel it is twenty-seven years ago, and that he is bringing your mother to see me for the first time. It is curious—almost terrible—to see history repeating itself.

(Forster 98)

Stephen too is not spared the visitations of the ancestral ghosts. In a clear echo of the famous scene in *Ghosts*, Forster describes Stephen's jollity, until now the reader's doubt having been that he is the illegitimate child of Rickie's father from another woman. The doubt stands temporarily confirmed in the following scene: Stephen has just come back home from one of his sojourns in the wilderness, after having had "a rare good time", only to find that everyone had gone out. "On the landing he saw the new housemaid. He felt skittish and irresistible. Should he slip his hand around her waist? Perhaps better not; she might box his ears" (Forster 124).

In Ibsen's play, Mrs Alving recounts Mr Alving's moral transgression: "I heard our maid come in from the garden with some water for the plants over there . . . . Shortly afterwards . . . I heard my own maid whisper: 'Let me go, Mr. Alving! Let me alone!'" (Ibsen 223). Scenes later, the following incident takes place: "(From the dining room comes the sound of a chair being overturned; simultaneously a voice is heard) Regina's voice [in a sharp whisper] Oswald! Are you mad? Let me go!" (Ibsen 244).

At the Cadford Rings, when Rickie meets Agnes and Mrs Failing, the latter, full of herself and Ibsen, as usual, informs him: "this place is full of ghosties . . . have you seen any yet?" (Forster 134). On Rickie asking her, "What kind of ghosties haunted this curious field", her cryptic reply is: "The D". We recall that the surname of Stephen's father was also to be suppressed with some degree of authorial nonchalance: "there is no occasion to mention his surname . . ." (Forster 231). That Mrs Failing could be referring to the initial of his father's surname can only be guessed. It is equally possible, in view of the references to Darwin elsewhere in the text, and the motif of inheriting genetic features permeating the text, that "the D" is Darwin. After all, Darwin had usurped the place of worship earlier occupied by the Christian God in the Sunday Church. But Forster evades, or so we think, and Rickie says simple-mindedly, "soldiers and shepherds . . . have no ghosts. They worshipped Mars or Pan-Erda perhaps; not the devil." In between these references to the ghosties/ghosts, Mrs Failing (that unfailing Ibsenite) disconcerts Rickie by letting slip references to Stephen as "your brother" and "the shepherd" until finally she breaks the news to him, that he is actually his half-brother (still withholding the fact that he is his mother's son). Forster does not want us to miss the allusion, even as the novel's hero-author Rickie gets unnecessarily alert to allusions: "Perhaps it was some literary allusion that he had not caught; but her face did not at that moment suggest literature" (Forster 136), Forster says in an authorial aside.

We know that through Mrs Failing Forster himself has so far been alluding to *Ghosts*.

Later in the novel he can no longer rest content with such indirections and quite explicitly makes one of the characters quote/misquote from the play. Here are Agnes and her brother discussing Stephen: Agnes says, "I'm glad he drinks. I hope he'll kill himself. A man like that ought never to have been born." To this Herbert adds: "Perhaps the sins of the parents are visited on the children . . . Yet it is not for us to decide" (Forster 259). Forster also uses his narratorial voice to make occasional ironic comments on certain Ibsenites. When Mrs Failing exclaims to herself: "Fresh air! . . . I will let in fresh air", the narrator remarks, rather sarcastically: "Thus reasoned Mrs. Failing, in the facile vein of Ibsenism. She imagined herself to be a cold-eyed Scandinavian heroine" (Forster 129–30). The allusion here is to Lona of *Pillars of Society*.

Having traced the allusions, we must now pause and ponder: what purpose do they serve in the novel? Does Forster simply want to popularise the ideas of Ibsen? Was he just another Ibsenite? After all, the offspring do inherit the lame foot of earlier generations. And Stephen does feel like embracing the new maid. Also, as Agnes successfully but only temporarily persuades Rickie to believe, Stephen "was the fruit of sin; therefore he is sinful". He was "illicit, abnormal, worse than a man diseased". And the narrator interjects, "And Rickie, remembering whose son he was, gradually adopted her opinion", but adds soon enough, "[Rickie] too became a sexual snob" (Forster 145), the implication of "too" being that both Agnes and her brother were sexual snobs. Similarly, from the beginning Rickie is portrayed as someone who does not "hate" anyone and is teased for it. He cannot stand the schisms in the college fraternity.

There are warnings enough for us, then, that we must not misconstrue Forster to be yet another Ibsenite and that all is not well with Ibsen or the Ibsenites. Through *Ghosts* Ibsen had succeeded in shocking the contemporary audience by a frank dissection of the very institution of marriage, questions of illegitimacy of birth, incest, and almost all forms of personal/sexual relationships. The vehemence of opposition to such frankness elicited numerous purblind defences. As Raymond Williams says, "Ibseni*sm* and Ibsen*ites* sprang up everywhere. Bernard Shaw wrote *The Quintessence of Ibsenism* . . . . What Shaw expounded in his book was hardly what Ibsen had written in his plays" (Williams 18). Forster, though, was uncomfortable with these versions of Ibsenism. He makes only a select few of his characters allude to Ibsen. He simulates *Ghosts*-like situations and characters, and makes these Ibsenites comment on them freely "in the facile vein of Ibsenism" and finally calls their bluff, as well as that of the real-life Ibsenites among his contemporaries.

That Forster interrogates the Ibsenites, whether or not he completely dissociates himself from them, becomes further evident when we find him attributing

Ibsenism only to three of the characters, Mrs Failing, Agnes, and Herbert, with none of whom can the authorial intentions be trusted.[5] On the other hand, Rickie's mother, Ansell, and Stephen Wonham, with whom the author's sympathies seem to lie, never allude to Ibsen. In between stands Rickie, who has been indoctrinated in Ibsenism no doubt, but he is half-believing, partly because he is his mama's boy and partly because of his Cambridge circle, dominated by Ansell. Soon after his disillusionment with his post-marital life and Agnes, and his discovery of Stephen, he too rejects Ibsenism.

The Cambridge companions

In Forster's fictional world, which can be construed partly through the authorial interventions, certain human values are indiscreetly espoused, whereas certain others are tested and rejected. In these moments of indiscretion might lie the alleged or actual weakness of Forster's art. However, the point is, imbued with the ideology of the Cambridge Apostles as he was, even while rejecting much of its abstract philosophical content, Forster felt impelled to accommodate aspects of it in the fictional framework of *The Longest Journey*. Furbank recounts how by 1906, "through the influence of Strachey and Keynes, the brethren had taken to discussing more everyday human subjects—a change that Forster thought greatly for the better" (Furbank I 78).

Sex was one human subject the *Society* already sometimes discussed at this early period. Same-sex desire, in particular, was talked about in a spirit of free and rational enquiry. The freedom, however, was only at the level of ideas. In so far as the brethren actually had any physical love affairs with one another, they kept the fact to themselves; it was not till a few years later, after a long drawn-out battle between Strachey and G.M. Trevelyan, that it became acceptable for the brethren to have same-sex "affairs" (Furbank, ibid.).

Notwithstanding the differences between the King's and Trinity sets of intellectuals within the Apostles,[6] much of the Apostolic ideology, not least its sexual content, undoubtedly found its way into the novel.[7] As Colmer says:

> In *The Longest Journey*, [Forster] is driven into using a number of artistic subterfuges to mask his real theme . . . Since the publication of *Maurice* in 1971 and the posthumous homosexual short stories in 1972, the meaning behind the artistic subterfuges becomes more apparent.
>
> (Colmer 83)

But instead of pursuing the point, Colmer says, ". . . this new way of reading the novel, although it may illustrate much that has always seemed obscure, still does little to clarify the confusion of themes and symbols within the novel" (Colmer 83). One wonders, for at least as far as the Ibsen motif is concerned, if "the confusion of the themes and symbols" will continue to obfuscate the central issues in the novel unless the subterfuges are taken into account. For example, the undercurrent of sexual dissidence, which runs strongly beneath the veneer of heterosexual-straight-familial love, promises to light up Forster's attitude towards interpersonal love. And it is here that Ibsen comes in. The work of Peter L. Hays can be useful here. In his *The Limping Hero*, he defines the "limper" as a:

> literary character who—actually lame or symbolically so—that is, actually or figuratively castrated . . . Lameness as a literary device is usually either symbolic of or a euphemism for a genital wound; the wound in turn, symbolizes a social disability. . .
>
> (Hays 4)

But, again, though Hays discusses Rickie, he does not see the significance of the limp in the context of the story (Hays 141–43).

In the main plot, Rickie's failure to become an artist is misogynistically ascribed to his wrong choice: his opting for heterosexual love and marriage, in spite of his early realisation, "As to women—oh! there they were dreadful . . . I realize that more and more" (Forster 51). Originally he had shared similar views with Ansell,[8] who had warned him in a letter "that men and women desire different things, man wants to love mankind; woman wants to love one man. When she has him her work is over." It was also Ansell's prophesy that "in time [Agnes] will get sick of this . . . And having made him thoroughly miserable and degraded, she will bolt—if she can do it like a lady" (86). Ansell writes in the same letter quoted here that woman "is the emissary of Nature . . . But man does not care a damn for Nature . . ." (87).

Such an attack on so-called natural sexual relationships is part of Forster's plot. All this woman-baiting begins to make a lot of sense as soon as the hints of Oedipal and same-sex love, more so the latter, are picked up on the way.[9] Rickie, the alter-ego of the queer author ("Forster", Furbank tells us, "by now, I think we can assume, knew perfectly well that he was homosexual by temperament"—circa 1906; Furbank I 78), also had intimations of the author's sexuality when he saw the athletic Gerald: ". . . there stood a young man who had the figure of a Greek athlete and the face of an English one . . . Just where he began to be beautiful the clothes [unfortunately for Rickie?] started" (Forster 46).

There are scenes, too, subtly depicting same-sex play between Rickie and Ansell (70). Thus, Rickie cannot stand the sight of Agnes and Gerald in embrace: "Gerald and Agnes were locked in each other's arms. He only looked for a moment, but the sight burnt into his brain" (Forster 45). Rickie, who was not "normal" (we might recall that Clive, Maurice's same-sex partner, becomes "normal" after a bout of illness), turned "crimson and afraid. He thought 'Do such things actually happen?' . . . It was the merest accident that Rickie had not been disgusted. But this he could not know" (Forster 45–46).

Eventually, however, he forgets his early intimations, even dismisses his "poor Shelley", and chooses to fall in love with Agnes, and pursues it at all events (Forster 66). But when he is with Agnes "with his head on her lap", Rickie tells her, "I *prayed* you might not be a woman." And then she kisses him. "He started, and cried passionately." Then he says, "I am too weak. . . what [Gerald] gave you then is greater than anything you will get from me." At this "she was [justifiably] frightened. Again she had *the sense of something abnormal*" (Forster 80; my emphases). One of the conclusions one could draw from such subterfuges is, perhaps, that Rickie, who had partially Oedipal and partly same-sex inclinations, looked for a mother figure in Agnes or a male friend like Ansell.

Ansell, who understood Rickie well, discusses with Tilliard whether Rickie's decision to marry was a step in the right direction. Tilliard says, "We're his friends, and I hope we always shall be, but we shan't keep his friendship by fighting . . . Wife first, friends some way after. You may resent the order, but it is ordained by nature." Ansell retorts in a tone sharpened by envy, the "point is, not what is ordained by nature or any other fool, but what is right" (Forster 85–86). Ansell's letters to Rickie take off from here. His pique undoubtedly springs from the fact that Rickie at this stage is moving towards "normal" love, and he takes it as a betrayal. Once he tells Rickie that he cared for Agnes because she "had the usual amount of arms and legs" (Forster 62). Whenever things go wrong with the lovers, he blames her more than him; in fact, he does not even recognise her existence: "[Mrs Agnes] has no real existence", he would say (Forster 182). But when he speaks genially about Rickie, Tilliard says, "For much as I like Rickie, I always think him a little effeminate" (Forster 85).

Once, planning to ask Ansell over to Ilfracombe, Rickie muses: Ansell was brutal and Agnes definitely jealous; he could understand Ansell's brutality, but he could not understand her jealousy:

> Let husband and wife be as sun and moon, or as moon and sun. Shall they therefore not give greeting to the stars? He was willing to grant that the love that inspired her might be higher than his own. Yet did he not exclude them both from much that is gracious? That dream of his when he rode on the Wiltshire expanses—curious dream: the lark silent, the earth dissolving. And he awoke from it into a valley full of men.
>
> (Forster 179)

The obvious allusion here is to the imagery Milton uses in *Paradise Lost* while describing the Adam–Eve relationship, Raphael's discourse on the love among angels, and Adam's later lament that Paradise was not all men. Through this Forster seems to attack accepted modes of heterosexual marriage. Rickie's world (and Ansell's, as indeed Forster's and that of the Apostles) was "full of men". The subject was taboo, but Forster in a spirit of freedom and truthful enquiry pursued it relentlessly and worked it into the texture of his plot. Writing in the shadow of the Wilde controversy, he engaged the characters in a subtle debate and came up with his own answers.

Ibsen and Ibsenism

Forster's reading of Ibsen, thus, was bound to be coloured by his own "moral" predilections around questions of marriage, notions of sexual guilt, sin, and sexual corruption/perversion. *Ghosts* may have been concerned with stylistic, dramatic, or universalist questions; but the iconoclastic social ideas made the noise, not the artistic ones. As Williams says, "These things made the scandal . . . they made Ibsen" (Williams 18). Even if we cleanse the play of Ibsenism, as does Williams, and insist that the meaning is central to Ibsen's idea that "we are . . . the creatures of our past", the play still remains a strong indictment of contemporary society, in certain ways welcome to Forster no doubt; but in certain other ways, much to his discomfiture. As a liberal, he could not have accepted any form of determinism—still less as a sexual dissident, inheriting the sexual repression of the Victorians. Living in Edwardian society, where sex beyond legitimate family was considered sinful, he felt the need to redefine "the sins of the parents" anew. Succeeding Ibsen, he had to redraw the contours of conventional morality.

Rickie talks about dead conventions, the "ghosties": "conventions are not majestic and they will not claim us in the end" (Forster 277). But then Ibsen's assault on "dead conventions" was also pronounced; as Mrs Alving says:

> It is not only what we have inherited from our fathers and mothers that walks in us. It is every kind of dead idea, lifeless old beliefs and so on. . . There must be ghosts the whole country over
>
> (quoted in Williams 50)

Yet his contemporaries, especially the Ibsenites, failed to grasp the ambiguity in the play and took the inheritance of syphilis to be the central theme. As Forster himself said in 1928, Ibsen is "not easily understood":

> [A]lthough he is not a teacher he has the air of being one . . . [He] further throws us off the scent by taking a harsh or a depressing view of human relationships.
>
> (*AH* 97)

In these comments, Forster's entire attitude towards Ibsen is summed up. In *The Longest Journey*, he seems to be grappling with two Ibsens: one the moralist, the other holding a "depressing view of human relationships". In appropriating *Ghosts*, he draws us into a debate with its author and the Ibsenites, only to subvert both: in *The Longest Journey* he is himself partly concerned with the ethical side of English sexuality.

First, Rickie and Stephen are shown as figures who are "visited upon" in more ways than one; and in many ways they threaten to prove the Ibsenite thesis of Mrs Failing, Agnes, and Herbert. But there appear in due course of time stark contrasts between developments in *Ghosts* and those in *The Longest Journey*. In the latter, Rickie and Stephen attain heroic heights by the Forsterian yardstick. Stephen was first rather mockingly attributed qualities of heroism by Mrs Failing (108). Rickie was to do the same with a fair degree of honesty (278); and Rickie himself is, of course, the aspiring hero-artist portrayed as a young man, whose "development" the book attempts to trace. Judged by conventional standards, like those of Agnes and Mrs Failing, both Rickie and Stephen may have been moral cripples. But not in the world envisioned by Forster. Rickie pronounces Stephen a hero hours before he dies trying to save his life, because "He was a law to himself, and rightly. He was great enough to despise our small moralities" (Forster 278). Stephen would fight against "all this wicked nonsense, against the Wilbrahams and Pembrokes who try to rule our world" (Forster 278). In saying all this and realising Stephen's heroism, Rickie rises in stature. As the novelist comments in his narratorial voice, "he was attaining love". Ansell also contributes to Rickie's heroism: "This evening Rickie caught Ansell's enthusiasm, and felt it worthwhile to sacrifice everything for such a man" (Forster 278). Two pages later, Rickie dies while trying to save Stephen's life. It would thus seem, at least in moments like these, that *The Longest Journey* foreshadows *Howards End* in its anxiety to connect people. Through the earlier novel, Forster expounds his theory of human relationships. "'Come with me as a man', said Stephen . . . 'not as a brother; who cares what people did years back? We're alive together, and the rest is cant'" (Forster 257). But as Forster himself comments in his authorial voice: "The rest was not cant" (Forster 257).

Ansell had suggested a formula in which we may sum up decent people. They must be serious, they must be truthful. They need not be serious in the sense of glum, but ought to be convinced that the earth was not a place "to beat time on". And about this Stephen was convinced: "he showed it in his work, in his play, in his self-respect, and above all . . . in his sacred passion for alcohol". The choice of the value-loaded adjective "sacred" is deliberate on the part of Forster, because he adds soon enough: "Drink, today, is an unholy thing" (Forster 266). Thus, contemporary definitions of "morality" were anathema to Forster's humanistic credo—as indeed they were to Rickie, Stephen, their mother, and Ansell. To Stephen even class distinctions did not matter. They were, in fact, "trivial things to him, and life no decorous scheme, but a personal combat or a personal truce". "For the same reason ancestry also was trivial and a man not the dearer because the same woman was mother to them both" (Forster 244). It does not matter to the likes of Ansell that Stephen was a tippler.

Nor did it to Forster, though Sheppard would have us believe that "the Kingsmen were all against alcoholism. In comparison, the Kingsmen appeared to be what Strachey called 'moral', though not in the traditional or conventional sense".[10] Forster, *au contraire*, did wonder how to reconcile the Kings' and the "Trinity" virtues. Thus, in attributing both certain Trinitarian traits and also certain other Kings' traits, such as the value of "personal intercourse" to Stephen and lauding these through Ansell, Forster was able to bring about a reconciliation between the two Apostolic sects in his fictional world. The task of incorporating this aspect of life into art was not difficult. But when it came to the task of expositing his ideas concerning interpersonal love, or, what social scientists call, homosocial love, which need not be confined to relations through blood kinship or marriage in a fictional framework, Forster found it daunting. "The love that dare not speak its name" became nonetheless an important theme in the novel and a component of "personal intercourse".

But then he had to contend with Ibsen, the moralist at large and a formidably popular figure, made all the more formidable by the Ibsenites who were all over the place. Thus, the device that Forster took recourse to was that of appropriation and subversion. Inheritance, not disease, is "the essential experience of *Ghosts*", says Williams. Forster introduces the theme of inheritance, including inherited deformity; but "personal intercourse", not inheritance, is the essential experience of *The Longest Journey*.

In *Ghosts*, Oswald Alving succumbs to the inherited disease and moral failing. The effort of Mrs Alving proved to be feeble against the inexorable forces that she was up against. The human relationship portrayed in the play is a gloomy one, according to Forster. This aspect of Ibsen he could not accept even while appreciating his art. The ". . . crux of Ibsen is that, though he had a romantic temperament, he found personal intercourse sordid". The main aim of his 1928 essay on Ibsen is to discount the Ibsen of the Ibsenites and discover the romantic-symbolist-poet and the dramatist. "The symbolism never holds up the action, because it is part of the action, and because Ibsen was a poet, to whom creation and craftsmanship were one" (Forster 1936, 100).

Forster's attacks on the institution of marriage, one of Ibsen's targets, are more problematic. Rickie blames himself for the failure of his marriage. Without Ansell he would have "renounced his mother and his brother and all the outer world, troubling no one . . . So Ansell himself had told [Agnes]" (Forster 260). Rickie fails because he allows himself to be "run" by her. As Ansell says, "Pembroke and that wife simply run him" (Forster 184). It is significant that he is finally "run over" by the train. But having been run by her and suffered a metaphorical/spiritual death, however temporary, and being run over by a train to save Stephen are two different things. Stephen's was a case apart, for he does not allow himself to be run by anyone, nor is he run over. In fact, he saves people from being run over. His basic understanding of human relationships is very clear: "You can't own people" (Forster 271). He was not one of the average men and could offer a critique of the modern morals too: "But romantic love is also the code of modern morals, and hence popular" (Forster 271). He does not believe in romantic love. He gets married with his eyes wide open; he wouldn't be ordered about, won't be "possessed" by anyone, let alone ghosts. When he goes out with his child, in the last lines of the novel, he does so musing about Rickie:

> The ear was deaf, and what thanks of his would reach it? The body was dust, and in what ecstasy of us could it share? The spirit had fled, in agony and loneliness, never to know that it bequeathed him salvation.
> (Forster 288)

We might recall that Forster described the main theme of *Peer Gynt* as "that of *salvation by being loved*" (quoted in Colmer 19; my emphasis).

The love between Stephen and Rickie was to burn forever like the paper trick Stephen had performed on the stream. The fire symbolism here is as powerful as that in *Ghosts*, praised by Forster in his 1928 essay (Forster 1936, 100). Thus it is that, "[Stephen] could . . . believe that he guided the future of our race . . ." (Forster 288).

Reconciling realism

Thus, if the evidence displayed here is any indication, long before Forster offered his discursive critique of Ibsen at the end of his career as a novelist, he had already critiqued the playwright imaginatively in *The Longest Journey*. Virginia Woolf was at once perceptive and off the mark when she compared Forster unfavourably with Ibsen. In 1927, a year before Forster's essay on Ibsen appeared, Woolf said in an article that the problem that both Forster and Ibsen faced was that of reconciling realism with vision. Forster worked with realism and minute observation, but "his reality must at certain points become irradiated: his brick must be lit up; we must see the whole building irradiated with light" (Furbank II 145). Ibsen, she said, achieved this; Forster did not quite succeed in it. Even though hurt, Forster was only too willing to accept this piece of criticism: that he lacked "the coordinating power that Ibsen had". The quarrel that ensued sidetracked the issue and the focus shifted to how "life" could be integrated into art and how best a novel could be judged "as a work of art" and not as a chunk of life. Forster need not have ceded any ground to Woolf, because, for him, incorporation of life into art was essential but not at the total sacrifice of art. One reason, perhaps, why *The Longest Journey* remained dear to his heart was that in it he could fuse so much of life, his own life, and art: the fusion of art and heart.

We can now examine variations on the Ibsen motif that Forster introduces in *The Longest Journey*. Rickie redeems himself when he finally realises that Shelley was less foolish than he had thought (Forster 261). He decides not to subscribe to the great sect which undertakes "the longest journey" with one friend or one mistress only. "He reviewed the watchwords of the last two years [at Sawston], and found that they ignored personal truces, and personal love" (Forster 269). Forster seems to subscribe to Rickie's theory that "In literature we needn't intrude our own limitations" (Forster 275). Nor is he "so silly as to think that all marriages turn out like mine". He is helped by both Ansell and Stephen—"one intellectual, the other very much the reverse"—to arrive at such redeeming wisdom. One of them tells him "You *must* write. You *must* go. Because to write, to go, is you." But all this is important in life to prove "that people are important" (Forster 275). So he dies while saving Stephen.

One need not be physically strong and manly but should have the strength of character to achieve the ideals Rickie, Stephen, or Ansell stood for. That is why "Gerald died that afternoon", without notice (Forster 56). Sudden deaths are a much-maligned affair in Forster. But seldom are the differences between such deaths noticed. Rickie, not tough like Gerald, who had always bullied him, is at least able to save a life; so does Stephen, who is as tough as Gerald. But Gerald dies a useless death, in spite of his Greek figure with the English face. Stephen's heroism manifests itself in several ways, but by following the Forsterian principles rather than the Ibsenian ones. "Come with me as a man", he beckons Rickie. In the last chapter he does what Rickie and Ansell had thought was expected of a hero like him. He twirls the likes of Herbert on the tip of his finger.

Forster's final comment on Ibsen, thus, seems to have been uttered in the last paragraph of chapter 31:

> Habits and sex may change with the new generation, features may alter with the *play* of a private passion, but a voice is apart from these. It lies nearer to the racial essence and perhaps to the divine; it can, at all events, overleap one grave.
>
> (Forster 257; my emphasis)

The voice overleaping the grave is what Rickie's life and death, in the final moment of sacrifice, symbolise. And the last chapter of the novel goes to show how.

Thus, Forster's achievement in *The Longest Journey* cannot be thought merely in terms of being a triumph over the limited Edwardian conception of art and morality but as art-and-morality. The treatment of sexually dissident relationships and attack on Victorian middle-class morality (however muted by narratorial subterfuges) was a daring undertaking in 1907, as Frieda Lawrence had noticed.[11] Similarly, but perhaps more importantly, the technical experimentation and innovation that Forster has made in the novel cannot be spoken of merely in terms of stretching the realist mode. The complex intertextual reading of Ibsen, the interweaving of the Ibsen text and the contemporary (mis)readings of Ibsen, is an integral part of the plot-as-theme. Forster is not only ironic in his Rortian humanism:[12] his role as the ironic narrator-interlocutor, constantly helping and commenting on, and undermining, the reader's reading of his text, as well as Ibsen's, is no less ahead of its time. Herein lies his modernism. The epic fabric of *Ulysses* may be missing in *The Longest Journey*: but its singular method of (f)using Ibsen—appropriating only to subvert him in order to be able to offer an alternative social-moral order based on love, sexually dissident as it may be—is definitely forward-looking rather than being Edwardian.[13] As a growth novel, it can stand comparison with Joyce's *Portrait*, which it pre-dates and with which it shares many thematic and artistic traits. However, an extended comparison of and an enquiry into their relative artistic merits have to be the subjects of another essay.

Notes

1 With the possible exception of critics like Richard Keller Simon, who calls it "complex", Trilling sees it as a failure to master technique, C.B. Cox argues that Forster failed to apply his liberal ideas to social reality, and John Harvey sees it "as an expression of a confused and inadequate vision of life" (Colmer 83). But contemporary reviewers found the novel "more provocative than satisfactory" (*Critical Heritage* 79) and complained of a "lack of straightforwardness" (ibid. 80).
2 For Joyce's early enthusiasm for Ibsen, see his definitive biography and the *Letters* edited by Ellman: "as he went by Baird's stone-cutting works in Talbot Place the spirit of Ibsen would blow through him like a keen wind" (quoted in Williams 153).
3 John Colmer describes the importance of Zola, Ibsen, and Wagner, "especially in advanced circles" (Colmer 19). Forster used to sign "Peer Gynt" for his university essays.
4 He said the book "at all events isn't Flaubert". See Forster's letter to Dickinson, quoted in Furbank I 148.
5 We find Rickie musing what was wrong with Agnes and Herbert. We also find how wrong Mrs Failing's Ibsenistic forecasts were to prove in the lives of Rickie and Stephen. History does not repeat itself except in the case of Rickie's daughter being born with a lame foot.
6 See Furbank I 104–06. He narrates the story of how John Sheppard presented a paper on the question of "King's or Trinity?"
7 See Strachey's letter to Duncan Grant, where he identifies some of the characters (in Furbank I 150).
8 Ansell is drawn upon H.O. Meredith, who too was one of the Apostles, as many commentators have found out.

9 "He worshipped his mother and she was fond of him" (29). Forster's love affair with his mother has been documented by Furbank.
10 Sheppard in his paper on "King's or Trinity?" (see Note 6) mentioned "the evident grief with which our brother Forster speaks of the cleavage and tells how serious the cleavage appears to him". He further said in his paper how "We should have been disgusted . . . by the scene [of] a room full of all manner of drink . . ." discussing the "immorality" of the Trinitarians (Furbank 105–06).
11 She told Forster in 1915, "man-to-man love—this sounds bold" (*CH* 97).
12 See Brian May 185–207.
13 Levenson says, "In the work of Forster it is possible to glimpse what the development of the novel might have been if at the turn of the century it had endured an evolutionary, rather than a revolutionary, change. Forster belongs neither with the Edwardians, Wells, Bennett and Galsworthy, nor with the lean modernists, Joyce, Woolf, Ford and Lewis" (Levenson 78–79).

Works cited

Colmer, John. *E. M. Forster: The Personal Voice*. Boston: Routledge & Kegan Paul, 1975.

Cox, C.B. *The Free Spirit: A Study of Liberal Humanism in the Novels of George Eliot, Henry James, E. M. Forster, Virginia Woolf, Angus Wilson*. Oxford: Oxford UP, 1963.

Forster, E.M. *Abinger Harvest*. 1936. Rpt. Harmondsworth: Penguin, 1967.

———. *The Longest Journey*. 1907. Rpt. Harmondsworth: Penguin, 1975.

Foucault, Michel. *The History of Sexuality I & II*. Trans. Robert Hurley, 1978. Rpt. New York: Vintage Books, 1980.

Furbank, P.N. *E. M. Forster: A Life, I & II*. Oxford: Oxford UP, 1977.

Gardner, Philip. *E. M. Forster: The Critical Heritage*. 1973. Rpt. Vikas: Delhi, 1974.

Ibsen, Henrik. *Ibsen: Plays*. Trans. with an Introduction by James Walter McFarlane. Oxford: Oxford UP, 1970.

Lago, Mario. "Introduction: Forster on E. M. Forster." *Modern Fiction Studies* 31.2–3 (Summer–Fall, 1985): 137–46.

Lamos, Colleen. "James Joyce and the English Vice." *Novel* 29.1 (Fall, 1995): 19–31.

Levenson, Michael. *Modernism and the Fate of Individuality: Character and Novelistic Form from Conrad to Woolf*. Cambridge: Cambridge UP, 1991.

Martin, Robert K., and George Piggford, eds. *Queer Forster*. Chicago: U of Chicago P, 1997.

May, Brian. "Neoliberalism in Rorty and Forster." *TCL* 39.2 (Summer, 1993): 185–207.

Richards, Bernard. "Re. of *Hellenism and Homosexuality in Victorian Oxford*, by Linda Dowling. Cornell: Cornell UP, 1994." *Essays in Criticism* XLV.ii (April, 1995): 166–72.

Williams, Raymond. *Drama from Ibsen to Brecht*. 1952. Rpt. Harmondsworth: Penguin Books, 1976.

3
REDEFINING BRITISH MASCULINITY IN *CAPTAINS COURAGEOUS*

Chetan

Kipling's American years were considerably productive, bringing him fame and wealth with the publication of the two *Jungle Books*, *Captains Courageous*, *The Seven Seas*, and *The Day's Work*. Some of his works embodied the elements of nostalgia apparent from the recapitulation of his Indian experiences in the tales compiled under *The Day's Work*, while others were popular for their exclusive thematic transition observed in the two *Jungle Books* and *Captains Courageous* categorised as children literature and fables. These works profoundly captured the themes of adventure literature instantiated with heroism, chivalry, morality, courage, competition, and rebellion. This chapter is an attempt to analyse *Captains Courageous* for its deviation from the dominant sea adventure stories of the late nineteenth century and how Kipling heeds to rapidly changing literary trends to integrate them with colonial boyhood culture. The chapter gives an insight into the methods Kipling adopted to collect information on the fishermen of Gloucester, Massachusetts. It also traces the thematic nodes which *Captains Courageous* borrows and rejects from *Treasure Island*—the most widely read nineteenth century sea adventure fiction. Besides, it focuses on the ways in which Kipling reshapes the concept of masculinity from the politics of imperialism to the reformation of young boys with idealistic traits of late Victorian culture.

Published in 1897, *Captains Courageous* is a story of a 15-year-old boy Harvey Cheyne, who takes pride in his father's wealth and fame. Harvey's father is a railroad tycoon of San Diego, California. The story begins with the fall of Harvey Cheyne from a ship in the Atlantic Ocean. He is rescued by a Portuguese fisherman named Manuel, a crew member on the boat of Disko Troop sailing for fishing from Gloucester. Ill-mannered Harvey adamantly tries to persuade Troop to take him back to the port for a reward from his father, but Troop refuses to concede and, thereby, sets an example that nothing can entice him from carrying out his professional duties. Consequently,

Harvey is bound to spend the next few months on the boat *We're Here* with Troop and other crew members. Harvey experiences several sea adventures and successfully overcomes many hurdles posed to the crew members by the sea. He learns the lesson of working in a team during adverse conditions and showing reverence to elders, and so comes to construct his own personal identity instead of simply being the son of a millionaire. He also realises that each man on the boat possesses unique qualities, proving his potential and justifying his presence on the boat. With increasing socialisation of Harvey on the boat, his belief in class hierarchy fades away and he begins to take Troop's commands unquestionably. Not only this, he becomes a good friend of Troop's son Dan and eagerly helps other crew members on the boat. By the end, when Harvey returns onshore and meets his parents in Gloucester, he has metamorphosed into a mature boy who believes in the practicality of life and is ready to shoulder his father's business.

It is difficult to not correlate *Captains Courageous* with the adventure literature that gained huge acceptance among young readers in the second half of the nineteenth century. In the 1880s, there was vigorous opposition to realist fiction for its novelistic embodiment of themes like love, marriage, romance, domesticity, families, and emotions as these did not address Britain's political and commercial mission to expand its colonial rule across the globe. On the one hand, the British Empire was at its peak with colonies in nearly every continent.[1] On the other hand, the country faced tough challenges from its rivals which diverted public attention from peaceful living to national interests. These themes were not captured by the authors of realist fiction except for a few references to colonies, natives, soldiers, and immigrants.

Hence, adventure literature gained huge popularity in Britain during the second half of the nineteenth century against the backdrop of the government's political, social, and imperial initiatives that prompted authors to incorporate them in their fictional narratives. With the opening of new schools and increase in the enrolment of children, there was an upsurge in demand of reading material. These schools and educational institutions became apparatuses to disseminate imperial and masculine ideologies. British writers such as R.M. Ballantyne, R.L. Stevenson, Jules Vernes, H. Rider Haggard, and G.A. Henty linked imperial ideals with masculinity: this fusion became one of the bedrocks of adventure literature and came to be endorsed widely by authors in the nineteenth century. The literary discourse between Andrew Lang and R.L. Stevenson highlighted an intense increase in the publication of adventure fiction. In the essay "Realism and Romance", Lang argued, "civilized people still long for adventure—not for nothing did nature leave us all savages under our white skins; she has wrought thus that we might have many delights, among others—the joy of adventurous living" (Lang 689). Stevenson also mentioned in his essay "A Humble Remonstrance" (1884) that "adventure appeals to certain almost sensual and quite illogical tendencies in man" (Stevenson 70). George Salmon justified the flourishing of adventure fiction on the ground that England could not provide fields of actions and therefore "Englishmen sought to gratify mentally a passion for romance which it was yearly becoming more difficult to gratify physically" (Salmon 248).

British adventure literature received a huge thrust from the country's overseas military expeditions launched to protect its colonial occupations and to safeguard its commercial interests. These military expeditions were demonstrations to prove Britain's military and naval strength. In the last quarter of the nineteenth century, the country fought several overseas wars such as the Zulu War (1879), the First Boer War (1880), the Mahdi Revolt in Sudan (1881), the British invasion of Egypt (1882), and the death of General Gordon (1885). These wars acted as catalysts for writers to encapsulate them in their literary output. For instance, Kipling fictionalised Britain's military expedition in Sudan in his novel *The Light that Failed*; several of his stories were also inspired from barracks in India. Alfred George Henty presented his protagonists in many of his novels as warriors fighting for the freedom of captured military officers. As in the case of *The Dash for Khartoum*, Henty worked to narrate Britain's attempt to reclaim the city of Khartoum from the Mahdist rebels.

This upsurge in adventure fiction was not solely driven by global engagements of Britain in the battlefield. There were other reasons too which bolstered the popularity of adventure books among readers. Among these reasons, the Education Act 1870 played a very critical role since the country's literacy rate jumped substantially in the last decades of the nineteenth century. In 1841, around 51 per cent women and 67 per cent men possessed reading skills. Over the next three decades, this rose to 73 per cent women and 80 per cent men (Altick 171). With increase in the literacy rate, demand for different kinds of reading material spiralled: weekly and monthly periodicals for adolescent boys and girls surged, newspapers and illustrated journals were widely read, and adventure novels witnessed unprecedented publication. In the year 1874, 644 new adult novels were available in the market, and this figure increased more than double to 1,315 over the next 20 years (1894) (Keating 32).

It is noteworthy that *Captains Courageous* does not touch upon the theme of colonial war nor is it a story of treasure hunting on an isolated island. It offers instead multiple interpretations ranging from bildungsroman narrative to conquest of inner frailties. Philip Mallet collated *Captains Courageous* in "The Naulakha Years" to suggest that the book showed Kipling's admiration for America, which provided him new material for his stories. It was also a kind of tribute to Kipling's interest in sea life. Martin Seymour Smith wrote in *Rudyard Kipling: The Controversial New Biography* that the book served as distraction after the quarrel between Betty and Carrie and it harkened to Dr Conland's memories of the fishing fleet in the 1860s. In his autobiography *Something of Myself*, Kipling too acknowledged his personal interest in framing a story around the lives of Gloucester fishermen and his desire to capture the beauty of the localised American atmosphere.

Along with these interpretations, it is worthwhile to explore Kipling's impulsive quest to gather research material for the story and how he planned its composition. Kipling invested a substantial amount of time and labour to know about the lives of Gloucester fishermen and to clear apprehensions about the book among his friends, publisher, and other writers. While working on the manuscript of *Captains Courageous*, he wrote several letters for either collecting information about the places mentioned in the story or to assure those people who were seemingly affected by the book directly. Among these letters, one was written to William Hallett Phillips on 18 February 1896 in which he requested for charts of the Newfoundland fishing banks and a book shedding light on cod fisheries. On receiving the charts, Kipling responded with exuberance and sent Hallett a copy of *The Jungle Book*:

> When they brought in a roll five feet long from the post office, looked like a gun almost but it was a chart of the Grand Banks and I shouted with joy. In the meantime, I send you a mean jungle book.
> (Pinney 231)

Kipling persistently searched for more information about Gloucester and different routes connecting it with San Diego. He wrote another letter to Fredrick Norton Finney on 2 March 1896 asking, "What would be about the shortest time in which the distance would be covered? Which are the best types of racing locos? And what type of frame and bogie are used under luxurious private cars?" (Pinney 232). One more letter was written to the novelist and story writer Elizabeth Stuart Phelps Ward on 19 May 1896 in which Kipling tried to explain that his story was primarily concerned with the Gloucester fishermen and their lives:

> I have never gone outside purely a fisherman's view of it . . . the scope of my story is very limited at the best—and it seems to me that your husband will have nothing whatever to change his course for.
> (Pinney 242)

With this letter, Kipling tried to clear confusions and doubts that might have arisen in the mind of Elizabeth's husband Herbert Dickinson Ward regarding the impact of *Captains Courageous* on his stories and writings. Besides, Kipling wrote letters to Frank N. Doubleday, William James, James N. Conland, and Charles Eliot Norton wherein he brought the topic of *Captains Courageous* for a host of reasons, including deliberations with the publisher, the American publication industry, and the printing of the book.

Although these letters highlight Kipling's intention to compose a sea adventure with specific reference to Gloucester fishermen, many critics have drawn a chord of similarity between R.L. Stevenson's *Treasure Island* and *Captains Courageous* on the ground that the boy protagonists in both the stories experience transformation in their attitudes towards life and society. Despite persistently reminding oneself not to stretch any coordinated point between the two books, the reader consciously places *Captains Courageous* within the analytical frame of *Treasure Island* because the scaffolding of both the texts was constructed on masculinity and their classification as adventure fiction.

Published from 1881 to 1882, *Treasure Island* is a sea adventure of a boy named Jim Hawkins who goes in search of a treasure hidden on a distant island. Hawkins comes to know about this treasure when he opens Billy Bones's sea chest which contains a map of the island where Captain Flint is believed to have hidden the treasure. The voyage begins when Hawkins shows the map to Dr Livesey and John Trelawney, who build a team of sailors to go with them in search of the treasure. Hawkins also joins them as a cabin boy. In this expedition, Hawkins experiences the most exciting adventures of his life, ranging from escaping death and exceptional display of his skills to returning with the treasure—a reward for skilfully overcoming challenges. Since the story embodies the trait of courage and bravery, *Treasure Island* is said to have echoes of medieval romance wherein a knight goes on a journey, overcomes challenges, defies his death, and returns victorious.

In the nineteenth century, intrepidity, fearlessness, and fortitude were associated with manliness and masculinity on which imperialism and colonialism were fundamentally erected. Wilderness, savagery, un-civility, and backwardness were the attributes of non-Western cultures which remained far from Euro-centric civilisational standards. Hawkins's voyage to the island can be easily paralleled with colonial expeditions of Britain in the African and Asian continents. Although Hawkins undertook the voyage to make his fortune by searching for the hidden treasure, he exploited the situation to prove his supremacy and masculinity. He learned how to face challenges and resolve problems:

> The scheme had an air of adventure that inspired me, and the thought of the water-breaker beside the fore companion doubled my growing courage.
>
> (Stevenson 200)

Although the journey to the island was a physical movement from one place to another, it was also a kind of psychological pathway that led Hawkins towards maturity, instilled confidence, and made him undertake responsibilities. This maturity, as Stevenson suggests in the novel, had multiple dimensions, each apparent from how Hawkins responds to the demands of the situation. For instance, Hawkins's manliness was not confined to physical dangers he placed himself in: rather, it was his comprehension of complicated British social structures. While Hawkins was born in a lower-class family, he quickly understood that Dr Livesey did not belong to his class. Throughout his journey, he remained conscious of his class and economic position. Hence, Stevenson consciously charted out a sea adventure replete with entertainment, physical violence, and dangers of venturing from the motherland, all of which led to the growth of the protagonist.

In contrast, Kipling reformed the frame of manliness and masculinity to adapt it to the demands of *Captains Courageous* by presenting not just a sea adventure but also an inward journey: Harvey finds his own individual identity rather than simply embracing his familial one. The novel reformulates the concepts of manliness and masculinity to highlight the importance of cooperation, friendliness, homogenisation, professionalism, learning of survival skills, accepting challenges, discarding social hierarchy in work, giving primacy to experience, and shedding egoism. Kipling consciously planned out the metamorphosis of Harvey from a spoiled and pampered boy to a crew member who eschewed self-abandonment and socialisation with people irrespective of their social standing. When Manuel saved Harvey and took him on board, he was intoxicated with the powerful financial status of his father. Harvey directed Troop and his colleagues to turn the boat to New York and earn rewards for saving his life. When he plunged his hand into the pocket and found nothing in it, he accused Troop of stealing his "ten dollars":

> Harvey dived into his pocket for the wad of bills. All he brought up was a soggy packet of cigarettes. "Not lawful currency, and bad for the lungs. Heave 'em overboard, young feller, and try again." "It's been stolen!" cried Harvey, hotly . . . A curious change flitted across old Troop's hard face. "What might you have been doin at your time o life with one hundred an thirty-four dollars, young feller?" "It was part of my pocket-money for a month." This Harvey thought would be knock-down blow, and it was indirectly.
>
> (Kipling 9)

He not only accused Troop for stealing money from his pocket but also looked down upon the fishermen as poor and uncivil people who looked for opportunities to supplement their purse with stolen wealth. Kipling goes on to undercut Harvey's egoism in his family heritage and the reputation of his father. On the boat, Harvey tried to influence crew members with his father's corporate power and wealth but soon realised that his father was unknown to them. This incident made him realise that an individual's success comes only through hard labour. Each fisherman got space on the schooner owing to his peculiar skills and willingness to perform hard labour. Troop also explained to Harvey that all the crew members shared space on the boat because of their exclusive skills.

Besides, Kipling seemed to have emphasised the exploration of the inner treasure instead of valuable gems and sapphires on an isolated island. This sea adventure has nothing to do with conquest of new lands and political control of natives. It is a journey to overcome frailties in Harvey, an attempt to discover oneself by staying with people of the lower class. Harvey's journey on the boat enables him to search for elemental, innate traits lying uncovered within him. These traits were crucial to become a gentleman. With the fishermen, Harvey understood that work ought not to be associated with class. Initially, after his rescue, Harvey refused to do any work on the boat and insisted to be taken back to New York:

> "Do you mean I'm to clean pots and pans and things?" said Harvey
> "An' other things. You've no call to shout, young feller."
> "I won't! My father will give you enough to buy this dirty little fish-kettle"—Harvey stamped on the deck ten times over, "if you take me to New York safe; and you're hundred and thirty by me, anyhow."
> "Ha-ow?" said Troop, the iron face darkening.
> "How? You know how, well enough. On top of that, you want me to do menial work"—Harvey was very proud of that adjective—"till the Fall. I tell you I will not. You hear?"
>
> (Kipling 10–11)

With his prolonged stay and personal experience of the relationship among the crew members, Harvey began to show interest in all kinds of works allocated to him. He became self-confident and got immense satisfaction in finishing allotted tasks. He felt proud of proving his utility on the boat and meeting the expectations of fellow shipmates:

> At the end of an hour, Harvey would have given the world to rest; for fresh wet cod weigh more than you would think and his back ached with the steady pitching. But he felt for the first time in his life that he was one of a working gang of men, took pride in the thought and held on sullenly.
>
> (Kipling 27)

In this fashion, Harvey comes to realise that expertise and skills separate a professional from an amateur. He begins appreciating his crew members' individual and specialised skills, forming thus a professional identity which appears as "a unified image on nearly all fronts—moral, aesthetic, intellectual and so forth" (Moss 115). His withdrawal from the pampered world of upper-class life to the life of struggle and hard labour taught him the merits of socialisation. His fall was the beginning of a heroic journey that orientated him towards introspection and allowed for rectification of his innate weaknesses.

Furthermore, Kipling seemed to have underscored in this novel the long history of the American and English fishing industry in Newfoundland and the Grand Banks, which were the bone of contention between France and England in the eighteenth century.[2] The domination of English fisheries at the Grand Banks increased substantially between 1765 and 1775 when "more than 200 bankers a year sailed from west country ports in England to fish the Grand Banks. During this period the 'bye-boat' keepers flourished and reached their greatest importance in the fishery" (Lear 50). The next hundred years were full of turbulence and persistent conflict for control of the area. Besides, the fishing industry recorded ups and downs in both production and value after the American Revolution. As history records show, the number of fishing vessels surged exponentially after the American Revolution: while this caused an overall rise in fish production, it also plunged market value amidst low demand.

Although Kipling avoided directly discussing the political and financial contours of the American fishing industry, he expresses his admiration for its initiative and intrepidity. Modernisation in techniques saw new kind of dories replace old boats, handlines become redundant, and the introduction of line trawls and gill nets. The steady growth of the fishing industry in and around Gloucester made this hitherto small, non-descript town a hub for exporting cod fish across the Atlantic. Kipling's fascination with this transformation may be gauged below:

> This Gloucester was a new town in a new land and he (Harvey's father) proposed to "take it in" as of old he had taken in all cities from Snohomish to San Diego of that world whence he hailed. They made money along the crooked street which was half wharf and half ship's store; as a leading professional he wished to learn how the noble game was played. Men said that four out of every five fish balls served at New England's Sunday breakfast came from Gloucester and overwhelmed him with figures in proof—statistics of boats, gear, wharf-frontage, capital invested, salting, packing, factories, insurance, wages, repairs and profits.
>
> (Kipling 145)

These lines indicate the economic potential of Gloucester and how the fishing industry turned out to be an employment generator for a large number of people. Cod fish served to people in New England and other parts of the world came from Gloucester and the Grand Banks. Moreover, business tycoons who took in prominent cities eyed Gloucester as a big opportunity to expand their operations. This transformation came, however, only with the many sacrifices made by the local men and women of Gloucester. Some women lost their husbands, while others sacrificed their sons in the yearly harvest. Besides, unlike other American cities Gloucester still did not have an industrial and modern infrastructure:

> Then up and spoke the orator of the occasion, another pillar of the municipality, bidding the world to Gloucester and incidentally pointing out wherein Gloucester excelled the rest of the world. Then he turned to the sea wealth of the city and spoke of the price that must be paid for the yearly harvest. They would hear later the names of their lost dead—one hundred and seventeen of them. Gloucester could not boast any overwhelming mills or factories. Her sons worked for such wages as the sea gave; and they all knew that neither Georges nor the Banks were cow-pastures.
>
> (Kipling 158)

Hence, going beyond the traditional ambit of the colonial sea adventure, *Captains Courageous* modifies set notions of masculinity, labour, and initiative so as to set equilibrium between the political and the personal. Kipling's extensive research on the lives of Gloucester fishermen was intended to supplement the novel with realistic elements. Kipling attempted to interpolate fiction with accurate details that rendered Harvey's journey with the fishermen a learning experience for the readers—and not just an entertaining adventure story.

Notes

1 John Bartholomew, a nineteenth-century Scottish cartographer, captured the immensity of the British Empire in *Atlas of the British Empire Throughout the World*, published in 1877. He compartmentalised the British possession of land under several heads: British Isles, India, Ceylon, Australia, New Zealand, Cape Colony, Natal, Transvaal, Canada, and minor possessions in Africa, Asia, and Europe. As per the book, British dominion was spread over an area of approximately 8,754,793 sq. miles and had control over nearly 284,110,693 people by 1877, making it the world's biggest empire.
2 The conflict between England and France for domination on the Grand Banks can be traced back in history to the Treaty of Utrecht (1713), which ended the long war between the two nations and placed Newfoundland in a new situation. After this treaty, the French government surrendered its colonial territory to England.

Works cited

Altick, Richard D. *The English Common Reader: A Social History of the Mass Reading Public, 1800–1900*. Chicago: U of Chicago P, 1957.

Belk, Patrick Scott. *Empires of Print: Adventure Fiction in the Magazines, 1899–1919*. New York: Routledge, 2017.

Berrong, Richard M. "*Captains Courageous* and Impressionism." *The Kipling Journal* 88.354 (2014): 25–39.
Ferrall, Charles, and Anna Jackson. *Juvenile Literature and British Society 1850–1950: The Age of Adolescence*. New York: Routledge, 2010.
Jensen, Albert C. *A Brief History of the New England Offshore Fisheries*. Washington: Fishery Leaflet 594, 1967.
Karlin, Danny. "*Captains Courageous* and American Empire." *The Kipling Journal* 63.251 (1989): 11–21.
Keating, Peter. *The Haunted Study: A Social History of the English Novel, 1875–1914*. Cambridge: Cambridge UP, 1989.
Kestner, Joseph A. *Masculinities in British Adventure Fiction, 1800–1915*. Surrey: Ashgate, 2010.
Kipling, Rudyard. *Captains Courageous*. New York: Amereon House, 1896.
Lang, Andrew. "Realism and Romance." *Contemporary Review* 52 (1887): 683–93.
Lear, W.H. "History of Fisheries in the Northwest Atlantic: The 500 Years Perspective." *Journal of Northwest Atlantic Fishery Science* 23 (1998): 41–73.
Moss, Robert F. *Rudyard Kipling and the Fiction of Adolescence*. London: MacMillan, 1982.
Pinney, Thomas, ed. *The Letters of Rudyard Kipling Vol. 2 1890–99*. New York: Palgrave MacMillan, 2004.
Salmon, George. "What Boys Read." *Fortnightly Review* 39.230 (1886): 248–59.
Stevenson, Robert Louis. "A Humble Remonstrance." *Selected Poetry and Prose*. Ed. Bradford A. Booth. Boston: Houghton Mifflin, 1968. 66–75.
———. *Treasure Island*, 1883. New York: Harper and Brothers, 1915.

4

READING POETRY THROUGH TRANSLATION

A brief note on a Hindi translation of Shakespeare's Sonnets

Rajiva Verma

As the title of this chapter suggests, its primary focus is not on the Sonnets themselves but on the process of reading poetry through translation, using the Sonnets as an illustration. Having said that, one must also acknowledge that it is not really possible to use Shakespeare only as an example to illustrate a point, for in such a case the illustration as vehicle can quite overwhelm the pedagogic or theoretical tenor, though no one surely will mind if this happens. I would also like to emphasise that I am concerned with the reading of poetry *through* translation rather than *in* translation. The reason for this is not some sort of professional decorum that lays down the rule that reading or teaching Shakespeare *in* translation should properly be the business of departments other than English, though this position can be justified strictly on intellectual grounds and not be seen merely in terms of territorial disputes among university departments. One can readily admit that where the language in which a text is written is not known, it is better to read a translation of it than not to read it at all, even though much is lost in translation, the loss being greater perhaps in the case of Shakespeare than any other comparable writer. Fortunately, a situation where Shakespeare has to be read or taught solely in an Indian language because English is not known at all is rather rare. It is far more common to find people who are bilingual, though with far greater facility in their own language than in English. It is in this situation of bilingualism that the reading of Shakespeare or any other English writer *through* rather than *in* translation becomes something much more than making the best of a bad job. Indeed, reading through translation can be not only enabling but vastly enriching in many ways, as I hope to show.

Before discussing the Sonnets in translation, let me share an anecdote with you. Many years ago, a skit was produced in St Stephen's College, Delhi as part of the founder's day celebrations. It was designed as a free adaptation in Punjabi of parts of *Romeo and Juliet*, particularly the quarrel in the first scene. As expected, the audience found the very idea of Shakespeare in Punjabi funny, though the scene in the original play was not really meant to be comic, though some laughter could have been expected during its performance in the Elizabethan theatre. At one point, there were loud guffaws when one of the characters addressed another as *khote da puttar* ("the son of an ass"). Now the last laugh here was on the sophisticated audience in the college hall, for *khote da puttar* is not at all a bad rendering of the usual Shakespearean equivalent of such an expression, "whoreson" (though the word is not actually used in *Romeo and Juliet*)—and I am not at all sure that this audience would have found that expression funny per se. A more accurate, but equally idiomatic, equivalent of "whoreson" could have been *randi da puttar* or *randi da chhora*, and I think one could make an easy guess that these expressions would have made the audience laugh even louder. There was of course an element of superiority in this laughter, arising from a sense of the absurdity of the very idea of Shakespeare in Punjabi. A less sophisticated audience, one which did not know the original play or the English language, would also, in all probability, have laughed at the expression. But in their case the laughter would not have been the laughter of superiority but simply the expression of delight that humanity at large takes in the use of such vigorous and earthly expressions—a delight arising from the sense of release from social inhibitions that the use of such expressions entails. Such is the delight that the Elizabethan audience would have got from the exchange of abuses between Hal and Falstaff in *I Henry IV* (2.5.208–229).[1] Thus, in a way, the putative response of the unsophisticated audience, totally unaware of the Shakespearean original of *Romeo and Juliet*, would be more authentic and accurate.

Looking back over the episode, I wonder if what really happened was that the audience in the college hall, sophisticated and ostensibly inward with the English language, had yet only rather shadowy, abstract notions of the words in that language and missed the subtler linguistic and cultural nuances. The only time they realised the full force of the words in the Shakespearean original was on this occasion, through the translated version, and they found the experience strange and funny. That need not of course be the inevitable response. A remarkable example of what translation can do to bring to us the full force of the original passage, indeed even to intensify it, is Harivansh Rai Bachchan's translation of Iago's speech about the old black ram tupping the white ewe as *tumhari ujli kaniya bachchiya par, kala mota sandh charha hai* ("a big black bull has mounted your pure white heifer"). The conclusion to be drawn from this episode is that while we are all bilingual, English is, for most of us, at best a second language—at least as far as the language of creativity is concerned. We may be more at ease with it in our intellectual discourse, but where discrimination of little and subtle nuances of words is required, we are more at home with our own languages. This is naturally even more strongly the case where, as in poetry, we are concerned not only with shades of meaning behind the words but also with their sound and rhythmic values. Therefore, the reading of the original text along with a translation of it may help us experience its resonances in a way that may not be possible if we read only the original text.

Shakespeare's Sonnets seem to be the obvious choice to illustrate the foregoing argument because they are unmatched in any comparable body of English poetry for variety and subtlety of language. Indeed, it is probably the case that it was the example of the Sonnets rather than the poetry of John Donne that set in motion the method of close reading associated with I.A. Richards and William Empson and, later, with the American New Criticism. Empson, I believe, embarked on his study of ambiguity in poetry after reading an analysis of one of the sonnets by Robert Graves and Laura Riding, and the analyses of lines from various sonnets in *Seven Types of Ambiguity* and in *Some Versions of Pastoral* are among the highpoints of those books.

The method of reading that I suggest would naturally be more effective if there were more than one translation to be read in juxtaposition with the original. Unfortunately, there is, as far as I know, only one translation of the complete sonnets in Hindi, namely *Shakespeare ke Sonnet* by Rajendra Dwivedi, published by Atma Ram and Sons in 1958 with a preface by Bachchan which contains some lukewarm praise. Dwivedi, who had master's degrees in English and Sanskrit, is extremely modest about his work, agreeing that like a fool he has rushed in where angels fear to tread ("देवदूत सकुचाते वहाँ झपटते मूर्ख सगर्व") but nevertheless hoping that his translation will pave the way for better ones in the future. It must also be stated that though his choice of the kind of Hindi to be used for the translation is not quite consonant with the kind of language that Shakespeare uses, or, for that matter, with any kind of actual spoken Hindi, he is a good scholar of Shakespeare and is familiar with the latest English criticism of the time on the subject of the Sonnets and acutely conscious of the subtleties and nuances of the language of the original.

Dwivedi's translation of sonnet 116 may be a good point to begin a discussion of his translation of the Sonnets, especially as an Urdu version of the same sonnet translated by A.C. Bahar is also in existence. Bahar's translation was published in 1960 and is as follows.

हमारा ये अकीदा है जहाँ सच्ची मोहब्बत हो
वहाँ कोई रुकावट दो दिलों में आ नहीं सकती
मोहब्बत वो नहीं है जो बदल जाए बदलने पर
खिज़ॉं में भी मोहब्बत की कली मुरझा नहीं सकती

मोहब्बत है किसी मज़बूत से मीनार की सूरत
जिसे तूफ़ान टक्कर मारकर लरज़ा नहीं सकते

मोहब्बत है वो इक ऊँचा सितारा जिसकी रफ़त की
हमें हो कुछ ख़बर लेकिन हक़ीक़त पा नहीं सकते

गुलाबी होंठ और गालों की रौनाई नहीं रहती
हँसी चेहरे नहीं रहते वलाराई नहीं रहती
मोहब्बत वक़्त की रफ़्तार से आज़ाद है लेकिन
मोहब्बत पर क़ज़ा की कारफ़रमाई नहीं रहती

मोहब्बत के सिवा दुनिया की हर चीज़ फ़ानी है
ये एक ऐसी हक़ीक़त है जो हर आकिल ने मानी है[2]

When we come to Dwivedi's translation, which was published two years earlier, in 1958, it is hard to believe that he has translated the same poem.

सच्चे मनों के मिलन में मानूँ नगण्य संचार
बाधाओं का ! प्यार नहीं कहला सकता वह प्यार
जो परिवर्तन पाकर परिवर्तित हो जाता साथ,
या झुकता अपहित होने को अपहारक के हाथ:

अरे, नहीं; सर्वदा अडिग वह एक बिंदु की माप,
जो निहारता तूफ़ानों को, कभी न हिलता आप,
प्रति पथभ्रष्ट नाव हित वह ध्रुवतारे के अनुरूप
अविदित जिसका मूल्य, यद्यपि ऊँचाई माप्य अनूप।

वह न काल किंकर है यद्यपि गुलाबी अधर-कपोल
कवलित होते उसके कुटिल पाश में पड़ अनमोल;
प्यार न निज लघु-घड़ियों-हफ़्तों में बदलता स्वरूप,
बल्कि प्रलय के दिन तक अडिग रखा करता निज रूप।

यदि यह बात गलत औ' मुझ पर हो जाए यह सिद्ध
मैं कदापि हूँ कवि न, न कोई व्यक्ति प्रेम-अनुविद्ध।

It must be admitted that both versions manage to give a feel of the Shakespearean form with three quatrains and a couplet, though the rhyme schemes are different. The second version is actually in couplets but by avoiding end stops and arranging the sense and syntax in units of four lines it does manage to give an approximation to the Shakespearean quatrains. Still one wonders why Dwivedi chose the couplet form at all when he had before him the example of a poet like Trilochan, who wrote more than 500 original sonnets in Hindi using both the Shakespearean and the Petrarchan form. The only explanation that Dwivedi gives is that the sonnet form had not yet found its roots in Hindi and that he chose a sonnet form of seven couplets that is neither Petrarchan nor Shakespearean but a 14-line poem nevertheless. He could also have pointed out the division into quatrains that I have just referred to, and to the fact that one of the original sonnets (Number 126) is also in rhyming couplets and has only 12 lines. In Bahar's version there are some faint echoes of the *ghazal* form as in the unrhymed third line of each quatrain, but the quatrain form is firmly established through the change of rhymes after every four lines. Both versions end with a couplet in the manner of the Shakespearean sonnet.

With regard to language, the first version is clearly closer to the original than the latter. Shakespeare's syntax can occasionally be tortuous, and many of his words may have been newly introduced into the language during his time and may have therefore sounded a bit strange, but his language, whether in the plays or the Sonnets, rarely strays from the rhythms of the spoken language. In contrast, Dwivedi's language in its diction as well as syntax is remote from any kind of spoken Hindi. Even native speakers of the language will have to struggle a bit to get the bare sense of the first line and a half and will find the syntax of the last two lines quite odd, especially the inversion in the clause "मैं कदापि हूँ कवि न". On the other hand, even students with a limited knowledge of English are likely to find the original of the first one and a half lines easier to understand, though they may have to look up the meaning of "impediments". Also, though there is an inversion of the "standard" English syntax here (which should of course be "let me not bring impediments to the marriage of true minds"), it is of a kind that is so common even in spoken language as to be almost unnoticeable. It is certainly not of the "मैं कदापि हूँ कवि न" type. Thus, we have here a rather interesting case of reading a text in translation where the student is not likely to make sense of the translated text without referring to the original. They will have to read the sonnet *through* translation and not merely *in* translation.

While the syntax and diction of the first version is closer in many ways to the language of the original sonnet, the same cannot be said when we consider the two versions with respect to figurative language. The first poem does not even try to tackle the metaphoric richness of the original poem but reduces it to a didactic poem in relatively bald language. Though it begins, like the original, with the first-person pronoun, it has nothing of its dramatic quality. Nor does it try to translate many of the crucial metaphors of the original. To take up the opening lines, for example, leaving aside for the moment the legal and religious associations of the words "impediments" and "admit" (whose echoing of the marriage service in the Church of England is missed by both versions), there is a vast difference between the *tone* of "let me not" (that is, "may I never admit", or "may I never be compelled or forced to admit") and the confident assertion of "हमारा ये अकीदा है". Moreover, the last line of the quatrain introduces the image of the flower which is not there in the original and which would have been more appropriate in the third quatrain. The second quatrain is a reasonable rendering of the original, though it misses out the image of the polestar, with reference to which sailors who have lost their way can get their true bearings. In the third quatrain, however, the loss of the metaphorical richness of the original is most conspicuous: gone is the image of Time as Reaper reaping a crop of rosy lips and cheeks with his sickle, or of idea of Time's Fool, or the reference to Doomsday. Similarly, the concluding couplet misses out altogether the persona of the speaker as poet. On the whole, I think it can be fairly said that Bahar's translation is a commendable effort with an easy and natural flow of verses, but it turns the original into a straightforward didactic poem with little of the dramatic quality or metaphoric richness of the original. The reader trying to understand the original with the help of this translation will get its broad paraphrasable content but not the complexities and metaphoric density.

In contrast, Dwivedi's translation retains most of the images of the original. The translation of "Time's Fool" as कालकिंकर is interesting and the reference to Doomsday is retained in the broadly analogous प्रलय. The bent sickle is hinted at in the phrase कुटिलपाश, though it is difficult to imagine what a bent or crooked पाश could be and the word अनमोल seems to be there only for the rhyme.[3] Still, but for its "poetic" language, the translation is a reasonably accurate version of the original.

One of the major difficulties of translating Shakespeare is that his imagination is so fertile and his associative faculty so quick and dynamic that even the native speaker of the language is often left lagging behind and missing out many elements of his rapidly shifting and often submerged imagery. This is illustrated very well by the following passage from *Antony and Cleopatra*:

> The hearts
> That spanieled me at heels, to whom I gave
> Their wishes, do discandy, melt their sweets
> On blossoming Caesar, and this pine is barked
> That overtopped them all.
> (4.13. 20–24)

The passage is of course an instance of the famous and much-discussed Shakespearean dog-sweets-saliva-flattery image cluster, where any one element in the cluster recalls all the other elements. Inconstant followers flatter you like dogs that lick your feet begging for food; the flattery is like the dogs' saliva, which in turn is likened to the melting of a candy and the resulting yucky gluey substance whose sickening sweetness is in turn associated with the sweet-smelling blossoms on a tree or plant representing Octavius, which then brings in, through contrast, the tall but bare pine tree whose trunk has been stripped bare (barked). It is interesting that the dog is still present in this last image through a pun on the word "barked", though this is probably of greater psychological than aesthetic significance.

In the passage just cited, a whole cluster of images is ushered in through a noun used as a verb ("spanieled"). Shakespeare often achieves similar effects through the use of a single verb. For example, one may examine the use of the word "fled" in the following passage from sonnet 71:

No longer mourn for me when I am dead
Than you shall hear the surly sullen bell
Give warning to the world that I am fled
From this vile world with vilest worms to dwell.

Dwivedi translates this quatrain as follows:

मेरे मरने पर मेरे हित करना बहुत न शोक
बस तब तक जब घोर कठोर घंटियाँ बजें अरोक
चेताती जग को मैं पामर जग से गया सिधार
पमारतम कीड़ों के साथ-साथ रहना निरधार

सिधार is not the same as "fled". It just means departed and is usually used to denote death, whereas "fled" connotes fleeing, as of a captive from prison. The word brings in an analogy between dying and fleeing from a prison, but in an interesting sardonic twist the fleeing from prison no longer brings the metaphysical comfort of the soul released from the bondage of the body. It is more akin to Hamlet's apprehensions about the dreams that may come in the sleep of death (3.1.58–70), or the "cold obstruction" and the rotting of the body that Claudio fears in *Measure for Measure* (3.1.118–132). In further elaboration of the analogy, the tolling of the sexton's bell during the speaker's burial is equated with the tolling of a prison bell to warn the world of a prisoner's escape, though it is not an escape to freedom but only to the even more constricted dwelling-house of the grave. There is also the injunction to the lover to mourn for the speaker only till the end of the burial ceremony, for that (by implication) is the way of the world. The word "सिधार" conveys hardly anything of this complex of thoughts and feelings that the word "fled" brings in. Words like "पलायन" or even "भागना" would have been closer to the meaning of the original.

There are numerous other instances where Shakespeare uses a verb or noun ostensibly in a straightforward literal sense while simultaneously exploiting its metaphorical resonances to enrich the texture of the verse. Take the words "plea" and "action" in sonnet 65, for example: "How with this rage shall beauty hold a plea/Whose action is no stronger than a flower?" It is well known that Shakespeare's language bristles with oblique and direct references to the law courts, and these words, while they can be taken non-metaphorically, are also metaphors derived from the legal terminology of suits (action) and pleading (plea). Dwivedi translates these two lines as: "इस प्रहार के आगे क्या टिक सकता है सौंदर्य,/ शिरिष सुमन से अधिक शक्त जिसका न रूप लावण्य?" As one would expect, Dwivedi's translation misses the legal metaphor and the word प्रहार would have been more appropriate in the second quatrain with its images of siege and battery (and of the "द्वारलौहमय" in the translation). He is more successful in translating those sonnets where metaphors derived from the world of law or business are more explicit and sustained (as in sonnets 45, 87, and 134, which he himself has cited in his preface, p. 31). It is interesting to note, though, that in the translation of Sonnet 46, he uses the term "जूरी–मंडल", which represents a departure from his usual highly Sanskritised diction.

Shakespeare's fondness for wordplay is another great challenge for the translator. Dwivedi admits that translating puns from one language to another is impossible and that he has therefore focused on translating the primary sense only, though in a few places he feels he has succeeded. He cites, as an example, the following lines from Sonnet 145:

> Those lips that Love's own hand did make
> Breathed forth that sound that said "I hate"
>
> "I hate" from hate away she threw,
> And saved my life, saying "not you".

Dwivedi translates these lines as follows:

> वे मधुर अधर, रचा था जिन्हें प्यार ने स्वयं संवार,
> " करूँ मैं घृणा" किए जा रहे इस ध्वनि का उद्गार,
>
> "करूँ मैं घृणा" में "घृणा" कह आगे विराम को छोड़,
> बचा दिया यह मेरा जीवन आगे—"तुम्हें न"जोड़।

His claim that he has managed to convey the wordplay of the original is not unjustified, even though he has missed the main pun in the poem, namely the play on the name of Anne Hathaway in this slight and playful and anomalous piece in octosyllabic lines. There is a more significant "miss" in the translation of Sonnet 138, where the pun on "lie" in the concluding couplet—"Therefore I lie with her, and she with me, /And in our faults by lies we flattered be"—does not get conveyed in the translation: "अतः झूठ कहता मैं उससे, वह मुझसे चुपचाप,/ मिथ्या कह अपने दोषों में हम सुख पाते आप।". The translation of this sonnet on the whole reads well, but there were limits to what it could achieve.

While the linguistic complexities of the Sonnets present a formidable challenge to the translator, cultural differences present an equal if not greater challenge. Dwivedi follows a pragmatic policy with regard to these. For example, he retains mythological allusions with their Western names in some cases but gives Indian equivalents in others. Thus, the names of Helen and Adonis and Phoenix are retained, as is that of Diana, but as डायना-कुमारी. On the other hand, "Philomel" is translated as कोकिल, "April" as मधु-ऋतु or वैशाख, "summer" as वसंत and "rose", occasionally, as कमल, and "Muse" as गिरे. This last term appears in the translation of Sonnet 101, where "O truant Muse" has been rendered as "अरे, प्रमादी गिरे". But the translation of this sonnet is important for another reason, for it weaves into it an allusion as well as the actual words from

Kalidasa's *Sakuntala* (Act 1) in the lines: "मधुराकृति मंडन चाहे न, बनेगी तो क्या मूक?" When one considers the fact that the idea of the relation between truth and beauty that the sonnet turns on goes back to Platonic thought, we have here a confluence of at least four minds: Plato, Kalidasa, Shakespeare, and Dwivedi. The translator cites several other parallels between Indian poetry, particularly Sanskrit poetry, and the Sonnets that establish a poetic affinity between the two traditions and add to the effectiveness of the translation. Most of these are either descriptions of beauty or expressions of the sorrows of separation. Some of these that Dwivedi cites in his preface are as follows:

विद्रुम के आगे हैं उसके अधर लालिमा-हीन
Coral is far more red than her lips' red
(sonnet 130, line 2)

निठुर शीत सा कितना दारुण यह था विरहअपार
पर तुम दूर, कीर-पिक कलरव अरे मूक लाचार

How like a winter hath my absence been
And thou away, the very birds are mute
(sonnet 97, lines 1, 12)

तदपि न मोहक राग खगों के और न मधुर सुगंध
मुझसे कहला सके न वे कुछ भी वसंत के गीत

Yet nor the lays of birds, nor the sweet smell. . .
Could make me any summer's story tell
(sonnet 98, lines 5, 7)

In many of these instances Dwivedi does seem to have succeeded in transforming Shakespeare's language into the idiom of Sanskrit/Hindi poetry. There are several other instances of Dwivedi's success as a translator. One of these is his rendering of Sonnet 20, especially its concluding lines:

ललनाओं के सुख हित तुमको उसने चुना, सुयोग,
मुझे प्यार दो निज, उनकी निधि हो उसका उपयोग।

While the pun on "pricked" is missing and was probably impossible to translate, the word "ललनाओं" is wonderfully felicitous. The translation of the sonnet beginning "They that have pow'r to hurt, and will do none" (sonnet 94) manages to catch quite well its complexity of tone and attitude, as in the second quatrain:

They rightly do inherit heaven's graces,
And husband nature's riches from expense;

> They are the lords and owners of their faces,
> Others but stewards of their excellence.

> उचित वही पाते हैं दिव्य गुणों का उत्तरदान,
> व्यय से रखते बचा प्रकृति की वे संपति निदान;
> अपनी मुख मुद्राओं के हैं वे स्वामी अधिराज,
> उनके गुण का वाहक सा है बाकी लोक-समाज।

Equally successful is the translation of Sonnet 138, even though, as pointed out earlier, the pun on the word "lie" in the final couplet could not be translated. In view of such examples and considering Dwivedi's sound and wide-ranging scholarship not only of Shakespeare but of Sanskrit and Hindi language and literature, one can only lament his unfortunate choice of idiom and diction, which were outdated even in the year of its publication in 1958. This could well have been a landmark in the history of Hindi translation had he chosen to use a more accessible Hindi and a more contemporary poetic idiom.

This essay began by arguing the value of studying Shakespeare and other English authors not only in translation but through translation: in other words, by studying the original text in juxtaposition with its translated version or rather the translated text in juxtaposition with the original. I would like to conclude by proposing that our pedagogy for teaching English literature needs to be modified to incorporate in our curriculum and syllabi the bilingualism that is such an inescapable part of our social and intellectual life. Reading through translation would help the vast number of students reading English literature in the hinterlands who may not be as proficient in English as their metropolitan counterparts but whose literary sensibility may be equally developed and whose knowledge of their own language perhaps better. Such a method of reading English texts would also help the students proficient in English to grasp through the example of their own "native" language the nuances and subtleties of the English text which they often tend to take for granted, as shown at the beginning of this essay. A start could be made by introducing one or two optional papers where texts in English are read in the manner shown earlier, in juxtaposition with texts in Hindi or any other Indian language of the student's choice. Students could also be required to do their own translation of texts. At a later stage one could think of introducing the study of English literature through an Indian language, provided it remains a study of the texts in the original language and not a study of texts in translation. The idea may appear sacrilegious at the moment, but this is a common practice in the study of so many foreign literatures. Most departments of English in the country are also already doing this: they are teaching a large body of works originally written in other languages not even *through* but only *in* translation.

The great leaders of our National Movement always professed a love for English literature but felt that the English language was enslaving our minds and therefore needed to be replaced. The great warriors of postcolonialism have been doing just the opposite. In the name of decolonising our minds they have jettisoned a large part of English literature from the syllabi of our universities and brought in a large number of texts from other languages, especially from Indian languages, but these are studied only in English translations. I hope this essay leads to a discussion of the intellectual and literary consequences of studying literary works in total isolation from the language in which they were originally written and, on the other hand, the value of translation in literary studies. A creative use of the bilingualism that is a pervasive part of Indian society and culture may greatly enrich the study of English literature.

Notes

1 All references to and quotations from Shakespeare are from *The Norton Shakespeare*, edited by Stephen Greenblatt and others (New York: W.W. Norton & Company, 1997).
2 I am grateful to my former colleague Dr Kusum Lata for a copy of this translation in the Dev Nagari script.
3 I wonder why Dwivedi had to change the vivid image of the reaper's sickle (हँसिया) to the more generalised (and literary) पाश (net or snare): Time thus becomes a clever and cruel creature that ensnares and devours, not a reaper that cuts the crop at harvest time as part of the cycle of nature, though in the original too the cruelty of Time is suggested by the fact that he harvests flowers in full bloom as much as crop that is ripe. The reaper with his sickle is of course a familiar figure in Indian culture too, but the association of this figure with the concept of Time is not too common. There is a vivid example of it in popular culture though in a song from the film *Mother India* (1957) which begins with the lines "जुन्हरिया कटती जाये रे/उमरिया घटती जाये रे", associating the reaping of crops with mortality and the approach of death. The song is presented in part as a harvest song that the protagonists (Nargis and Raj Kumar) sing while cutting a crop of sorghum (jowar) which is quite clearly visible in the scene. But generations of film goers and film music fans have mistaken the first word जुन्हरिया, which is a local name for jowar, for चुनरिया, which is quite meaningless in the context.

5
TEACHING GENDER AND SEXUALITY IN TRANSLATED LITERATURE[1]

Ruth Vanita

In this essay, I discuss the way Indian-language texts in English translation function when taught in different types of courses at universities in the West. My reflections are largely based on my experience of teaching in the United States for two decades. My teaching, whatever the text, always includes discussions of gender and sexuality, concepts of which require a different kind of translation because they change over time and place. Continuities and discontinuities in Indic concepts of gender and sexuality are inflected by language, culture, period, and region. In my classes, this type of conceptual translation interacts with language translation.

Indian-language texts in English translation may be taught in four types of courses. These types are:

1. An Indian literature course in which the students have learnt or are learning the original language but are not fluent in it, so they read the original along with one or more English translations. This type of course may also be a translation studies course.
2. A world literature course in which the students do not know an Indian language, and they read Indian texts in translation along with texts in translation from other languages, including European languages.
3. An English literature course in which the students do not know an Indian language, and where Indian texts in translation are read along with European and American texts written in English.
4. An Indian literature course in which the students do not know an Indian language, and where all the texts are translated into English from Indian languages.

He, she, and the optative voice

In the first type of course, students have learnt the original language but are not fluent in it, and the English translation is read along with the original

DOI:10.4324/9781003049777-6   64

text. This kind of course for advanced undergraduates or graduate students is taught only at a few major universities in the United States. I taught such a course on Urdu poetry at the University of Chicago. The translation works as a supplement to the original text and helps the student negotiate unfamiliar linguistic and cultural territory as well as consider the difficulties, often impossibilities, of translating gender and sexuality.

Exploring the way gender and sexuality work in language is most rewarding in this type of course, which inevitably becomes also to some degree a course in translation studies. One question we examined is the extent to which gender is emphasised or underplayed in love poetry. In English the use of first and second person ("I" and "you") has been a common way to avoid gendering love poetry, but this is hard to do in the third person. In Hindi/Urdu, the optative voice is often used to avoid gender even in the third person. A very large number of film songs avoid gender in precisely this way, and once they outlive the films in which they occur, they can be sung by anyone to anyone. Consider one of the most iconic film songs:

Insān kisī se duniyā meṅ
Ek bār muḥabbat kartā hai
Is dard ko lekar jītā hai
Is dard ko lekar martā hai

This translates fairly easily into English: "One loves but once in this world/ One lives with this pain and dies with this pain."

After this, however, distortion becomes inevitable in English translation:

Pyār kiyā to ḍarnā kyā
Pyār kiyā ko'ī chorī nahīṅ kī
Chhup chhup āheṅ bharnā kyā . . . .
Un kī tamannā dil meṅ rahegī

———

Chhup na sakegā 'ishq hamārā . . .
Chāroṅ ṭaraf hai un kā nazārā
Pardā nahīṅ jab ko'ī khudā se
Bandoṅ se pardā karnā kyā . . .

The first problem is that of pronouns. The ungendered pronoun in the original has to become "he" or "she" in translation, thus losing the song's grand universal claims. A translation that tries to preserve the ungendered quality of the original sounds awkward:

[When] One loves, why fear?
One has loved, not stolen—why suppress one's sighs?

> My/our love cannot be hidden
> It's seen all around
> Desire will remain in my heart
> Nothing's hidden from God
> Why hide from humans?

The second problem has to do with the way verbs work. In the refrain *Pyār kiyā*, the word *pyār* (love) acquires force from being the opening word. "One loves" or "I have loved" weakens this and also reduces the universal to the individual case. "Why fear", asks a question, where *ḍarnā kyā* is more declarative, foregrounding the infinitive form and dismissing fear. I struggled with translating this particular song for my book on courtesans in Bombay cinema and commented on the way Bombay film songs unsettle gender, because they often ungender both the speaker and the addressee (Vanita 2017, 12).

Conversely, when reading eighteenth- to nineteenth-century Urdu *rekhtī* (poetry with female speakers and addressees), I noticed how translation masks the gendered verbs in the original. My first-ever translations of several of these Urdu verses appeared in *Gender, Sex and the City*, my book on the literary culture of Lucknow in this period. For example:

> Maiṅ mailī kuchailī hūṅ, nahā lene de mujh ko
> Us bāt kā kuchh tere se inkār hai gu'iyāṅ
> (Qais, p. 40, verse 24)

> I'm dirty and untidy, let me have a bath
> Would I ever refuse you that thing, girlfriend?
> (Vanita 2012, 165)

Given the overwhelming heterosexist bias we as readers suffer from, we tend to unconsciously translate the ungendered "I" and "you" in a flirtatious verse such as this into male and female. Such heterosexualisation is not possible with the original where the verbs remind one of the speaker's gender. Likewise, the addressee is called *gu'iyāṅ*, a dialect word used only for a woman's female friend (still used in rural Uttar Pradesh), while in English either a man or a woman could have a "girlfriend".

On the other hand, the polite third person allows Urdu poets to leave the lover's gender ambiguous:

> Līye Inshā ne bose do hazār un ke laboṅ se kal
> Du-gāna de ke sīdhe hāth meṅ 'anāb kā joṛā
> ("Insha", p. 74: verse 77)

In such cases, and Urdu poetry is replete with them, translators simply heterosexualise the verse by turning the lover into a "she". I avoid that by using s/he, but this is awkward:

Yesterday Inshā took two thousand kisses from her/his lips
Having given in her/his right hand two doubled jujube fruits.
(Vanita, 2012, 169)

Translation from manuscript to printed text has also suffered this heterosexualisation because manuscript writers often write the letter *ī* and the letter *e* in exactly the same way, so that, for example, *ga'ī* (she went) and *ga'e* (he went) are indistinguishable, introducing a radical gender ambiguity.

Translating sex for English speakers is even more difficult. There is no equivalent for the word "sex" in Hindi and Urdu. This is true of premodern English poetry too. *Yaun* is an ugly modern coinage, which cannot be used in poetry. *Bāt karnā*, to talk/speak/converse, is a lovely common idiom for having sex, still used today in the Hindi heartland. It corresponds to the older English "conversation". But English readers today are likely to miss the double entendre if one uses the word "converse" to translate *bāt karnā*.

The euphemism "to sleep with" translates directly, but here the double pun gets lost:

Ham do gharī bhī sāth tere so rahe na hā'i
Bāton men yun hi chār pahar rāt kat ga'e
("Insha" p. 358, verse 343)

I couldn't sleep with you for even a short time, alas
Four watches of the night passed just in talking.
(Vanita 2012, 164)

In English the pun in the first line is evident—the verse could mean "I couldn't go to sleep with you" or "I couldn't have sex with you". But the pun in the second line cannot be translated because "the night passed in talking" or even "the night passed in conversation" refers just to speaking in modern English. In the original, it could mean the night passed talking to each other, or it could mean the night passed having sex (with the result that we could not go to sleep together).

Words for "love" present another problem. English has basically only one word. Hindi and Urdu have at least a dozen. *'Ishq* refers to romantic passion alone. *Muhabbat* and *ulfat* are often romantic love but not always. *Pyār* and *prem* can be any kind of love. *Sneh* is affection; *vātsalya* is parental love. Translating *'ishq* just as "love" loses some of its force; for example, in *Pyār kiyā to darnā kyā*, the idea that love is free from fear does not refer to romantic passion alone but *chhup na sakegā 'ishq hamārā* does. In English one cannot convey this shift, because one has to translate both as "love".

Losing *rasa*

Two other types of courses are (a) world literature courses, where almost all the texts are translated into English, and (b) English literature courses, wherein many of the texts are written in English but some are translated into English.

The second type of course, widely taught in universities now, is the one I find deeply problematic. Translation always loses what may be termed the poetry of a text, that which makes it literature—its *rasa*. One may argue that this does not matter because the vast majority of literature courses today focus on content, not on aesthetics or style. Although this is true, my experience is that the two cannot be entirely separated, and that even when the focus is on content, as in a course that I teach called Gender and Sexuality in Twentieth-Century Fiction, a minority of students certainly and most students arguably do respond at some level to the strange effects of beauty. They respond to the *rasa*, the taste and pleasure of language.

Take an average sentence:

> leṭe-leṭe hī aṅgrā'ī lekar badan toṛtī Nanda ne ekdam karvaṭ badalkar Harsh kī qamar meṅ bāṅhen ḍāliṅ aur use phir baiṭhā liyā.
> (Yadav 52)

> still lying down, and languorously stretching, Nanda suddenly turned on her side, put her arms round Harsh's waist and pulled him down again.[2]

Consider the untranslatable elements of the sentence: the doubled verb so common in Hindi, *leṭe-leṭe*; the word *aṅgrā'ī*, which conveys the voluptuous turning and twisting of parts (*aṅg*) of the body; *badan toṛnā*, literally breaking the body but metaphorically twisting the limbs in a pleasurable way; and *karvaṭ badalnā*. Among the pleasures that these phrases produce are the crunchy, almost onomatopoeic, consonants. This cluster of words indicates a writer at the top of his form, and the pleasure is inevitably missed by students who read a translation. But when they read such a translated text side by side with a text written in English, the rewards of language, the *rasa*, are clearly experienced in the latter. Here, for example, is a sentence taken completely at random:

> The bony face, the dark, cropped hair, the narrow eyes, sentient now, seemed to belong to a clever boy, not even raffish, not even a dandy, just hard and clever (Murdoch 165).

The picture conjured up here depends on adjectives native to English and shows the author's mastery of language. "Clever", for example, with its range of cultural connotations, is not replicable in Hindi.

In an English literature course, the translated Indian-language text is thus put at a disadvantage and students leave with the unarticulated, even unconscious, impression that the English writers are more accomplished writers. This is true even when the students may know the Indian language but are reading the text in translation and not in the original. Their interest in the translated Indian text has to depend largely on content, not form or language, whereas their interest in the English-language text is inflected by *rasa*, the pleasures of aestheticised emotion.

The problem of unequal ground is sharply heightened in the case of poetry. Take the example of the famous verse that opens the *Satsai*, Biharilal's collected works:

> Merī bhava bādhā harau rādhānāgari so'i
> Jā tan kī jhā'īṅ parai syām harit duti ho'i
> (30)

Here is Rupert Snell's rather lovely translation:

> May Radha the sublime, whose golden glow
> greens Krishna's raincloud-blue,
> clear from my path the hindrance of the world. (Snell 3)[3]

Here's my translation:

> Remove the distress of existence from me, all-knowing Radha,
> Whose body's gleam, falling on the Dark One, makes him radiant green.

Several translators have wrestled with this verse, but anyone will admit that no translation can reproduce the layered wordplay and delights of the original.

Nāgari, Radha's epithet, is untranslatable. It means a denizen of the city, suggesting someone courtly, knowing and sophisticated, and is unexpected because Radha is a rural woman. The epithet alludes to Krishna being an urbane, courtly city-dweller, and the verse gestures towards Mirabai's famous epithet for Krishna, *Giridhar Nāgaar*. Because of her association with Krishna, Radha too becomes urbane; also, of course, as an incarnation of Goddess Lakshmi, she is knowing and knowledgeable in herself.

The philosophical term *bhava bādhā* is equally hard to translate. It indicates the obstacles and distress created by the very fact of existence. Although somewhat similar to Ghalib's "Ḍuboyā mujh ko hone ne na hotā maiṅ to kyā hotā?" (Being has sunk me, had I not been what would have been?), the Hindu image in *bhava bādhā* is that of separation from the divine due to bodily existence, mirrored in Radha's separation from Krishna after he leaves the village for the city.

Merī bhava bādhā, translated directly as "my distress of being", gives the incorrect impression that the poet is referring to his personal problems. This is because of a different conception of individuality in the two cultures. In Hindi, *bhava bādhā* is a common phrase, and readers understand that the poet's distress is existential and shared with all living things. The use of "my" in English personalises whatever follows. Hence Snell's translation, "clear from my path the hindrance of the world", and my translation, "remove . . . the distress of existence from me", both of which try to convey the impersonality of the distress but in doing so lose the compression of the original.

This is complex enough, but it is the couplet's second line that is impervious to poetic translation. When the shadow of Radha's body falls on Krishna, the dark one, he turns radiant green. Why this happens is not explained but is evident to any reader who knows that Radha is golden-coloured and Krishna (here termed Syam, the dark one) is blue. The mingling of yellow and blue produces green. In English, his turning green might suggest that he becomes jealous. In Hindi, the meaning is entirely different—green is the colour of fertility, life, and joy. Krishna blossoms with greenness when Radha's light falls on him. One of Krishna's names is Hari, echoed in the word *harit* (green), meaning the joyous and joy-giving one. These words also reverberate with the verb in the first line, *harnā*, to take or destroy, when the poet asks Radha to destroy or take away the obstacles of existence.

The *rasa* of the verse arises in part from word-choice: for example, the dialect word *jhā'īn̐*, which means not only shadow, reflection, or gleam but also darkness, trickery, and echo. Radha, though golden-complexioned, is also Maya, the goddess of enchantment and illusion, and echoes Krishna's darkness. The play of light, darkness, and colour in the couplet emblematises the interfused union of the two: Krishna, the dark one, needs Radha in order to be Hari, the green, joy-giving one.

One can explain all this to students, but explanation cannot reproduce the pleasurable shock of compression in the original nor, of course, the assonance and alliteration. Compare, for instance, the effect of lines from Bihari's slightly senior contemporary John Donne's 1633 Sonnet 14. These lines also appeal to the divine with eroticised devotional figures of speech:

> Take me to you, imprison me, for I,
> Except you enthrall me, never shall be free,
> Nor ever chaste, except you ravish me.

The puns and paradoxes and the sliding of vowels in "you enthrall" that reproduces, as it were, the experience of being irresistibly drawn, take hold of the reader with an immediacy not reproducible in translation. Even though modern students may require explication of the double meanings of "enthrall" and "ravish", the poetic power speaks directly to them. A student who reads one poem in translation and the other in English is almost certain to find Donne more memorable than Bihari.

Many translated texts or none

Two other kinds of courses I teach are (a) those in which many texts are translated from different European and Indian languages and (b) those in which all the texts, including the Indian ones, are written in English. Both types of courses avoid placing Indian texts in translation next to British or American texts written in English, thus avoiding evaluation of the former by standards developed in a Western critical tradition based on and adapted to the latter.

In my course, Stories East and West, most of the texts are translated, and some are written in English (by both Indian and Western writers). We read Plato's *Phaedo*, the *Kathopanishad*, extracts from the *Panchatantra* and Aesop's Fables, short stories translated from European and Indian languages, and some written in English, Hesse's *Siddhartha* and Narayan's *Guide*, and extracts from Thoreau and Gandhi, among other texts. We focus on similarity and difference in genre (dialogue, novel, essay, fable) and discuss how ideas circulate between so-called East and so-called West.

When reading texts translated from European as well as Indian languages, there is less room for invidious comparisons. Students read works written in English by both Indians (Kamala Das, Mulk Raj Anand, Narayan) and Britishers and Americans (O. Henry, Maugham, Mansfield, Ozick) and thus realise how English has become an Indian language.

But in a course like Gender and Sexuality in Twentieth-Century English Fiction, I teach only texts written in English and include texts by Indian writers such as Suniti Namjoshi and Vikram Seth. In the books by Indian writers, students encounter a non-Western or rather a mixed Eastern–Western world.

For example, when they read Namjoshi's *Conversations of Cow*, students appreciate her facility with the language and the fun she has as she playfully converses with Indian and Western literary and philosophical traditions; here is an example from the end of the book: "The Cow of a thousand faces and a thousand manifestations who walks rough-shod over fields and forests, and falls asleep when her day is done . . ." (Namjoshi 125). While glossing some of the names, such as Surbhi, Suniti, and Bhadravati, does enhance students' understanding, the writing is transparent enough for them to enjoy the book even without this extra knowledge. The book stands up to those written in the UK, America, and New Zealand. What I will not do is include texts translated from Indian languages in a course like this one.

The texts I select are all from traditions of which I have some understanding and which I am equipped to teach at the undergraduate level. I was once asked whether I might be interested in teaching a postgraduate course where students write on books and films, each in a different European language that the particular student knows, while the teacher has little or no knowledge of the critical or creative traditions of those languages. I declined, saying that it would require too much work to acquaint myself with the traditions of so many languages and the contexts for the texts.

The teacher replied that the course is easy to teach because she does not always bother to read the text in translation and because the films are often not available with subtitles. She grades papers on the basis of their internal coherence without checking for accuracy in the papers' references to or analyses of texts. This type of teaching is unfortunately becoming increasingly common. I know of several doctoral dissertations in the U.K. and the U.S. written on such topics as Indian film songs or folk songs, where neither the supervisor nor anyone on the committee knows any Indian language or anything about Indian musical or cinematic conventions. Thus, the student can get away with mistranslations and with analyses that may be entirely off the mark.

Only Indian texts in translation

The fifth kind of course is one in which students do not know an Indian language, and we read only an Indian text or texts in English translation. Here, the translated text stands on its own without unfair comparison to texts written in English.

A popular course of this type is my course, Talking to God: the Bhagavad Gita. After an overview of philosophical, religious, historical, and reception contexts, we conduct a close reading of the *Gita*, discussing interpretations by different philosophical schools, such as Dvaita, Advaita, and Dvaitadvaita, and also by figures like Shankaracharya, Tilak, Gandhi, and Sri Aurobindo. We briefly consider the text's influence on the Western literary and philosophical tradition, reading short excerpts from writers like Emerson, Thoreau, T. S. Eliot, and Yeats.

All translations have shortcomings. I use Graham Schweig's translation because it is gender-neutral (for figures like the devotee and the Self), poetic but not archaic ("you", not "thou") while staying close to the original, and the translator is conscious of the pitfalls of using Christian terminology to translate concepts and thus flatten out complex terms. Thus, dharma remains dharma and does not become "duty" or "righteousness", as it does in many translations; *dehī* is "embodied", not "soul". *Sattva*, *rajas*, *tamas*, and dharma all remain as is. *Shraddhā*, unfortunately, is translated as the Christian "faith", and the translator makes a conscious and, in my view, inaccurate choice to translate *bhakti* as "love" instead of "devotion", which dilutes the meaning of *prīti* (love) when it appears, but I remind the students of these problems as we read.

From engaging in discussions of concepts, some students develop an interest in language and ask questions about the original words, so I keep the Sanskrit text at hand to answer such questions.

Conclusion

My argument should not be interpreted to mean that I am opposed to translation. I have myself translated many works of fiction and poetry. These are intended for general as well as scholarly readers. My argument is only about the placement of texts for students: reading translated texts in tandem with texts written in English has the effect of making the former seem less powerful than the latter.

Notes

1 All translations in this essay are by me, except as otherwise indicated.
2 This is a slightly modified version from my translation of the story in Vanita and Kidwai ed., *Same-Sex Love in India*, 329–35; 330.
3 Used with Snell's permission.

Works cited

Bihari Satsai. Varanasi: Nagari Pracharini Sabha, Vikram Samvat 2056.
Khan, Insha Allah. "Insha." *Kulliyat-e Insha*. Ed. Khalil-ur Rahman Da'udi. Lahore: Lahore Majlis-i Taraqqi-yi Adab, 1969.
Murdoch, Iris. *A Fairly Honourable Defeat*. 1970. Rpt. Harmondsworth: Penguin, 1978.
Namjoshi, Suniti. *The Conversations of Cow*. London: The Women's Press, 1985.
Qais, Muhammad Siddiq. *Qais ka muntakhab Divan-i Rekhti*. Ed. Abdulhafiz Qatil. Hyderabad: Anjuman-i Taraqqi-yi Ta'lim, 1961; 1984.
Snell, Rupert. *Poems from the Satsai*. Cambridge, MA: Harvard UP, 2021.
Vanita, Ruth. *Dancing with the Nation: Courtesans in Bombay Cinema*. New Delhi: Speaking Tiger, 2017.
———. *Gender, Sex and the City: Urdu Rekhti Poetry, 1780–1870*. New Delhi: Orient Blackswan, 2012.
Vanita, Ruth, and Saleem Kidwai, eds. *Same-Sex Love in India: A Literary History*, 2000. New Delhi: Penguin, 2008.
Yadav, Rajendra. "*Prateeksha*." *Rajendra Yadav: Pratinidhi Kahaniyan*. Ed. Mohan Gupt. New Delhi: Rajkamal Paperbacks, 1985.

6

RADICAL UNLEARNEDNESS IN PROLETARIAN SCHOOLING

Dilemmas of discipline and teaching in D.H. Lawrence's *Education of the People* and *Fantasia of the Unconscious*

Divya Saksena

In keeping with the themes of this Festschrift volume, this essay examines Lawrence's *Education of the People* along with *Fantasia of the Unconscious* to elicit his articulations of the complexities and dichotomies implicit in the education of what he called the "proletariat" and reconcile them with his demand for a "radical unlearnedness" (595). I will also briefly consider educator-tutor characters such as Birkin, Ursula, and Gudrun in his fictional works like *Women in Love* to demonstrate the working of his educational theories of discipline and intuitive learning. Approaching Lawrence as an early exponent of modernism, this essay explores the secular humanist connection that is evident in, and which forms the basis of, so much of his fictional writing. This is his reaction away from indoctrination, towards the pursuit of personal relationships and the "star equilibrium" between individuals, and so flying in the face of the social establishment of his times.

Lawrence, like his contemporary Forster, offers an internal response to a world gone externally wrong, a world traumatised and torn apart by political and military conflict on an unprecedented scale. Both authors experiment with taking the impulse towards fragmentation to its farthest potential so that the return to unity and harmony may become possible. While sensitively perceiving the end of form in the collapse of order (the Yeatsian idea of how "Things fall apart, the centre cannot hold"), each writer still tries to retain some essence of aesthetic form. For, as Iris Murdoch puts it, "[since] literature is the main carrier and creator of wide-ranging understanding . . . [a] great artist sees the vast interesting collection of what is other to him and does not picture the world in his own image" (Murdoch 25ff). Certainly, Lawrence compels his readers to imagine and reflect upon the fragmented, more "objectionable" aspects of human nature and personality—the threat of formlessness and chaos. In his non-fiction writing (perhaps more directly than through the characters he creates in his fiction) readers engage with, rather than evade, what Murdoch calls the "anxious avaricious tentacles of the self" (Murdoch 385). Consequently, these works obligate recognition of an imperative need to discover, or develop from within oneself, the capability to see the world in its fullest possible "reality". It also calls for a greater tolerance of negatives and contradictions, somewhat in the sense of Keats' Negative Capability. Both Forster and Lawrence's statements often resonate with Keats' praise of the poet's power of existing "in uncertainties, Mysteries, doubts, without any irritable reaching after fact and reason . . . With a great poet the sense of Beauty overcomes every other consideration, or rather obliterates all consideration" (*NAEL* 889–90).[1] Through the aesthetic encounter with their writing, it becomes possible to discover or re-discover the aesthetic ability to maintain an individual selfhood and to function in a world that at the same time appears full of absurdities. In such a world, traditional or gender-based relationships and connections become vexed and sexuality and sexual attraction are no longer just a straightforward "Victorian" male/female issue.

When he started his career as a teacher, one strong criticism against Lawrence was that he preferred to concentrate on a minority of bright or promising pupils in his class, tending to ignore the majority. The opening line of his poem "Last Lesson of the Afternoon" echoes a teacher's despair—"When will the bell ring and end this weariness . . ."—as much as the boredom of the students. In practice, as in theory, he sought a golden mean that would somehow provide discipline and a general education for the masses (whom he considered mediocre at best), while also addressing the special needs of individual advanced learners. In his Foreword to *Fantasia of the Unconscious*, Lawrence offers a clear definition of this endeavour with reference to his own writings:

> I don't intend my books for the generality of readers. I count it a mistake of our mistaken democracy that every man who can read print is allowed to believe that he can read all that is printed. I count it a misfortune that serious books are exposed in the public market, like slaves exposed naked for sale . . . I am no "scholar" of any sort. But I am very grateful to scholars for their sound work. I have found hints, suggestions for what I say here in all kinds of scholarly books, from the Yoga and Plato and St John the Evangel and the early Greek philosophers like Herakleitos down to Frazer and his '*Golden Bough*', and even Freud and Frobenius. Even then I only remember hints—and I proceed by intuition . . .
>
> (Lawrence 11–12)

Lawrence was no scholar or administrator "of any sort" but by intuition a passionate teacher all his life.

In *Education of the People*, Lawrence continually tries to figure out how to discipline the young mind of a student and yet leave it free to find its own wisdom, how to juxtapose vocational utilitarianism that he accepted as the need of the masses with the individual intuitiveness that he saw as the foundation of a high culture in the future. In *Fantasia of the Unconscious*, Lawrence describes some of the ways in which selfhood and self-awareness may be damaged by utilitarian needs in childhood: "The warm, swift, sensual self is steadily and persistently denied, damped, weakened throughout all the period of childhood. And by sensual . . . we mean the more impulsive reckless nature" (117). Lawrence's attempt is to show that much of the problem with mass education arises out of the urging of students towards either utilitarian vocational learning or pure, abstract "knowing". Hence, to seek any "pure, perfect knowledge" is to make pre-conceptual the learning process that should be intuitive. For him, this makes characters like Miriam in *Sons and Lovers* and Gudrun in *Women in Love* the victims as much as the representatives of the purely mental consciousness that he opposed so vehemently. His advocacy is for Ursula's holistic response to Birkin and to the:

> curious hidden richness, that came through his thinness and pallor like another voice, conveying another knowledge of him . . . rich, fine, exquisite curves, the powerful beauty of life itself. She could not say what it was. But there was a sense of richness and liberty.
> (44)

This is what Lawrence demands of educators—facilitating an ineffable, elusive, yet strangely comprehensible "radical unlearnedness".

Understandably then, in *Women in Love*, in the chapter "Classroom", Birkin tells Ursula that the children drawing pictures of catkins need to use their crayons to fill in the colours of the flowers, instead of pencilling their hard shapes and outlines. "I'd chalk them in plain, chalk in nothing else, merely the red and the yellow", he declares. "Outline scarcely matters in this case" (36). Ursula makes no claim to artistic talent, while, by contrast, her sister Gudrun is a practising artist whose relationship with Gerald Crich progresses under the aegis of her tutoring his youngest sister Winifred in art. However, Lawrence makes it clear that it is Ursula's spontaneity, which she shares with Birkin, and not Gudrun's pre-meditated and coldly analytical mentality that he endorses. When Birkin enunciates his educational philosophy that ". . . You've got to lapse out before you can know what sensual reality is, lapse into unknowingness, and give up your volition. You've got to do it. You've got to learn not-to-be, before you can come into being" (44), it is Ursula, not Gudrun, who can recognise and share, even participate in, Lawrence/Birkin's passion for spontaneity.

However, can learning take place without organisation, pre-meditation, and discipline? In *Education of the People*, Lawrence confronts the great dilemma of discipline—to punish or not to punish the child. For individuality to flourish, the child must be left strictly "alone". The superimposition of ideals, "personality and mind . . . are a deformity in a child" (620). Yet, for any sort of educated development to proceed, discipline and punishment are inevitable in some measure. Lawrence acknowledges the power of punishment even as he asserts, "Do not ask me to transfer the pre-mental dynamic knowledge into thought. It cannot be done. The knowledge that *I am I* can never be thought: only known" (34). True education and learning must be achieved intuitively by individuals, not hammered into an amorphous mass of humanity through the relentless application of logical processes.

Questions may arise—is Lawrence elitist in the educational policies he advocates? Are his theories of education and culture practical? In seeking to define his ideal teacher, does Lawrence fall prey to his own *bête noir* of preconception and idealisation? Perhaps, not quite so. Educators, he says, must be "the priests of life, deep in the wisdom of life" (606). It is Birkin/Lawrence and "life-priests" like him who can guide students to appreciate "the shimmer, not the shape of things" which leads to "radical unlearnedness". With a conviction that is as genuine as it is self-reflexive, Lawrence articulates and follows through on a seemingly didactic but inherently fluid philosophy of education: "mankind is one and universal. Therefore, each individual is a term of the Infinite" (635).

For Lawrence, life and beauty that should lead the individual to that "national, communal and personal efficiency" originate in the cosmic will, in the blind intuitive will to live at all costs. As he encountered the works of nineteenth century philosopher-scientists like Darwin, Carlyle, Mill, and Schopenhauer, Lawrence also wrestled with the problem of reconciling his new consciousness of materialist realities with traditional attitudes to religion. Jessie Chambers, in her memoir,[2] emphasises the impact of the new rationalist and sceptic attitudes propagated by the philosopher-sceptic Leslie Stephen, the father of Virginia Woolf (see Annan), on Lawrence. She describes how troubled he was by "the nebular theory of the Universe, and . . . the discrepancy between such a hypothesis of the origin of things and the God postulated by the Congregational Chapel" (Chambers 83–84). As he felt himself drawn further away from indoctrinated religious reverence, and began to encounter what he called the amoral, artistic "demon" within him, Lawrence was intensely conscious that this internal divide had to be understood, if not quite healed or overcome. Since Jessie Chambers, as indicated in her memoirs and her letters to Lawrence, was unable or unwilling to accept his vision of his divided self, Lawrence took his theories about the human condition elsewhere.

On 3 December 1907, he wrote to the Reverend Robert Reid, articulating his confusion with religious dogma: "I was constantly endeavouring to give myself, but, Sir, to this day I do not understand what this 'giving' consists in, embodies, and includes" (Letters 39). Here is early confirmation of Lawrence's growing commitment to the life of the human body, his idea that an ideal society should consist of individuals existing in perfectly balanced, multidimensional connections. Here too is his early affirmation of an all-embracing secular humanism as the core foundation of education. It is not quite the supercharged New Liberal optimism of Hobhouse, Herbert Samuel, and Bernstein with whose ideas Lawrence was undoubtedly acquainted, yet it is akin to his contemporary Forster's *Two Cheers for Democracy* in that it locates its power in the human dimension. Interestingly, as Asquith often reiterated, this was not a new gospel (see Herbert). Nor was Lawrence interested in re-inventing the wheel. One point of divergence is that while Forster investigates the lives of distanced historical figures like Alexander and Plotinus, Lawrence is, in his own words, "naturally introspective, a somewhat keen and critical student of myself" (39). For him, the origin and conclusion for his theory of liberal/secular humanism is himself. The starting point for a student is his/her own self.

In the same letter, Lawrence informs Reid that he no longer believes in the idea of a spiritual ecstasy pursuant to doctrinal conversion or the idea of being "saved"; he does not concur that "the Holy Ghost descended and took conscious possession of the 'elect'—the converted one" (39). For him, any doctrine of life and learning must situate itself in the human world of the body, of physical realities and material experience through sensory perception:

> I believe that a man is converted when first he hears the low, vast murmur of life, of human life, troubling his hitherto unconscious self. I believe a man is born first unto himself—for the happy developing of himself.
>
> (39)

In another personal moment of "conversion", he confesses to Louie Burrows in November 1906 and to Jessie Chambers on 28 January 1908 that a truly "intimate" relationship for him comprises physical contact alongside a deep spiritual connection. Like Forster's appeal to "connect" contradictory poetic and prosaic oppositions, Lawrence too desires an amalgamation of "the kissable and embraceable part" with "the deep spirit within" (Letters 42–43). Already Lawrence is anxious to emphasise the personal, individual, and particular aspects of life over the "sweeping general interests" he considers so detrimental to a truly humanitarian society. In his earliest available letter to Blanche Jennings[3] dated 15 April 1908, Lawrence mentions the noticeable change in Alice Dax, their common contact, "a softness, an increasing aesthetic appreciation of things instead of mere approval on utilitarian grounds, or . . . a strong, crude emotion?" (44). He contends that the "improvement" in Dax derives from her new commitment not to generalities but to particular human interests: "—in Woman, for instance, instead of in a woman and some women; *in humanity rather than in men* . . ." (44–45, emphasis added). Here is the genesis and the kernel of his philosophy, his insistence upon the individual as the core of all societal systems and his demand for an "aesthetic culture" (45) rather than a utilitarian or purely cerebral/mental view of life.

Similarly, after watching Sarah Bernhardt perform in "La Dame aux Camelias", he is fascinated by her ability to bring to aesthetic life an inanimate piece of dramatic art, because her essentially physical human presence becomes the site for aesthetic interpretation and the communication of a near ecstatic experience. Lawrence writes to Jennings on 25 June 1908 that Bernhardt is "the incarnation of wild emotion which we share with all live beings, but which is gathered in us in all complexity and inscrutable fury. She represents the primeval passions of woman, and she is fascinating to an extraordinary degree" (59). Lawrence's repeated use here of the pronoun "she" suggests a coalescing of the real-life Bernhardt with the persona she portrays on the stage, as well as with the elusive traits he attributes to woman in the abstract. As Wilde puts it:

> The meaning of any beautiful created thing is . . . as much in the soul of him who looks at it, as it was in his soul who wrought it. Nay, it is rather the beholder who lends to the beautiful thing its myriad meanings, and makes it marvellous for us, and sets it in some new relation to the age.
>
> (*NAEL* 2. 1757)

Just as Pater, in his interpretation of "La Gioconda", may have "put into the portrait of Mona Lisa something that Leonardo never dreamed of" (*NAEL* 2. 1756), so too Lawrence in his response to Bernhardt puts in something of his own. He also discovers something hitherto unknown within himself. As Bernhardt's performance transmutes the written word, and her ordinary self, into a frighteningly intense presence that is inexplicably superior to mundane "reality", Lawrence's own experience of her portrayal of human passions somehow transforms his present mundane existence into something magical and ineffably superior. He sees the experience of passion in its raw physical state (depicted as variations of love) as integral and crucial to his development of his aesthetic vision as an artist. It supports his confidence in his destiny as an artist and in his ability to "give good help sometime to the march of the procession" (58), through his irrevocable commitment to the larger community of humanity, and demonstrates his commitment to an all-encompassing secularism. Through Lawrence's letters to Jennings we may come closest to understanding this development of his vision. On 17 July 1908, in their ongoing debate on religion,[4] comes his first statement of the "star-existence" philosophy he later enunciated so powerfully through

Paul Morel and Rupert Birkin, positing that perfection in the human world demanded an ongoing "trembling balance" of constant, delicate adjustments between individuals always situated in a series of intermeshed, dynamic relationships. Eventually, for him love between individuals was to be a kind of secular faith, a religion in itself.[5] Education was to be based upon, and the outcome of, such a secular faith, the "star equilibrium" with each student that a teacher ought to strive for. Perfection of the learning process, for Lawrence, is thus quite an achievable objective based upon mutual balance between the teacher and the taught.

In enunciating his theories of education for the people, Lawrence also rejects the abstract, pure art or philosophy that does not perform a social function. For him, the aesthetic value of art cannot be dissociated from its social and instructional (though not utilitarian) aspects, which become operational in the influence of art upon individuals.[6] Like Forster, he hopes to be an effective ("influencing") artist, but he intends to do so without losing his personal, individual objective of looking towards an eternity, not of "singing" but of "being". Later, in his expository writings like *Fantasia of the Unconscious* and *Apocalypse*, he would reiterate his insistence upon the efficacy of "being" rather than the process of "becoming" in his call for "effectual, not conscious", human beings. The present moment was to attain paramount importance for him, not hedonistically but in valuing each moment for its special experience and contribution to personal growth. Ultimately, like Forster, Lawrence is strongly in favour of a "wholeness" of life experience, against the "halfness" or "partness" that he saw as causing the "Judas" of betrayal in human relationships.[7] For him, the value of physical contact resides not merely in the sexual aspect but in the establishment of a tangible community of living people, regardless of age or gender, which in turn leads to a reinforcement and regeneration of the individual spirit. More importantly, it makes possible through physical contact a reunification of the individual soul with the cosmic "reality" that primitive man knew and which Lawrence sees as lost to modern humanity. Although yet his "phraseology is vague and impossible", he, "joining hands with the artists" as a special community of humans, declares that "there must be some great purposeful impulses impelling through everything to move it and work it to an end . . . and submission to the great impulses comes through feeling—indescribable—and, I think unknowable" (99). Like the young Forster at Alexandria, contemplating the Neo-Platonists and their "immortal eloquence" and struggling to articulate his own response to it, Lawrence at age 23 knows and understands/accepts that he is still feeling his way in the articulation of his aesthetic beliefs. Certain truths, for him, must remain beyond the pale of mental "understanding". Always his effort is, and will be, to reiterate the ineffable, "unknowable" value of "feeling" and of instinctual rather than mental knowledge.

As Boulton notes in his chronology to the *Letters*, after Lawrence eloped with Frieda[8] on 15 June 1912 he urgently spelled out to his friend Arthur McLeod his discovery of this doctrine of human love as the equivalent to, if not substitute for, human life itself (Letters: 418). His letter of 3 July 1912 to Edward Garnett reveals how Frieda and her love combine for him oppositional feelings of ecstasy and agony, pain and relief. She integrates all the qualities he has observed and sought in a woman and assists him towards a wholeness of being, for he shares with her the positives as well as the negatives of their relationship.[9] Among others, he feels, she has brought to him a sense of self-discipline that he lacked, with the realisation that discipline, like learning, must begin with the self.

The dilemma of discipline in education (and thereby in schools) is one that Lawrence centres again upon the individual. He clearly resists the prevailing tendencies of educators to impose physical restraints and controls upon students, including parents and teachers alike in the establishment of the learning process. To best educate a child, he argues, rule number one should be to "leave it alone". Thereafter, as the child begins to evince interest in its surroundings, it must be allowed free movement to facilitate learning through exploring itself and its surroundings. As Sarah Bouttier argues, "the acquisition of knowledge [is] described in 'Education of the People' as a connection of points in space" (Bouttier 4). By connecting the two physical centres—"volitional" and "sympathetic"—into a "perfect circuit", a child voluntarily learns to apprehend and understand the world around it. The process is not perfect, accompanied by many failures and frustrations, which the child must learn to deal with on its own. Excessive parental sympathy or excessive external control alike will cause deviations from the path of natural learning. Movement, not stasis, should be the base of education from the very beginning, literally, from the cradle—as Bouttier observes, "movement is the process of education, but also its primary goal".

Discipline is also at the core of Forster's proposition of mediating opposites[10] to "only connect the prose and the passion", perhaps to create a more effective Anglo-India. Forster's option was to suggest a viable new "exalted" alternative to the existing order based upon political fragmentation (see Crews on Forster). By contrast, Lawrence prefers to face head-on the problems in education that he perceives as factors in the deterioration of human relationships (and through them of society). His insistence is upon the individual as the starting point, the foundation and the objective of learning. Therefore, even an individual failure is, according to his thinking, preferable rather than a cohort of clones being communally nose-led by political leaders or moral watchdogs. Such agents encourage levels of brainwashing and ideological training bordering on the totalitarian, even when this is allegedly based on ideals of love and universal brotherhood. Much like Forster, Lawrence celebrates the mismatched, the odd, and the irregular as the source and location of the truly beautiful. However, Lawrence adopts a more extreme vitalistic position in which reside the problems that so many experience with his philosophy. Hence, although readers of his non-fiction writings can identify with ideas that are exciting, exotic, and intensely charged with their own experiences, they often struggle to relate to Lawrence's concepts of the aesthetics of education. Often, the allegation is that he is too vague, too didactic, and that the vision he puts forward can be used in negative ways—for instance, it could be applied equally to the democratic as well as the fascist cause. Although such vitalism is usually acceptable, for many readers it becomes necessary to search for more nuances as they mature themselves—as, for example, in its presentation by Albert Camus. Camus' writings present a very similar return to the primal springs of vitality, as he too upholds the value of natural intuition and experience against an excessively intellectual apprehending of reality. Nevertheless, Camus' work comes much later and offers a more nuanced version of humanist thought when compared to Lawrence's didactic-sounding arguments or Forster's seemingly facile desire for resolution in exaltation. This relates to Lawrence's rather distanced romanticising of the life of the miners (prior to the First World War) as a source of the "pure" life, still retentive of innocence and unconditional human warmth that so-called modern industrial society had lost or destroyed. Perhaps, he tries to mythologise a past in which he never really participated. A similar romanticism also tinges Forster's wish for Anglo-Indian unification in *A Passage to India*. Although differences stem from the quality of the life experience of both authors, both are at one in their anxiety to not only communicate their views but also see them become operational in the lives of real people, free of stultifying social practices and institutions.

Writing to Sallie Hopkin on 25 December 1912, Lawrence describes again how love has been, intellectually and psychologically, the catalyst that brings together several facets of his concept of humanism through the integration of diverse facets of his own personality: "Once you've known what love *can* be, there's no disappointment any more, and no despair . . ." (492). The exhilarating and liberating spontaneous fusion of body, mind, and spirit reflects Schiller's observation that:

> instincts are the only motive forces in the world. If hitherto truth has so little manifested her victorious power, this has not depended on the understanding, which could not have unveiled it, but on the heart which remained closed to it, and instinct which did not act with it.
>
> (Schiller 770)[11]

Founded upon mutual honesty, human love is for Lawrence complete and final; it is the foundation and core of all learning and it brings him the wisdom of truth that reinforces his faith in the future.[12]

Such a "true" wisdom, like that of the Yeatsian sages, like the emotions that accompany a true aesthetic experience, usually remains silent because it cannot be easily articulated or communicated. But for Lawrence, such wisdom is and always should be the consequence of natural, voluntary learning, based upon mutual love and balanced connections between individuals. "The great emotions like love are unspoken. Speaking them is a sign of an indecent bullying will" (54). From this wisdom, there comes a spontaneous sense of morality—the starting point of true learning—and, thus, an intuitive knowledge of what is right or wrong for each of us. It is this affirmation of a wisdom that comes from within that Wayne C. Booth refers to as the factor that converts him to Lawrence's beliefs (see Booth Introduction). Hence, morality should not be blindly implemented as a standard of perfection, in a communal manner, regardless and uncomprehending of the subtle differences between individuals and between different sets of circumstances and conditions. Beauty emerges through learning. Moreover, like morality, beauty exists not only in the bright and "pretty" side of life and humanity but also in the beast, the darker passions, which are both seductive and challenging to the human soul. The whole, and not any part(s) of it, has to be embraced for a true experience of aesthetic and educational value, which may become the medium through which we may know others and, eventually, the cosmic and moral dimensions of our own selves.

Notes

1 Extracted in *The Norton Anthology of English Literature (NAEL)*, vol 2, 889–90.
2 Chambers, Jessie. *D. H. Lawrence: A Personal Record* (first published 1935 under the pseudonym "E.T"), 2nd edition, ed J.D. Chambers, (London: Frank Cass, 1965).
3 See Boulton 43.
4 See also *Sons and Lovers*, 353–54, 365.
5 His statement that "Religion, work, love all link us on to an eternity—the one of singing, the other of influencing, the last of being. You think the middle one best—I like both the last two . . ." (62) reflects his first formulations of what would be his lifelong optimism and philosophical tenets.
6 Lawrence appears there to position himself against the Aesthetes for whom art mattered for art's sake, as well as against the later Romantics. His term "eternity of singing" echoes W.B. Yeats's use of the singing motif in poems like "Sailing to Byzantium" and "A Dialogue of Self and Soul". I take it also to refer to the hymn-singing aspect of institutionalised religion that he was beginning to resent openly by this date.
7 See letter to Dorothy Brett, dated 27 January 1925 (according to Harry T. Moore). In Trilling, Diana ed. *The Selected Letters of D. H. Lawrence* (New York: Farrar, Straus & Cudahy Inc, 1958), 233–35.
8 "The most wonderful woman in England" (37). See Boulton 365; 479–80. The almost platonic terms "gratitude" and "good to me" suggest the societal and materialist nature of his relationship with Louie Burrows.
9 Letter to Sallie Hopkin on 23 December 1912 in Boulton, 490.
10 Hence the famous appeal to "only connect the prose and the passion" in *Howards End* and the fusion characters like Aziz in *A Passage to India*.

11 See Schiller, Friedrich, Letter VIII in *Aesthetical Essays of Friedrich Schiller* (Amazon Kindle Edition: Public Domain Book), 769–801.
12 Evidently in 1901 Frieda had translated some works of Schiller from German into English. Whether or not she brought her reading of Schiller to bear on Lawrence's writing is not certain. What does appear to be certain is that, independently, or through her, Lawrence is now able to articulate his theories about instinctual knowledge more confidently. As he tells her, she has made his sexual passion a "calm" and "steady sort of force", and "no longer a wandering thing" (403). Therefore, he promises her: "I try, I will always try, when I write to you, to write the truth as near the mark as I can get it" (403).

Works cited

Annan, Noel. *Leslie Stephen: His Thought and Character in Relation to His Time*. Cambridge, MA: Harvard University Press, 1952.
Asquith, Herbert Henry. "Introduction." *Liberalism: An Attempt to State the Principles and Proposals of Contemporary Liberalism in England*. Ed. Herbert Samuel. London: Grant Richards, 1902.
Bernstein, George L. *Liberalism and Liberal Politics in Edwardian England*. Boston: Allen and Unwin, 1986.
Booth, Wayne C. "Confessions of a Lukewarm Lawrentian." *The Challenge of D. H. Lawrence*. Ed. Michael Squires and Keith Cushman. Madison: U of Wisconsin P, 1990.
Boulton, James T., gen. ed. *The Letters of D. H. Lawrence*. The Cambridge Edition of the Letters and Works of D. H. Lawrence. Cambridge: Cambridge UP, 1979.
Bouttier, Sarah. "The Geometrics of Education in D. H. Lawrence." *Études Lawrenciennes* [En ligne] 47 (2016), mis en ligne le 23 novembre 2016, consulté le 03 décembre 2018. <http://journals.openedition.org/lawrence/255>; DOI: 10.4000/lawrence.255
Chambers, Jessie. *D. H. Lawrence: A Personal Record* (first published 1935 under pseudonym "E.T"), 2nd ed. Ed. J.D. Chambers. London: Frank Cass, 1965.
Crews, Frederick C. *E. M. Forster: The Perils of Humanism*. Princeton, NJ: Princeton UP, 1961.
Forster, E.M. *Two Cheers for Democracy*. New York: Harcourt, Brace and Company, 1951.
Gerson, Lloyd P., ed. *The Cambridge Companion to Plotinus*. Cambridge: Cambridge UP, 1996.
Hobhouse, L.T. *Liberalism*. London: Thornton Butterworth, 1934.
Lawrence, D.H. "A Study of Thomas Hardy." *Phoenix: The Posthumous Papers of D H. Lawrence*. Ed. Edward D. McDonald. New York: Viking Press, 1936
Lawrence, D.H. *Touch and Go*. 1919. Rockville, MD: Wildside Press, 2004.
Medalie, David. *E.M. Forster's Modernism*. New York: Palgrave, 2002.
Murdoch, Iris. *Existentialists and Mystics: Writings on Philosophy and Literature*. Ed. and with a preface by Peter Conradi. New York: Allen Lane, 1998
Samuel, Herbert. *Liberalism: An Attempt to State the Principles and Proposals of Contemporary Liberalism in England*. London: Grant Richards, 1902.
Schiller, Friedrich. "Letter VIII." *Aesthetical Essays of Friedrich Schiller*. Amazon Kindle Edition, Public Domain Book, 2008.
Trilling, Diana, ed. *The Selected Letters of D. H. Lawrence*. New York: Farrar, Straus & Cudahy Inc, 1958.
Wilde, Oscar. "The Critic as Artist." *The Norton Anthology of English Literature*, 7th ed., vol. 2-B. Ed. Carol T. Christ and George H. Ford. New York: Norton, 2000. 1752–60.

7
HOLDING ENVIRONMENTS
An enquiry into institutional minds

Sonali Jain

Introduction

In India, while educational policy frameworks have attracted attention, hardly any study has looked at how the human psyche affects institutional management and performance. The dynamics of higher educational institutions are a key consideration in discussing the future of higher education. This chapter sets out to study under a wide net all-women's undergraduate colleges in Indian metropolises as exemplars on the psychoanalytic couch. As far as possible, most group and individual processes in these educational institutions are placed under the classical psychoanalytic lens, and how the unconscious plays a major role in teaching and learning is examined. The theoretical framework is provided by the works of Sigmund Freud, Melanie Klein, Manfred Kets de Vries, Nancy Chodorow, Sudhir Kakar, Salman Akhtar, D.W. Winnicott, and Wilfred Bion. I argue that colleges serve as "holding environments" in Winnicott's terminology.

My argument is informed by organisational concepts like leadership, interpersonal behaviour, group processes, and the role of money as emotional currency. One may believe that in educational institutions such as colleges, the mind does not move beyond the conscious. This is where I maintain that psychoanalysis is of immense significance and one must "give the unconscious its due". This enquiry is into the institutional minds of faculty and staff and does not address the student body. Such a study is definitely required; however, it is beyond the scope of the present analysis.

The chapter is structured as follows: "The Setting" describes the system of higher education in India and situates institutions in their social, cultural, and economic diversity. The next section is titled "The Inner Theatre", in which various personality types are discussed. Subsections of this section highlight individual traits and processes: "Narcissism and the Charismatic Leader", "Idealisation and Devaluation", "Envy and Gratitude", "Loners". Winnicott's idea of "A Holding Environment" forms the subject of the next section. The following section deals with "Group Processes". Issues related to culture are discussed in the section "Cultures and Identities". This is followed by a section on "Money as Emotional Currency". Some concluding remarks are made in the final section.

The Setting

In the higher education system in India, a variety of institutions, including single-campus universities and specialised technical institutions, fall within the definition of universities. While many colleges are co-educational, a substantial number are all-women's colleges. Streaming is done at the entry point, with programmes in Humanities and Sciences being separate. Another feature is the existence of a ubiquitous Commerce stream. The bias against girls studying science at the higher level merits independent study. There is a definite gender bias, in most cases right from school. Girls are not encouraged to study science, largely because of existing patriarchal stereotypes. (See, for example, Jain and Varma 2002.)

Several all-women's colleges are located in Indian metropolitan cities and have well absorbed different cultures, ideologies, and identities. While students come from different parts of the country and have a middle-class or lower-middle-class socio-economic status, teachers are largely based in cities and do not quite share a regional or socio-economic bonding with students. The students fall within the 17–21 age group and are young adults who can often challenge their teachers more than school students. While the Institutions[1] that I am referring to do have some male faculty, their ethos is largely shaped by their female faculty.

The curricula, teaching strategies, teacher actions, and decisions are formed by considerations of a bigger decision-making body. However, each college is responsible for its own students, their needs, the backgrounds, and interests. Pedagogy includes how teachers interact with students and the social, intellectual and emotional environment the teacher seeks to establish. The psychological growth of both teacher and student and a sensitivity with which to approach the processes of teaching and listening remain vital.

The Inner Theatre

Sigmund Freud impeccably argued that neurotic symptoms can be used to decode why people behave the way they do. As conspicuous signifiers of a person's inner world, the part that remains concealed from reason, he believed, as "the royal road to an understanding of the unconscious". I would like to point out here that each participant in a college has to deal with his or her "inner theatre". Each has to analyse how his or her conscious behaviour reveals itself at the workplace.

Manfred Kets de Vries, a pioneer in the psychoanalytic study of organisations, has emphasised the importance of the inner theatre, which ". . . can foster creativity and cooperation among their colleagues and subordinates" (Kets de Vries xix). It is a play between teachers and students which contributes to its individual and group processes. Educators need to reflect on the following issues: is the leader a balanced, dependable person? Are all members of the staff intelligent, logical individuals fostering creativity and a sense of aliveness in each other? How should one cope with highly destructive behaviour? The art of listening needs to be inculcated in teachers as much as in students.

What really happens in institutions is in the intra-psychic and interpersonal world of people at work, much beneath the conscious. Those underlying behaviours of teachers and students need to be comprehended in terms of pedagogic freedom, anxieties, defence mechanisms, and conflicts. The personality of a student is still in the making while at college; however, that of the teacher has already been sculpted.

As Nancy Chodorow remarks:

> According to psychoanalytic theory, personality is a result of a boy's or girl's social-relational experiences from earliest infancy. Personality development is not the result of a conscious parental intention. The nature and quality of the social relationships that the child experiences are appropriated, internalized, and organized by her or him and come to constitute her or his personality. . .The conscious self is usually not aware of many of the features of personality or of its total structural organization.
>
> (Chodorow 47)

Narcissism and the Charismatic Leader

Narcissists may broadly be defined as those who take their own selves as love objects. In this chapter I study narcissism as a part of human behaviour as first articulated by Freud (100-02) and how it has worked in the given educational context. I analyse with examples of some charismatic women leaders in higher educational institutions.[2] One must note that usually they become leaders in their mid-careers. While some may owe their position to political allegiance, by and large they are quintessential teachers, dynamic and devoted to teaching—which wins them much respect among students. A good grip over the subject gives them an added sense of respect, admiration, and even awe. Added to this may be the factor of personal charm, which remains embedded within the collective unconscious.

More often than not, it heightens a sense of "healthy narcissism" in faculty when the highest administrative post reaches them. Most faculty, when they take on the role of administrators, usually show a good measure of hard work, self-esteem, and vision that extends beyond the immediate.

Unconsciously, sometimes in the leader there is a pressing work ethic which goes beyond even a good measure of work. This could be understood as a strong need to satisfy a punitive super ego and thus to excel. Any institutional achievement is both consciously and unconsciously taken as a personal success. However, workaholism can be examined more deeply and sublimation as a defence mechanism may also be applied. As Salman Akhtar defines it, sublimation is "the capacity of the sexual instinct to alter its original aim into a non-sexual aim that yield socially valued activity" (*Dictionary* 273–74).

Before we look psychoanalytically at the phenomenon of charisma, we may recall John Bowlby's theory of attachment, which dealt with attachment of the child with one primary caregiver throughout life. The study of the process of bonding and the breaking or disruption of personal relationships can provide insight into the nature of charisma. Based on Bowlby's theory, David Aberbach has developed a theory of charisma:

> Charisma in its various forms and intensities . . . may be linked with the breach or disruption of affectional bonds, especially in childhood. Loss is not the exclusive cause of charisma but is evidently an ingredient . . . In its outstanding manifestations, charisma is an aesthetic phenomenon and, as in the case of other forms of creativity, it may arise from unresolved childhood grief.
>
> (Aberbach 846)

I apply these ideas to charismatic leaders in higher educational institutions. Usually, the charismatic leader possesses an unusual insight into societal attachment behaviour arising from her experience of childhood loss or separation with the caregiver. It is often the case that the attachment behaviour activated by loss in the charismatic leader has not found a satisfactory outlet in other human relationships. She may therefore reach out to abstract objects such as the Institution, Society, or even Knowledge. This possibly gives her an opportunity to create a relationship with colleagues through which she aims to find the "resolution, the love and wholeness that were lost, attenuated or never had in private life" (Aberbach 845). This relationship may have a pathological element but may well indicate the striving for health.

Idealisation and Devaluation

Very often, the attitude of colleagues towards the leader or colleagues in other important positions in the Institutions is that of either idealisation or devaluation. To begin with idealisation as defence:

> We all idealize people important to us, beginning with our first caretakers, assigning powerful imagery to them. Through this idealizing process, we hope to combat feelings of helplessness and acquire

some of the power of the person admired . . . It's a two-way street, of course: followers project their fantasies on to their leaders and leaders mirror themselves in the glow of their followers.

(Kets de Vries 44)

However, it is to be noted that it is not only the leader who is idealised. Such equations exist between other members of the faculty as well. For instance, teachers who sincerely follow and stand by a political ideology without ambition/personal gain or attempt at acquiring power may also be much idealised by other faculty. Such faculty are seen to work for the Institution, not for personal gain, but here too at the unconscious level narcissism and competition do come into play.

In a case of devaluation, colleagues unconsciously use splitting and the paranoid-schizoid position in their inability to sustain ambivalence. Splitting is a mechanism that views events or people as either all bad or all good. When viewing people as all bad, the individual employs devaluation: attributing exaggeratedly negative qualities to the self or others. They may feel victimised and cannot tolerate the "injustice".

Ambivalence was used by Freud to indicate the simultaneous presence of love and hate towards the same object. According to Melanie Klein, love and hate start off as clearly differentiated emotions in the infant's life. If one were to see any "victimised" faculty member through this paradigm, as an infant, also wishing to seek the mother, it would be clear that both good and bad aspects of the self are split in her and later projected as love and hatred to the mother—in this case to the leader and the others around. During the paranoid-schizoid position, she shall have experienced the world, especially the leader as good or bad, according to her experiences.

Envy and Gratitude

Among peers there is much envy and jealousy as well. As Melanie Klein argues:

> Envy is the angry feeling that another person possesses and enjoys something desirable—the envious impulse being to take it away or to spoil it. Moreover, envy implies the subject's relation to one person only and goes back to the earliest exclusive relation with the mother.
>
> (Klein 212)

Peers do not accept hierarchy, and many want to be the power around the throne by occupying positions such as Bursar or Heads of Committees. Several have no agency at their homes, remaining steeped in patriarchy and anti-feminist values. The only place they can assert themselves is at the workplace: in meetings and so forth, trying to act according to rules, posturing fair but at the same time creating a "mini parliament" strongly opposing the leader. Some are of a controlling disposition and observe the interpersonal relationship with the head of the Institution, only in terms of dominance and submission. They deal with the sense of inferiority that hounds them by trying their level best to compete and feel superior, in an authoritarian and not in an egalitarian manner.

This perception extends to the classroom situation as well. There are many teachers in these Institutions who do not hold any power outside of their roles as academics. What Krishna Kumar observed as the "paradox of the teacher's personality" in the context of school education appears to apply here too. Teachers, devoid of agency at home and not asserting themselves elsewhere, turn authoritarian when faced with powerless students. They are thus "meek dictators" (Kumar 73).

In several Institutions, peers are delighted when they take charge at positions such as Staff Association/Staff Council Secretary, Superintendent of Examinations, University Co-ordinators, all important stations. This may serve to assuage the feeling of envy.

In India there is a huge premium on permanent positions in higher educational institutions. Largely, younger faculty idealise leaders enormously: a lot of it is gratitude about the job, whatever be the nature. Temporary, ad hoc, and contractual faculty often take on additional work and the environment becomes exploitative, even if inadvertently. Here, I must add that it is not a slave–master equation (in the sense of Hegel and Lacan) where each confronts the other and seeks supremacy over the other. Leaders can also feel like "good internal objects" to some who seek reassurance, support, and affirmation.

According to Melanie Klein:

> A full gratification at the breast means that the infant feels he has received from his loved object a unique gift, which he wants to keep. This is the basis of gratitude. Gratitude includes belief in good objects and trust in them. It includes also the ability to assimilate the loved object—not only as a source of food—and to love it without envy interfering . . . Gratitude is closely bound up with generosity.
> (Klein 215–16)

Loners

Once you label me, you defeat me.
—Jean Paul Sartre

Some colleagues may be loners, with a partially schizoid tendency, not seeming to care very much about relating to others. They may not dislike people in the Institution but may appear to be better by themselves, not caring too much about traditional ways and processes of bonding. When spoken to, they may respond but retreat into their shell quickly. They could restrict social relationships out of fear that contact may become disruptive and painful. Fear of rejection causes schizoid and avoidant behaviour.

Body weight or being overweight is another difficult issue for many women. There is a current cultural distaste for obesity, especially among women (see, e.g., the review article by Rothblum). Faculty are usually preoccupied with patriarchal stereotypes of good "edited" bodies. It takes courage to embrace one's body the way it is, recount struggles with body image, and not feel ashamed of one's body. Sometimes, competition with better, more graceful peers or even the leader becomes very challenging. Nevertheless, Institutions do not discard anybody on this account. A holding environment, which is discussed in the next section, is provided for all no matter how they look.

A Holding Environment

The Institution strives to provide what D.W. Winnicott describes as "a holding environment" in all experiences:

> Holding Environment is a term coined by Donald Winnicott (1960) in connection with the ordinary function of a mother holding her infant. Holding in this context meant not only the actual physical holding of the infant, but also the total environmental provision (43) . . . Such an environment meets psychological needs and is reliable. It does not abandon nor does it impinge. It facilitates growth.
> (*Dictionary* 130)

Change is inevitable, yet change is not easy. It can happen only when participants feel safe and protected, and willing to experience in a new space. The Institution creates a transitional space, a secure, confidential space where there can be possibilities for "playing and reality" for both students and faculty. The Institution makes them feel motivated, and of course, the greater the need to change, the greater the keenness for self-exploration. Listening to others is a sensitising process. However, it must be noted that mere realisation does not go too far; changing deep-rooted behaviour patterns and thought is another matter, and here the term "holding environment" is significant.

When I use the term "holding environment", I cannot ignore mental illness and health. Some Institutions have counselling centres or low-fee therapy clinics, a space where patients begin to form a relation with anguish to reach health. Psychodynamic counselling, as an engaged perspective, locates illness as part of being human and encourages a connection with loss as pivotal in a journey towards healing. In painful and traumatic experiences, the individual loses her capacity to think and disturbing feelings are kept out.

Psychodynamic counselling of the kind that some centres provide enables the building of a relationship with the silent and expressed parts of the self. The most encountered difficulties that a counsellor comes across may include separation anxiety and fear of independence on the part of the patient. The patient may be a victim of sexual abuse and incest. Students often take recourse to drugs and go through withdrawal and prolonged sadness. There may be repeated academic failure and an inability to concentrate. Students who reach out for counselling may complain of loss of appetite or binge eating as a way to manage negative feelings, narcissistic rage, and conflicts around intimacy.

Institutions manage to hold extreme cases of psychosis—wherein faculty may get quite disturbed or may have several breakdowns at work. Such members may be impulsive and reckless, self-centred, abusive, aggressive to the point of violence, sometimes particularly targeting the leader, analytically seeing her as the tyrannical father. Such a person may even leave the Institution; however, doors are not closed forever and the person may return in a much-improved psychological state.

Group Processes

There are many regressive group processes at work as well. I draw upon Bion's group assumptions of dependency, fight-flight, and pairing. In bigger group processes the syndrome of dependency is at work. The faculty assumes that the leader, "on whom it depends for nourishment, material and spiritual, and protection" (Symington and Symington 139), shall provide what was offered earlier by parents. In the Institution, leaders (whether they are the formal chairs of committees, elected or self-assumed) often try to blend with unconscious wishes of the group. There are leaders in an Institution who believe they are omnipotent—all powerful, which is once again a very primitive form of defence.

In other situations, the fight-flight syndrome may be observed. It is assumed that the workplace is dangerous and therefore fight-flight as a defence mechanism must be resorted to. Faculty splits into camps of friends and enemies. Common fight reactions are "Aggression against the self, against peers (in the form of envy, jealousy, competition . . .) Flight reactions include avoidance of others, absenteeism, and giving up" (Symington and Symington 138).

Bion's third unconscious assumption is that of pairing. "Pairing up with an individual or group perceived as powerful will help a person cope with anxiety, alienation and loneliness" (Symington and Symington 139). To cite an example, one faculty member in an Institution, despite her loud, defiant, and almost hysterical behaviour, stuck to one of her peers, because deep in the unconscious she was a frightened child, scared of abandonment.

I further argue that the struggle for dominance and power is based on sexuality in the unconscious. It may be noted that in most Institutions under study the non-teaching staff comprises mostly men. For instance, in one Institution a member of the non-teaching staff had intense romantic feelings, sexual in the unconscious, for the head of the Institution. It was not just he who felt for her, the Accounts Officer had her photograph as wallpaper on his computer. Another member of the staff, not directly vocal about his feelings, called her "mother", thereby denying sexual feelings.

The Chief Officer was a new recruit in this particular Institution. A man somewhat obsequious and polished and at the same time pompous, he earned the dislike of all among the non-teaching staff because of his proximity to the Principal. It is interesting to observe that he reacted positively to this stressful situation and as a measure of gratitude became very loyal to authority. He became more receptive to the attitudes of others and much less defensive, helping the Institution to work better collectively.

Cultures and Identities

Even though the Institution represents only a microcosm of Indian society, it is not homogeneous and thereby no generalisation is easy. I quote Sudhir Kakar:

> How can one generalize about a billion people—Hindus, Muslims, Sikhs, Christians, and Jains—who speak 14 major languages and are characterized by pronounced regional and linguistic identities? How can one postulate anything in common among a people divided not only by social class but also by India's signature system of caste, and with an ethnic diversity typical more of past empires than of modern nation-states?
>
> (Kakar 2006)

Discrimination against historically disadvantaged classes is a well-known feature of Indian society. In many Institutions there may not be ostensible discrimination against faculty belonging to the depressed classes. However, there are cases of poor teachers lacking in effort, which may not be because of being marginalised. There is a case of one such faculty member in a college who felt victimised because of her class and wrote a letter alleging discrimination based on caste and social class. A person with a paranoid disposition, she engaged in the three primitive defences of splitting, projection, and denial, blamed others for her own shortcomings, and made a routine hue and cry over small issues. Under Indian law, the charge of discrimination that she levelled is a serious one, and the sequence of events was highly disruptive for the Institution:

> At the heart of the paranoid disposition—as with the other prototypes—there's a frequently negative childhood experience.

As children, paranoid individuals may have been exposed to an extremely intrusive parenting style that fostered feelings of inadequacy or helplessness. Shame and humiliation may have been used by parents as controlling devices.

(Kets de Vries 113)

Elaborating more on cultures and identities, the younger faculty often get fashionably dressed and espouse independent political thought and ideology in their roles as academics and feminists. This comprises right-wing academics as well, who otherwise do not believe in equality or autonomy for women or in liberal notions of justice. Often, topics of discussion are family, particularly maids and their absence, food, and designer outfits. Some faculty may pay a lot of attention to glamour. They might be active on social media, well turned out in fashionable clothes, with much hype around feminism. Sometimes, away from actual classroom teaching, the concentration of such academics is on the academe as well as their own peer groups outside the Institution. The economically privileged students, especially, identify or want to identify with them.

As Laplanche and Pontalis write:

Identification is defined as a psychological process whereby the subject assimilates an aspect, property or attribute of the other and is transformed, wholly or partially, after the model the other provides. It is by means of a series of identifications that the personality is constituted and specified.

(Laplanche and Pontalis 205)

Money as Emotional Currency

It is vital to reflect on the role of money in Institutions. To begin with, issues of governance with the faculty in committees, as well as with non-teaching staff, arise primarily from the structure of student fees. Student fees for regular students are low and funding comes largely from government sources. Moreover, Institutions run many extracurricular societies and funds have to be disbursed for extracurricular activities and good productions. This is where many leaders differ majorly in their personalities.

In 1908, Freud listed parsimony among the major traits of obsessional personality and traced its origin to the pleasure felt by the anal phase child in retaining faeces. Freud declared that money and faeces were equated in the unconscious. This proposal was supported by his early pupils such as Ferenczi, Jones, and Fenichel, and the faeces–money equation became an established psychoanalytic dictum.

In Higher Educational Institutions, usually, a senior member of the faculty is appointed Bursar, and it becomes a position of power, inadvertently or otherwise. The final authority of course rests with the leader. A narcissistic leader may pursue extracurricular activities with fervour, and, indeed, they require both money and person power. According to the self-psychological perspective, showing off one's laurels or wealth is a means to seek affirmation and applause from others. This helps maintain a positive self-image. As Salman Akhtar points out, it provides a sense of vitality and coherence to an otherwise fragile self ("Review" 89). In some cases, it could be an overcompensation for a personal loss.

Money has come to symbolise an elusive source of security in later life. In leaders who may be very tight-fisted and feel themselves controlled by the presence/absence of money all the time, "money is invested early on with the power to negotiate an easy by-passing of emotional deprivation and loss and to allow the acquisition in phantasy of what is painfully lacking in reality" ("Review" 90).

An important theme is the childhood experience of dependency and the potential perils attendant upon it. I close this section with a quote from Rose and Carrington:

> As the availability of money can be crucial to survival, we can see that its threatened absence has the potential to evoke the kinds of feelings we infer from witnessing a feeding baby. In maturity in later life, when we have established an ongoing economic security, we are unlikely to experience the same kind of panic. However, we can infer that the absence of money, because it signifies survival, always has the potential to evoke this panic. Threats, arising from dependency, will inevitably become part of the meaning of money because of what its lack will signify . . . where the absence of money turns from phantasy to reality and, thus, threatens, and sometimes brings total annihilation of, the individual.
>
> (Rose and Carrington 41–42)

Conclusion

It has been argued in this chapter that it is crucial to give due importance to unconscious processes inside HEIs, since these affect the functioning of the Institution. Whether a person is labelled "normal" or "abnormal", the same psychological processes are at work. Not much work along these lines has been done in the educational sector. Psychoanalytic study of organisations has emerged as an independent field of study in recent years, but its application has largely been confined to the corporate sector.

All-women institutions are common in India and many other Asian countries. They become necessary as, even in metropolitan cities, many parents will not let young girls study in a co-educational school. This breeds its own dynamics: many teachers in practice enforce the same patriarchal code as many of the parents. The psyche of the participants is necessarily shaped by the patriarchal social system. There are crucial issues that must be considered while discussing the gendered mind–body struggle at the workplace. Most of the female faculty exhibit male processes of culture and socialisation, though the setting is asymmetrical in gender terms.

While the face of education is changing, institutions like those studied here play a major role in shaping students in their formative years. Students will continue to choose going to college over other means of learning because development is much more all round. Thus, it becomes imperative to understand the psychodynamics of institutions. As observed here, the Institution, in spite of all the differences, does aim to provide a holding environment to all its members.

The concept of the Container was coined by Bion in 1962 for the maternal mind which receives the projections of the child and, by that very act, makes it possible for the latter to discover its needs. Symington and Symington have elaborated the concept as follows:

> . . . Bion's concept of the container is frequently equated with Winnicott's idea of holding or holding environment. We wish here to differentiate them clearly. Bion's concept differs in three ways. The container is *internal*, whereas holding or the holding environment is external or in the transitional stage between internal and external; the container is non-sensuous but the holding environment is predominantly sensuous; the container together with the contained is active.
>
> (Symington and Symington 58)

The individual and group examples recounted here indicate that, although there is room for all kinds of emotional experiences, most Institutions are not containers in the sense of Bion's theory.

As argued here, it is not possible to comprehend the dynamics of institutions without recognising the unconscious processes at work. Institutional mechanisms need to be worked out so that educational institutions can achieve the aim of containing the emotional experiences of all participants.

Notes

1. For the rest of this chapter, an "Institution" or "College" is understood to be of the kind described in this paragraph.
2. While the analysis here is based on observation of several charismatic leaders, no identifying details are presented in order to protect their privacy.

Works cited

Aberbach, David. "Charisma and Attachment Theory: A Crossdisciplinary Interpretation." *The International Journal of Psychoanalysis* 76 (1995): 845–55.

Akhtar, Salman. *Comprehensive Dictionary of Psychoanalysis*. London: Karnac, 2009.

———. "Review of *Money as Emotional Currency: Psychoanalytic Ideas*. Ed. Anca Carrington." *International Journal of Psychoanalysis* 13.1 (2016): 89–94.

Chodorow, Nancy J. *Feminism and Psychoanalytic Theory*. New Haven: Yale UP, 1989.

Freud, Sigmund. "On Narcissism: An Introduction." *The Standard Edition of the Complete Works of Sigmund Freud*. Ed. James Strachey et al., XIV. London: The Hogarth Press and the Institute of Psychoanalysis, 1957. 67–102.

Kakar, Sudhir. "Culture and Psychoanalysis: A Personal Journey." *Social Analysis: The International Journal of Social and Cultural Practice* 50.2 (2006): 25–44.

Kets de Vries, Manfred F.R. *The Leader on the Couch: A Clinical Approach to Changing People and Organizations*. San Francisco: Jossey-Bass, 2006.

Klein, Melanie. *The Selected Melanie Klein*. Ed. Juliet Mitchell. Harmondsworth: Penguin, 1986.

Kumar, Krishna. *Political Agenda of Education: A Study of Colonialist and Nationalist Ideas*. New Delhi: Sage, 2005.

Laplanche, Jean, and Jean-Bertrand Pontalis. *The Language of Psycho-Analysis*. Trans. Donald Nicholson-Smith. New York: W. W. Norton, 1973.

Rose, James, and Anca Carrington. "Money and Childhood Phantasies." *Money as Emotional Currency: Psychoanalytic Ideas*. Ed. Anca Carrington. London: Karnac, 2014. 37–53.

Rothblum, Esther D. "The Stigma of Women's Weight: Social and Economic Realities." *Feminism & Psychology* 2.1 (1992): 61–73.

Symington, Joan, and Neville Symington. *The Clinical Thinking of Wilfred Bion*. London: Routledge, 1996.

Winnicott, Donald Woods. "The Theory of the Parent-Infant Relationship." *The International Journal of Psychoanalysis* 41 (1960): 585–95.

8
THE CHALLENGES OF *SKILLING* THE UNDERGRADUATE ENGLISH LANGUAGE LEARNER FOR THE GLOCAL MARKET

Anjana Neira Dev and Sameer Chopra

The undisputed importance of English as a crucial soft skill in the contemporary Indian socio-economic environment cannot be denied. In terms of academic success and the fulfilment of professional aspirations, it merits consideration for teachers of English engaged in pedagogical interactions in the undergraduate classroom. This chapter will discuss the challenges and opportunities for both teachers and learners as they negotiate the transactions that are predicated upon the shared belief that the successful handover of knowledge and skills will empower learners in both tangible and intangible ways. The intangibles are increased self-confidence as the learners are able to communicate with greater facility in both speech and writing; the tangibles include high scores and success in job searches and upward professional mobility in the work space.

This chapter also draws inspiration from a pioneering work on the teaching of English in Indian universities, a collection of essays edited by Svati Joshi (1994). In the Introduction to the collection she notes:

> Our growing sense of dislocation within our discipline and an even greater sense of bedevilment at the contradiction and crises of the time we are living in have left us with many questions concerning our academic engagement and its relation to our historical situation as well as the nature of political and cultural processes in our contemporary society.
>
> (Joshi 1)

While the essays in this volume are concerned with recontextualising pedagogy with reference to history and culture, our concern is with the nuts and bolts of daily classroom interactions which are doubtless affected by the surrounding socio-political and economic milieu. As Joshi says:

> English continues to be the language of the metropolitan ruling elite that is located in state apparatuses and the professions. English still remains the language that regulates access to higher education, and is linked to class interest, economic benefits and with the production and reproduction of major forms of social power and cultural privilege.
>
> (Joshi 2)

The first perspective from which this issue can be studied is *the role of the teacher as facilitator*. Most contemporary approaches to ELT emphasise the seminal importance of the teacher being able to reconfigure the way s/he conceptualises her/his role vis-à-vis learners in the classroom. In her illuminating discussion on the techniques and principles of Communicative Language Teaching (CLT), American linguist Diane Larsen-Freeman argues for a dynamic, democratic learning space wherein students are given many an "opportunity to express their ideas and opinions" and, in turn, the "teacher acts as a facilitator in setting up communicative activities and as an advisor during the activities" (Larsen-Freeman 126–27), rather than an authoritarian, distanced figure who, as the sole repository of knowledge, transmits it to her/his learners in a unidirectional way. Thinking back to our personal experiences of language acquisition at the secondary school level, we remember it being primarily constituted of a deductive teaching of grammar: newer and more advanced rules would be introduced at every level of instruction, and we as students were expected to understand, absorb, and use them with mathematical precision. In retrospect, this approach is limited on two counts: firstly, it focuses on grammar as an abstract entity that can be taught in isolation from real-life communicative situations; secondly, other *functional* areas of language—especially listening, speaking, reading, and writing—are more or less ignored. It is assumed that once the student masters grammar, s/he would automatically be able to read, write, and speak well. To borrow terms from the discourse of ELT, such a technique prioritises *linguistic competence* over *communicative competence*.

In contrast, an effective language lesson must get the students to learn language by actually *using it* and not merely being instructed *about it*. It is critical that they are active, pleasurably engaged, and self-motivated throughout. To ascertain that the teaching methodology is activity-oriented, the teacher should enable a thorough involvement of learners in meaningful, focused, yet fun-filled tasks, activities, and exercises. Using innovative materials that go beyond the textbook (worksheets, role-plays, games, audio-visual exercises) goes a long way in breaking monotony and keeping learners curious and engrossed. At the same time, one must not completely sidestep the significance of some direct instruction: grammar explanations, for instance, are very helpful in introducing important concepts, which can then be reinforced through creative activities and exercises. Equally, it is crucial that teaching materials are designed keeping the level of learners in mind; the learner should not find the materials either excessively challenging or easy, lest s/he loses interest. Finally, while a focus on activities generally contributes to learning positively, it sometimes takes away from the gravity of that process. It is imperative that productive language learning takes place in the classroom at all times; in other words, it should not be just "fun and games". This is achievable through carefully and conscientiously planning a lesson's/task's objectives well in advance and anticipating solutions to some of the problems that arise from inadequate and inconsistent participation.

The greatest impediment to fully implementing such an eclectic and experimental pedagogy in a typical classroom of Delhi University is its sheer size in terms of numbers. With an average strength of over 50, executing CLT strategies earnestly not only becomes laborious and time-consuming but also sometimes simply untenable for the teacher. Inevitably, the methodology becomes more standardised and homogeneous and less responsive to the linguistic and socio-cultural diversity of learners. In order to circumvent this problem, an institutionally backed paradigm shift in favour of ELT is necessary. For reasons outside the scope of this chapter, most English departments in postcolonial India are steeped in a hierarchical matrix, one that considers literature and theoretical analyses more valuable than language and communication. This is rather unfortunate, given that the learning needs of a majority of our students, especially in relation to the market, are communicative and not academic.

As we need to take on board the actual beneficiaries of the research that goes into creative pedagogy, the Indian undergraduate classroom has a distinguishing variable that is a major determinant in the success or otherwise of all academic initiative and endeavours. This variable is *heterogeneity*, perhaps the foremost pedagogical challenge routinely faced by English language teachers. Besides their socio-economic background, learners are variously distinguished by their language-learning ability and knowledge, learning styles, mother tongues and knowledge of other languages, confidence, motivation, and self-discipline. In theory, diversity is a much-cherished, perhaps even incontestable, ideal: it invigorates the teaching-learning space, rendering it more dialogic, interactive, and relevant to the individual needs of learners. When it is accompanied with large class sizes, however, as is almost invariably the case in the context of publicly funded higher education in India, it sometimes becomes a hindrance. The primary problem we have regularly had to contend with is that of ensuring a productive and stimulating learning environment for *all* our learners: textbook exercises are usually standardised, with little room for manoeuvring; even the teacher's own initiatives for learning enhancement, such as worksheets and role-play tasks, are often perceived as too easy or difficult, depending on the linguistic capabilities of the learner. This generates boredom and complacency on the one hand and feelings of inadequacy and low self-esteem on the other. Large and diverse classes also make it difficult for the teacher to closely monitor her/his learners' progress in a consistent fashion. Consequently, a small group of proficient and confident learners tend to overshadow their peers in terms of participation and the achievement of learning objectives. In such a scenario, summative and formative assessments are not entirely successful in realising their diagnostic and corrective aims: the volume of the teacher's correction work de-incentivises her/his personal investment in a qualitative improvement in language proficiency among learners over a sustained period of time.

These problems are pervasive in the Indian university system and have no easy solutions, mainly because they are more *structural* than *situational* in nature. Nevertheless, the teacher should continually strive to overcome them, to the extent possible, for her/his learners. In fact, viewed differently, heterogeneity in the classroom can provide unique opportunities for creative experimentation, professional development, and action research, precisely because the teacher has to perpetually seek newer ways of making her/his classes interesting and meaningful in the face of strong resistance from the institutionalised barriers discussed earlier. In our experience, varying one's topics and texts, and their difficulty levels, greatly helps tackle the problem of fluctuating participation and reaching out to all the different constituencies in the class, especially with regard to their proficiency and performance in the language. It is similarly important to create and adapt tasks in such a way that they are open-ended, making room for a number of different individual responses emerging from learners' pre-existent skills and opinions. Accumulating ideas for a pre-reading exercise with the help of a brainstorming map on the blackboard is one such very effective strategy. In addition, the teacher should consciously utilise activities that set into motion most, if not all, forms of "multiple intelligences" theorised by Howard Gardner: verbal-linguistic, visual-spatial, musical-rhythmic, bodily-kinaesthetic, and interpersonal, among others (Gardner 8–9). As long as an activity is able to sufficiently pique the curiosity of learners, which happens more frequently when it provides audio-visual stimulation, they tend to respond despite the specific linguistic challenges it poses. In fact, the perceived weakness of previous knowledge of linguistic structures and even vocabulary can be turned into an opportunity for learners to experience a sense of discovery and achievement as they are encouraged to master new digestible bites of knowledge in a friendly, non-judgemental space. Engaging learners in pair and group work also encourages more evenly distributed patterns of learner involvement: lower or middle ability learners, for instance, can be made to collaborate with the more advanced ones. This not only partially resolves the encumbrances emanating from learners' diverse intellectual needs but also facilitates interpersonal camaraderie among them. Finally, employing activities with a compulsory-cum-optional component can potentially turn the heterogeneous classroom into a more affirmative and equitable space for all: according to one of its chief proponents and practitioners, Penny Ur, this technique entails "tell[ing] the class . . . to do a certain minimal part of the task, the rest . . . [being] optional—that is, available to those who understand/ can do it/have time/ wish to do more" (306). The teacher ought to be conscious all along that those unable/unwilling to perform the optional, that is, more sophisticated, parts of the task aren't made to feel "lesser", lest it ends up reinforcing the hierarchies among learners even further.

As mentioned earlier, howsoever well-intentioned and skilled the teacher and motivated the learners, the visible outcome of classroom interactions remains the grade or mark on a printed page, one that becomes the sole indicator of the success or failure of an entire semester of pedagogical transactions. While there is plenty of research that continues to be undertaken on innovative and effective strategies for assessment and evaluation, *the impact of the reality of expanding class sizes* is another concern that merits serious consideration. The purpose of assessment is to augment quality, while that of evaluation is to assess it. When we are in the language classroom, both play a very significant role in helping teachers and learners arrive at a common understanding of goals and targets and the success/failure in achieving them. Assessment can also be defined as evaluation that has a value attached to it, a grade or a mark—a judgement of strengths, weaknesses, opportunities, and threats. In order to achieve this, we use various strategies that can be called tests: focused assessment, designed to elicit certain behaviour based on which one can make inferences and give a grade/mark/judgement. These strategies are used firstly at the formative stage, in the course of the semester, when we use the learners' performance in tests and exams to help us in our teaching and make decisions about content, strategies, approaches, and so forth. Then we do what is called "summative assessment" at the end of the semester when we rank and grade students, leading to certification. The first set of strategies is assessment *for* learning, a pedagogic evaluation to find out what learners have and have not learnt and to improve teaching and learning. The second set of strategies is assessment *of* learning, a judgemental evaluation conducted to examine whether the learners have learned something or not and to grade them accordingly.

If we agree that learning is collaborative and knowledge co-constructed, then feedback becomes a vital part of scaffolding the syllabus so that we can gradually hand over control to our learners, who should then be able to perform independently the tasks that they were previously being guided through. This feedback will ensure that the learners are made familiar with the paradigms that the teacher deploys while assessing and evaluating their inputs, both verbal and written. This feedback happens while teaching and during class hours—a deliberate, planned effort, involving the whole class in assignments—where the need is to go beyond correction of mistakes (spelling and grammar) to help learners understand what they need to do, continue doing it or effect relevant changes, and valuing what they have already achieved. A question that can be asked at this stage is: how will students learn what a good/correct/appropriate answer is versus its opposite? The evaluation of assignments and examinations can be done only after we are clear about what we are testing—content and/or proficiency. Once we have our goals in place, sharing them with the learners is crucial for their shared pursuit and successful achievement. In addition to goals, a challenge that comes from the large size of the class and its inevitable heterogeneity, as discussed earlier, is how to create a set of "valid" and "reliable" criteria that cater to the range of responses that our questions, both spoken and written, will elicit. Since it is rarely practical to give individual feedback and experience shows us that writing long comments on learners' assignments does not necessarily translate into desired outcomes, it would be useful to think of ways in which we can give feedback that is meaningful and relevant for the learners. A method that we have tried out with a fair amount of success is to list all the kinds of errors that students have committed on a particular assignment and then discuss these while returning it. This fulfils at least two very important objectives. Firstly, no single student or group of students is made to feel inadequate in front of the class as everyone is at the receiving end of the feedback. Secondly, it allows the teacher to discuss the errors at a metacognitive level, helping the students to think about and internalise the reasons why some kinds of writing do not generate a positive response from evaluators. This also makes the whole exercise of evaluation transparent and will hopefully result in the learners being able to become critics and judges of their own writing—perhaps one of the most beneficial skills a language teacher can impart to her/his students.

Assessment is not and should not be a final statement of a learner's abilities but an ongoing process that allows the learner and the teacher to collaboratively engage in helping the former improve her/his performance. The hierarchical, punitive model of assessment, a legacy of a pedagogical paradigm that reflected the manner in which socio-economic relations were organised, needs to be dismantled: this necessary shift relates to the entire theory and practice of English teaching. Experience of admissions to college that are currently based exclusively on summative assessment, the marks achieved by a student at the end of Class 12, is a stark reminder of the pitfalls of underestimating and ignoring all the formative assessment that goes into making learners develop a certain sense of themselves as located at a specific juncture of the scale of success and failure. The multiple intelligences model, a highly regarded concept in educational psychology, is blithely ignored when we exclusively focus on summative assessment and forget that our learners are not statistics and numbers but individual human beings who negotiate the challenges of life in distinct ways and at different speeds. A teacher's idealism is the greatest antidote to the tyranny of administrative barriers, and it is imperative that we use the constructive learning opportunities afforded by formative assessment judiciously in order to give every learner the opportunity to excel so that it is success and not failure that becomes a self-fulfilling prophecy.

Technology has become an ineluctable part of every sphere of our lives *and its pervasive role in the contemporary English as a Second Language (ESL) context* merits comment. Through the 1990s, there was a rapid emergence of programmes and software, collectively termed "computer-assisted language learning" (CALL), specifically geared towards enhancing creativity and interactivity of the subject. With greater access to the Internet and increasing user-friendliness, ELT activities also became widely available on web pages. These developments were motivated by a strong push in the direction of "blended" and "extended" learning, concepts that focus on the seamless amalgamation of digital technologies and teaching methodologies on the one hand and the use of the former in broadening the horizons of the formal curriculum on the other (Motteram and Sharma 84). The turn of the millennium only furthered the scope and impact of this revolutionising of language pedagogy: wikis, video sites like YouTube, social-media platforms such as Facebook and LinkedIn, e-books (both text-based and audio), massive open online courses (MOOCs), and a host of other applications not only support the emphasis that CLT places on authentic materials and communicative learning tasks but are also frequently deployed as tools to stimulate learners' interest and participation. Such widespread availability of a range of media has almost irreversibly altered the publication practices of traditional textbooks: most of them are now accompanied by CD-ROMs that provide audio-visual supplementation to the exercises they contain. Digital technology mediates learners' engagement with the various language skills in myriad ways, and an overview of this will give us a context in which to understand the phenomenon:

> *Reading and writing*—A vast amount of reading and writing exercises, including ready-to-use and downloadable worksheets, are available online. Additionally, written exchanges between learners and teachers, feedback mechanisms, and even evaluation strategies have become speedier and more effective with the help of email and online course management portals. Chat messenger services are used to set up fluency-based tasks such as group discussions, written records of which are later analysed, for instance, to address common grammatical inaccuracies one commits during routine discursive exchanges. The teacher can also hold blog-writing competitions (in class or as homework), allowing learners the encouraging opportunity of showcasing their work to a wider audience as well as peer-reviewing each other's entries.

Listening—Over time, listening activities have acquired tremendous sophistication and ease of usage with faster networks and learners no longer require access to a dedicated language laboratory, provided the classroom itself has provision for adequate equipment. Podcasts, TED Talks, radio-shows, interviews, audiobooks, and even mobile phone recordings can easily function as "texts"—the teacher's ingenuity lies in making these a basis for designing tasks that keep the learners involved and motivated throughout.

Grammar and vocabulary—Along with elementary grammar-check tools that almost all word-processing software come equipped with, there are more specialised ones, such as "Grammarly", that learners can use to edit and proofread their submissions. Technology is also particularly useful in presenting drills in the classroom—unlike humans, computers can deliver targeted practice for grammatical structures and functional patterns with tireless precision. At more advanced stages, teachers can make use of concordance programmes and linguistic corpora, types of indexes that search "for occurrences of a word or combinations of words, punctuation, affixes, phrases or structures within a *corpus* (a large collection of text) and can show immediate context of the search item" (Sokolik 417). Search results of this kind can be used to isolate and reinforce accurate usage patterns (did + first form of verb, for instance)—promoting a greater understanding and internalisation of complex grammar rules in naturally occurring sentences rather than reductive, decontextualised examples—as well as in the preparation of teaching materials. As for vocabulary, technology has enabled the digitisation of dictionaries, which can easily be found online or downloaded on one's computer/phone.

Speaking and pronunciation—Attempting to find ways to do meaningful spoken practice in the classroom can be distinctly challenging because learners are often much more inhibited about accuracy and fluency while speaking than writing. Speaking, to that extent, is the most "public' of acts: learners often feel, and legitimately so, that it is the one skill they are likely to be most judged on in real-life situations in the workplace and elsewhere. Understandably then, technology has faced some resistance in being able to intervene in the persistent hesitation many non-native speakers of English experience in expressing themselves confidently. Nevertheless, through integrated speaker and microphone devices, Voice over Internet protocol (or "Internet telephony"), Voice Recognition (forms of software that interpret spoken dictation and carry out voice commands), and presentation tools such as Microsoft PowerPoint and Windows Movie Maker, such encumbrances are gradually being overcome. Most online dictionaries these days have an inbuilt audio-pronunciation option, a feature that has significantly transformed, and rendered more approachable, the complex and at times daunting field of phonetics.

Evidently, technology seems to have become normalised in ELT, but one must be mindful that this trend is by no means universal as digital divisions are pervasive, especially in the developing world. Our experience of teaching English in the contemporary Indian tertiary education sector brings to the fore yet again a serious schism between theory and practice: most colleges of Delhi University, for example, simply do not possess the infrastructural wherewithal to fully exploit the potential of technological innovation in ELT. Until such a lacuna is rectified, and our institutions become more amenable to using technology to foster a genuinely autonomous and learner-oriented ethos, some reliance on the teacher's discretion is inevitable and, we would argue, desirable. S/he should be able to clearly evaluate whether a particular lesson/concept is actually enriched by technology, since one of the drawbacks of the digital boom we are currently in the midst of is the lack of quality control of online content. As Greene notes:

> there is an attraction in . . . CALL instruction for software applications that demonstrate the power of computers to do graphic design rather than to learn English. . . This is evidence to the extent to which the "wow factor" controls the . . . post-secondary EFL agenda.
>
> (Greene 241)

In order to avoid such a pitfall, the use of technological aids must be strongly aligned with the predetermined objectives of the course. In other words, it is the course that should drive technology and not vice versa. In a situation where technology seems not wholly appropriate to the needs at hand, it can, and indeed must, be modified and made to function in co-existence with non-digital materials like books, worksheets, posters, charts, and games. In this way, the other limitations that accrue from an excessive reliance on technology in the formulation of one's pedagogical choices, such as diminishing interest in reading and the rise in intentional and unintentional plagiarism among learners, can also be counterbalanced.

The final point of concern is the match or mismatch between *ability and aspirations and the demands of the job market* and the impact of this on the lives of individual learners, on the professional satisfaction or otherwise of teachers, and, in fact, on the future of English studies in India. The development of English in the undergraduate classroom presupposes an acquisition of the basic skills of that language in the formal teaching-learning environment of school and to some extent in the personal and relatively informal environment of home and/or the virtual world of interactions in which most young people participate. In both instances, the learner has been exposed to English in a variety of situations and has used it for not only its instrumental function of fulfilling basic needs of food, drink, and comfort but also, in many instances, for its regulatory (persuading, commanding, and requesting), interactional (building and maintaining relationships), personal (self-expression), representational (exchanging information), heuristic (learning about and exploring the environment), and imaginative (creating imaginary scenarios and planning and reacting) functions. The learner who enters the college classroom is assumed to have at best 12 years of learning and practice in the use of English and in some cases a minimum of six years of such acquisition and usage, even if the exposure to English began in middle school. If we can safely assume that a major part of our self-image derives from how we come across to others and the way they respond to us, in the marks we get and whether we succeed or fail in fulfilling our targets, then our aspirations are also a product of these factors. The problem arises when the criteria used to assess and evaluate our command over the use of English change as we move from the informal to the formal domains of life and also when we move from school to college.

It is this assumption that underlies the construction of syllabi and pedagogic planning. Current trends and wisdom pertaining to the formulation of the undergraduate curriculum have as their focus outcome-based frameworks that attempt to make tangible what the learner will take away from an academic programme of study. They foreground a particular set of skills and knowledge units that the learner will imbibe and be able to apply when needed. This application is largely restricted to her/his ability to perform well in formal evaluation challenges, namely summative semester-end examinations and ongoing internal assessment tests, assignments, projects, and so forth. The real challenge to this model comes from the learner's prowess in using this learning in the world outside the educational setting, in the job market.

When we think about the English language curricula, it becomes imperative to investigate and take into account the range of language skills in the domains of speaking and listening, reading, and writing that the graduates should imbibe in the course of their formal education and then be able to use with confidence in a real-world scenario. This is the chasm that our learners are constantly teetering on the brink of, when they face in the first instance the challenge of writing their biodata and applying for jobs. However helpful the range of templates available to them electronically, learners mostly find it difficult to meet this challenge and, despite qualifications, interest, and ability for a particular job, fail to get past the first post. Even if this hurdle is crossed, they find it difficult to compete with those peers who may be fortunate enough to have a richer linguistic skill set during interviews and group discussions. Even after joining work, many of our graduates struggle with the communication challenges of their jobs, and this leads to frustration, loss of confidence, and stagnation. Feedback from industry and employers is rife with complaints about how unemployable our learners are when it comes to basic "soft skills" of communicative competence.

Now that we have identified the problem, what is the way forward? What are the efforts that can be made by the teacher, the institution, and the curriculum to facilitate the easy transfer of knowledge by the learner from the classroom to the office? Foremost among these is a need to identify the range of job opportunities that a learner has the interest and the qualifications to pursue. The next step is to find out and list the kinds of linguistic skills that these potential jobs require so that they can be performed optimally. This done, the teacher as facilitator will need to help the learner with a personal SWOT (strength, weakness, opportunity, threat) analysis so that s/he knows which areas need work and strives accordingly. In a research report titled "English Skills for Employability: Setting Common Standards" (Prince and Singh 2015), a detailed study was carried out to address the problem of why "far too many students are graduating without sufficient skills to enter the workforce; they are unemployable" (Prince and Singh 4). As the background and rationale to the study indicate:

> With 55% of India's population below 30 years of age, as per the National Vocational Education Qualification Framework vision document (AICTE-NVEQF Vision Document 2011), many policy making bodies view English as a key skill that can transform the employability of India's youth . . . Special emphasis on verbal and written communication skills, especially in English, would go a long way in improving the employability of the large and growing mass of disempowered youth.
>
> (Prince and Singh 66)

With this end in mind, the report has developed a very useful "Indian National Skills Qualification Framework" (Appendix 2 of the Report) that lists communication as a "Core Skill" at every level.

It would be utopian to believe that the job market will adjust its demands to the available skills; it is the aspirants who need to equip themselves to fit the demands of the market if they want to be a part of it. At this stage, the graduate must realise that their goals need adjustment and their skills need strengthening. In both instances, it is the learner, with the help of the teacher, who needs to find the best fit and make the appropriate effort. Once this is achieved, the chasm can be crossed, and the dreams of a professional life that are in tune with one's personal desires and interests will remain intact in the (often harsh) light of day.

Works cited

Gardner, Howard. "The Idea of Multiple Intelligences." *Frames of Mind: The Theory of Multiple Intelligences*. New York: Basic Books, 1983. 3–11.

Greene, D. "A Design Model for Beginner-level Computer-mediated EFL Writing." *Computer Assisted Language Learning* 13.3 (2000): 239–52.

Joshi, Svati, ed. *Rethinking English: Essays in Literature, Language, History*. New Delhi: Oxford UP, 1994.

Larsen-Freeman, Diane. *Techniques and Principles in Language Teaching*. New Delhi: Oxford UP, 2000.

Motteram, G., and P. Sharma. "Blending Learning in a Web 2.0 World." *International Journal of Emerging Technologies & Society* 7.2 (2009): 83–96.

Prince, Emma-Sue, and Manish Singh. *English Skills for Employability: Setting Common Standards. A Research Report*. British Council, Trinity College London and City Guilds Manipal Global, 2015.

Sokolik, Maggie. "Digital Technology in Language Learning." *Teaching English as a Second or Foreign Language*. 4th ed. Ed. Marianne Murcia-Celce, Donna Brinton, and Marguerite Ann Snow. New Delhi: Cengage Learning, 2000. 409–21.

Ur, Penny. *A Course in Language Teaching: Practice and Theory*. Cambridge: Cambridge UP, 1996.

9
EVIDENCE-BASED DECISION-MAKING IN OUR TEACHING
Why is it important and how do we do it?

Rama Mathew

Introduction

While this topic seems to be a very important one for any teacher at any level, I would like to locate it within a context that makes it all the more relevant and important. The context is a seminar and a workshop that were held at different times in Bharati College of Delhi University. Dr Promodini Varma, the Principal of the college, initiated these and invited me to present a paper and conduct some sessions. The passion with which Promodini conveyed teachers' voices and concerns had made it genuine and understandable to someone like me who didn't teach students in an undergraduate college. I could relate myself to the everyday concerns of teachers in the classroom, especially assessment. Classroom-based assessment interestingly has a lot to do with what we teach, how we teach in the classroom, and the meaning we convey to our students of what it is to perform well and not-so-well, which may have important implications for university-based exams.

I will try to capture in this chapter what we discussed then that is relevant even today and try to go beyond it to see how it might be useful to other teachers in other contexts. The focus of the chapter will be the idea of evidence-based teaching and assessment. Unless we look for evidence quite carefully and even set up tasks and activities that tell us of how things are unfolding in the classroom, a lot of "student learning" (and teacher learning therefore) or lack of it will go unnoticed and result in our making wrong decisions about our next steps. We will therefore need to be extra cautious about our role and also be very sympathetic to our learners so that we can get the best out of them.

That's only part of the story; there is also the notion of the teacher as an educational connoisseur and critic that goes beyond the mundane job of teaching and assessment we carry out—which neither we nor our students seem to enjoy much, let alone learn from it. How can we become more astute and serious observers and evaluators of our own and our colleagues' work? How do we make our work motivating and sustainable (beyond ensuring job security and decent salaries) to ourselves and to our students? More importantly, how can we involve our learners in being equal partners in the business of teaching and learning? How, how, how?

I hope to take the readers on this intriguing journey as I myself do when people like Promodini offer such exciting opportunities. I owe a debt of gratitude to her and also to Sonali Jain, who provided me a platform to reflect in writing on past and present thoughts and waited patiently as I struggled with this write-up.

This chapter is therefore a tracking of my journey as a teacher and assessor rather than a scholarly write-up on sound evaluation practices, highlighting as I go along what I have found useful and interesting, which I believe others might find useful and interesting. I hope to reflect on what my work in my long career of 40 years entailed, especially the years I spent in Delhi University, where I had an opportunity to meet and work with tertiary-level teachers on issues of pedagogy and assessment of not only English but also other subjects. Dr Promodini Varma, the Principal of Bharati College, allowed me into her college corridors to figure out what concerns teachers vis-à-vis students deal with when they go about their everyday teaching and assessment, and I clearly remember the way she steered the discussions/workshops/seminars I was part of, with her own deep engagement with basic classroom issues. Another significant dimension to my life got added when I was a university representative on the college Governing Body and later on became the default Chairperson, since a regular one had not been elected. The discussions we had during the meetings, which sometimes spilled over to out-of-office hours as well, provided a fuller picture of the (professional) life teachers led.

I need to provide here a glimpse of who I am and where my interests lie. I come from an Education and ELT background and strongly believe that teachers can and should be trained regardless of the level they teach. While a pre-service training programme ending with a degree or diploma is a well-known route to becoming a teacher in school, it's not so for higher education. This is not to say that once they have been through a programme of study, they will forever have the wherewithal for being good teachers. A continuing professional development scheme would have to be put in place for teachers to keep growing and developing. Similarly, just because there is no pre-service training programme for college/university teachers, it doesn't mean that they don't believe in or get any "training". There are any number of workshops and seminars that are organised at the college and university levels. The most popular among them are the UGC orientation programmes and refresher courses. I have had the opportunity to teach on these programmes several times. Although I haven't been very happy with my experience on the UGC programmes (probably not many of the teacher-participants either), the ones organised at the college level appeared to have emerged from a felt need (such as the one on conducting tutorials in Bharati College) and left both me and the teachers slightly more satisfied. More importantly, one got the feeling that the "unanswered issues" could be addressed subsequently. There was thus a sense of continuity and some "looking forward to". These were not therefore one-off programmes. I was happy about this deep inside my heart, and I think Promodini felt the same way.

In this chapter I will try and present a picture of what is involved in teaching generally and how we can do it well. The ideas I present are not all mine; I draw on three main scholars/experts in the field whom I hold in very high regard: N.S. Prabhu, Dick Allwright, and Elliot Eisner, not necessarily in that order. Although their views on teaching and assessment don't all converge, there is a common strand that runs through their writings which enables a coherent understanding of the issue at hand.

Macro issues

To begin with we'll examine what the larger canvas of university education vis-à-vis student learning and the resultant job situation is. Prabhu talked of a double paradox in higher education in 1979, which is relevant to this day. Teaching takes place because students want certification, mostly for employment, but the education system is unable to maintain a relationship between certification and real ability. Employers, on the other hand, demand real ability and have started ignoring certification. In fact, employers are forever unhappy that the university graduate is ill-equipped for the job s/he qualifies for and complain that they have to train them afresh. Given this paradox, it does not matter whether the teacher teaches well or badly, since the system defines teaching in terms of how many "classes" a week (sometimes including tutorials) the teacher has to teach and success is usually measured in terms of exam-passes. "A pragmatic teacher therefore does in the classroom what it is easiest for him/her to do, and the pragmatic learner takes the shortest route s/he can to examination passing" (Prabhu 20). It is ironic that this situation is largely true even today after 40 years!

This then is what we can call the macro-situation in higher education. Prabhu had then recommended an innovative strategy for reform through *Remote Control* as opposed to *Direct Contact*. He advocated this particularly in the area of English language proficiency, which the regular exams didn't assess, creating a huge impediment for employers and others who looked for proficient undergraduates. He analysed the pitfalls of the system (i.e. Direct Control) which was quite incapable of producing desirable results. I would like to urge everyone interested in this issue to read the full article for its coherent and persuasive argument for the alternative strategy which would have a positive washback on the system (though he didn't use the term "washback"). The question of why our end-of-term exams of language courses don't test students' language proficiency is intriguing.

Micro issues

Thinking of more micro issues concerning teaching and learning, we probably agree that learning occurs when students are:

> thinking, problem solving, constructing, transforming, investigating, creating, analyzing, making choices, organizing, deciding, explaining, talking and communicating, sharing, representing, predicting, interpreting, assessing, reflecting, taking responsibility, exploring, asking, answering, recording, gaining new knowledge, and applying that new knowledge to new situations.
>
> (Cameron et al. 6)

Add to these cognitive mental processes, those in the affective domain. The affective domain includes the manner in which we deal with things emotionally, such as feelings, values, appreciation, enthusiasms, motivations, and attitudes. If we agree that these cognitive and affective abilities (at required levels of complexity) are important for any learner in the education system, then we will need to enable and facilitate (instead of hindering!) these processes as much as possible inside and outside classrooms. The immediate question that comes to mind is: are we doing it? How do we know?

What do we want students to learn, and how do we find out what they have learnt?

We will need to be fairly certain about why we do what we do in class knowing fully well that, in fact, students don't all learn what we think they should learn or what the official curriculum demands.

I can't resist sharing at this point the exciting article Dick Allwright wrote a long time ago titled "Why don't learners learn what teachers teach?—The interaction hypothesis". He did this interesting "experiment" over a period of time, which involved asking learners what they had learnt from a language class. He was astonished to see that about half the class was unable to clearly say what the lesson was about, although it was based on the lesson from the textbook each learner had in front of them; moreover, they had alternative ideas about what the lesson was about. He says in his paper:

> Assuming good faith on the part of these students we could only conclude that, in some important sense, the lesson had in fact been about different things for different learners. The obvious question was: "Where might such differing perceptions come from, and how

> might they be related to what learners actually learn from a language lesson?"
>
> (Allwright 3)

Allwright put forward the interaction hypothesis, which suggests that language lessons are best seen as instances of collective interaction. I must hasten to add here that this is mostly applicable to any class, not just a language class. The article goes on to argue how this hypothesis may be researched in the classroom by taking several steps, first by asking the learners to tell us what they think they learnt from a class. Although this may seem problematic in that many of us may not be happy to equate students' self-report data with actual learning, it has the potential for taking informed next steps. Suffice it to say at this point that trying to understand individual, differential "uptake" is a messier affair than administering a standard test based on the intended syllabus or teacher's lesson plan to everyone to assess how much of that each one has learnt. However, it is of great significance if we wish to understand what it is that each learner learns from the same input/lesson. Moreover, this allows consciousness-raising about language learning among learners, in itself a very important objective. Next, we could look for interactive evidence of these occurrences in classroom data. This is where audio and video recordings can help to get an authentic record of things that can be interpreted along with other sources of data such as interviews of teacher and students, so that we can begin to look for those learning opportunities that afforded differential uptake to different students. Clearly teaching and learning is not a straightforward enterprise: the more we probe and problematise the relationship the more complex it gets. Therefore, it is a choice one needs to make about whether to leave it as a simple equation, that is, teaching = learning, or try and understand the nuanced phenomenon more and more. Summative exams are notorious for making it appear like the equation that renders everyone's job rather simple and straightforward. Things that happen inside the classroom defy these simplistic explanations.

Although there may be some problems in pursuing this line of inquiry, and Allwright discusses them, there seem to be distinct advantages to the way this line of researching can be pursued. We won't be able to discuss the details of the proposal further but teachers, regardless of whether they are language or other subject teachers, are strongly urged to read this article and see its relevance to their classroom.

One thing that is clear from the foregoing discussion is the importance of evidence to find out what *is* happening in the classroom. Although evidence is usually linked quite directly with assessment/evaluation and research, it is an integral part of our everyday teaching. We, teachers, are all the time looking at the class, our students, the general atmosphere and assessing it as we make the next move. To take a very basic example, when we observe that a student is not quite paying attention to what we're saying/doing (s/he may be looking bored, looking out of the window or talking/laughing with the neighbour, and this list is endless), we pause and say something to the student to draw her/his attention: it could be a comment, a question to check his/her understanding or just a stare to show that we are aware of the situation. This move which is not planned but happens spontaneously is actually based on evidence. How we assess the evidence and what decision we make on the spur of the moment of course depends on the teacher and can vary from one teacher to another.

The more we look for evidence before making any assessment the more reliable our decisions will be. And better still, the more our students know what evidence leads to what decisions, the more aware they become of their learning and can gradually self-direct their learning.

Let's think for a moment that we are very sincere teachers and do a lot of serious planning. We are convinced that our "lectures" or simply put, classes, do have a lot of opportunities for our learners to engage in some deep cognitive and affective processes. Thus everyone benefits from them, albeit to different degrees and even in different ways, given that we have learners at different levels and with different "personal agendas". John Schumann (cited in Allwright 8) suggested long ago the notion of "personal agenda" (a personal view of what one wants to learn and how s/he wants to learn it), that in fact determines the "uptake", that is, what learners actually get from the class.

Therefore, looking quite consciously for evidence enhances our role as teachers and clearly sends out a message to students that we are not carrying out work in an ad-hoc or arbitrary way. This is a very strong message in my view. I must quickly add here that this is also part of our life outside our class, where we make decisions continually based on evidence, however commonplace that occurrence may be. Contrast this with "taking things for granted" such as "students from poor home backgrounds can't learn" or making decisions based on past experience, such as "I learnt well from long lectures and therefore lectures are good" or that "using mobile phones is a big obstacle in learning" and so forth. Lack of evidence can clearly pose a threat to understanding the situation afresh and making decisions that are justifiable in each situation.

It helps to look at the nature of the evidence we usually gather. Some evidence might be *tangible* and *retainable*, such as a written assignment, a chart, and a paper–pencil test, while the other is *ephemeral*, which is an oral response/question, something you see, but it is fleeting and the evidence is gone. Another useful distinction is that of *primary* and *secondary* evidence. Primary evidence is produced by the person whose evidence you are interested in, and secondary evidence is a step removed in that the person or someone else provides an account based on what they have seen/heard. Observing student behaviour or looking at their performance on tests for example, not to forget that it may be based on a (subjective) judgement the observer is making, is retainable and is definitely of value. However, asking the student to say what s/he learned from the lesson, that is, students' self-reports—which is secondary data—can also be of practical significance as we can use this as a starting point for gathering more tangible evidence subsequently. For example, we can think of other ways of capturing the ephemeral using audio/video-recording, direct observation of the class by another observer and so forth.

Further, students' perceptions of what they learned (and by corollary what they didn't learn) can guide us to plan further steps and can help tap those behaviours/abilities that a standard assessment tool may not be able to capture. Involving the students in articulating their learning during and after the class has the added advantage of helping them to become more aware of the strategies they use to listen, read, speak, think, solve problems, and so forth. This way, they will plan their "personal agenda" beforehand and take responsibility for their learning. Students' sense of quality in performance and expectations of their own performance are increased as a result of their engagement with the assessment process.

So far, we have focused on learning processes that take place in the classroom as the lesson goes on and how both teacher and students can keep track of or monitor what is going on that is actually contributing (or not) to learning. Therefore, this teaching, of which informal assessment is an integral part, especially the kind that feeds back to learning in a seamless way, is something all of us teachers engage in on a daily basis. We can extend this notion of monitoring progress to conducting formative assessment in a slightly more formal way as well. Here it is necessary to distinguish between two main kinds of assessment. The first is assessment for learning (AfL), where the purpose is to track progress of teaching-learning by giving feedback so we can ensure that learners are making progress the way they can. This obviously would be more individualised, and learners will have an opportunity to learn according to their individual styles and preferences.

The other kind of assessment, commonly known as assessment of learning (AoL), is where we find out how much the students have achieved/attained in relation to a given syllabus, and most often a prescribed textbook. This gives a good indication of how many students have done how well on a pre-determined exam/test, which also fulfils the role of certification. This is what Prabhu drew our attention to as requiring a reform, since these summative exams do not focus on what the learner can do with the language in terms of reading, writing, speaking and listening in different contexts for different purposes. Be that as it may, these exams/tests come at the end of a course and therefore we can't do much with the low scores except that the students can apply for a re-evaluation of their answer scripts where the system allows it, for any inaccuracies in scoring/marking. This is the one-off snapshot taken by an outsider that students depend on for certification vis-à-vis future decisions about employment/higher level courses.

Where do we go from here?

So far, we've tried to understand the teaching and assessment process based on evidence in a rather "scientific" way, the way educational research of a conventional sort operates. I would like to present another refreshing and non-parochial viewpoint here, not so common in education or ELT circles. This is the notion of "Educational connoisseurship and criticism for evaluating classroom life", presented in a seminal article of the same title by Elliot Eisner in 1977.

Let's first understand what connoisseurship and criticism entail. Connoisseurship is what we normally understand when we think of art, tea or wine-tasting. Eisner's own description of a wine-connoisseur will illustrate the meaning well:

> The wine connoisseur has through long and careful attention to wine developed a gustatory palate that enables him to discern its more subtle qualities. When he drinks wine it is done with an intention to discern, and with a set of techniques that he employs to examine the range of qualities within the wine upon which he will make his judgments. Body, colour, nose, aftertaste, bite, flavor—these are some of the attributes to which the wine connoisseur attends. In addition, he brings to bear upon his present experience a gustatory memory of other wines tasted. The other wines, held in the memory, form the backdrop for his present experience with a particular vintage. It is his refined palate, his knowledge of what to look for, his backing of previous experience, with wines other than those he is presently drinking that differentiate his present level of discernment from that of an ordinary drinker of wine. His conclusions about the quality of wines are judgments, not mere preferences. Judgments, unlike preferences which are incorrigible, can be grounded in reasons, reasons that refer back to the wines' qualities and to other wines of the same variety.
>
> (346–47)

Connoisseurship therefore is the art of appreciation, while criticism is the art of disclosure. A critic, apart from being a connoisseur, aims at "providing a rendering in linguistic terms of what it is that he or she has encountered so that others not possessing his level of connoisseurship can also enter into the work" ("Connoisseurship" 347). Applying these two notions to education, Eisner argues how the range, richness and complexity of educational phenomena occurring within classrooms are wider than what can be easily measured. Reflecting on questions such as: what is the underlying meaning one can discern from the way the teacher and students conduct themselves in class? Who has the floor? Who decides when to do what? Whose agenda is being pursued? Do some people give up in the process? What is the "hidden agenda" as opposed to what is officially declared? Does the class have a sense of movement? What new learning can one glean from this class? These according to him are some of the qualities, ideas and practices that an educational connoisseur might attend to. More importantly educational connoisseurship is not just the job of an outsider, but of educational practitioners. If one knows how to see what one looks at then one can get a lot more insightful data/evidence about the phenomenon under consideration. For example, do we as teachers know how to distinguish plain noise from constructive noise, students' restive behaviour from deep engagement/struggle with a task at hand?

The important point about educational connoisseurship and criticism is that we can refine our ability to recognise what is subtle and complex in our workplace if we don't become oblivious of things we are familiar with due to years of experience. There is a danger of functioning at minimal levels which will not allow us to address challenges and bring about change. "What is even worse", according to Eisner, "is . . . we often come to believe, because of the habit reinforced by convention, that the way things are is the way they *must* be" (351, emphasis original).

While good criticism needs the artful use of language, that is, language that is fluid, poetic and imaginative, one also needs to understand the values and history beneath educational practices. The critic must be in a position to perceive the superficial and apparent and also the subtle and the covert that is not easily visible to the educationally naïve eye. "A lecture is not intrinsically bad and a discussion intrinsically good regardless of the number and types of interactions in a discussion" ("Connoisseurship" 354). It is interesting that Eisner also strongly recommends that this job of criticism be done not by outside experts or professional writers but by teachers who have a deep understanding of educational theory and educational history and with sufficient experience as classroom teachers.

Eisner admits that the type of connoisseurship and criticism he is describing has not been an accepted tradition (even to this day) in education institutions although it has existed in literature, drama, art, poetry, cinematography and music. Even modern or more evolved research traditions in education have relied on a scientific paradigm where getting "hard" evidence, that is, tangible and retainable, has been the uncontested approach. It is only recently that we have started looking at "thick" descriptions, self-reflections, and impressionistic views as valid and reliable evidence. We can also take the help of video/audio recordings to capture the ephemeral phenomena and look at it critically at leisure.

An important dimension that Eisner does not discuss in his 1977 paper but talks about in detail in his later book—*The Enlightened Eye: Qualitative Inquiry and the Enhancement of Educational Practice* (1998)—is the need to look for multiple types of evidence to ensure corroboration, also called triangulation in research terminology. The most important source of data undoubtedly is direct observation of teachers and classroom life, carried out by a colleague who is well-versed with the ethos and history of the classroom and the institution. This can be enriched by talking to the teacher and students and listening to them sympathetically. Since connoisseurship is aimed at getting a holistic picture of what is going on, any data that contributes to that understanding is a rich resource: student work, teacher-made tests, portfolios, written assignments and so forth. It would be interesting to ask questions of the data to get to the bottom of the phenomenon under consideration: Are teacher's expectations of student behaviour/performance shared? Negotiable? What message is being conveyed through the assignment given/not given? What is the time taken between assignment submission and returning of students' work? What kind of feedback is given? Is it written/oral, just grades, qualitative comments/scores or what? Can they revise and resubmit their work? Is there provision for peer/self-evaluation or is it always the teacher whose verdict is final? Are the criteria for assignment marking negotiable? Is there always a right/wrong answer to questions? Do all students get the same task to complete? What does that mean? These and other questions show a concern to arrive at a deeper understanding of the situation from multiple perspectives and ensure credibility.

A last but important aspect of connoisseurship and criticism is interpretation, which is different from description of classroom life and asking questions about it as illustrated above. Description deals with what *is*, interpretation focuses on *why* or *how*. "The sense we make of social situations, the meanings we assign to action, and the motives we infer from what we see are typically built up over a period of time" (*Enlightened Eye* 98). Interpretation involves using ideas from educational theories, often competing ones, to explain what is described in the context in which it occurs, to explicate, to unwrap.

What we have said so far

Teachers are the best candidates for being educational connoisseurs and critics, with a caveat: they will need to be good observers, with a discerning eye and mind, and know what to look for, but at the same time look for the unexpected and the not-so-common in our daily business of teaching and learning in our classrooms. What Paulo Freire put forward in his book *Pedagogy of Freedom* on what is teaching provides an apt ending:

> First of all, to teach is not to *transfer knowledge* but to create opportunities or conditions so that learners construct their knowledge. In this process of creating opportunities for learning, the teacher cannot assume the role of a "subject" who is giving shape to the "object", i.e. the learner; both are being formed or reformed in the educative

process. Therefore, "there is no teaching without learning" . . . (and) "whoever teaches learns in the act of teaching and whoever learns teaches in the act of learning." In essence, then, teaching is learning and learning is teaching; by corollary, both teacher and learner are simultaneously in the process of learning and teaching.

(cited in Mathew 33)

Works cited

Allwright, Dick. "Why Don't Learners Learn What Teachers Teach?—The Interaction Hypothesis." *Language Learning in Formal and Informal Contexts: Proceedings of a Joint Seminar of the Irish and British Associations for Applied Linguistics held at Trinity College, Dublin.* Ed. David M. Singleton and David G. Little. Dublin: Irish Association for Applied Linguistics, 1984. 3–18.

Cameron, Caren, Betty Tate, Daphne Macnaughton, and Colleen Politano. *Recognition without Rewards.* Winnipeg, Man.: Peguis Publishers, 1998.

Eisner, Elliot W. "On the Uses of Educational Connoisseurship and Criticism for Evaluating Classroom Life." *Teachers College Record* 78.3 (1977): 345–58.

———. *The Enlightened Eye: Qualitative Inquiry and the Enhancement of Educational Practice.* New Jersey: Prentice-Hall, Inc., 1998.

Freire, P. *Pedagogy of Freedom: Ethics, Democracy and Civic Courage.* Oxford: Rowman and Littlefield Publishers, Inc., 1998.

Mathew, Rama. "Giving Choice and Voice." *Teacher Plus*, September 2017: 32–34. <www.teacherplus.org/giving-choice-and-voice/>.

Prabhu, N.S. "Alternative Strategies in Educational Reform: An ELT Practitioner's Views." *Journal of Indian Association of Programmed Learning and Educational Innovation* 3 (1979): 39–44. Rpt. in *Perceptions of Language Pedagogy.* Ed. Geetha Durairajan. Hyderabad: Orient Blackswan, 2019. 17–25.

10
DEVELOPMENTS IN TEACHING COLLEGE ENGLISH AT THE UNIVERSITY OF DELHI

Mukti Sanyal

This chapter attempts a subaltern history of English language teaching or ELT at the University of Delhi. It expresses a view from below as seen by those tasked with teaching the great "unwashed masses", rather than from the point of view of the policymakers, against the backdrop of developments in the field within India. In doing this, it highlights the very problematic relationship that the two "Englishes"—literature and language—have had for some teachers who wish to serve the cause of language teaching more. At the University of Delhi, as I suspect at most universities in India, literature teaching has always been seen as a more expertise-oriented and challenging profession than teaching language. Language teaching is usually treated as a poor cousin, probably because it is aimed at the students from the Hindi and other regional medium schools and is seen as requiring little or no expertise or skills.

The chapter attempts to delineate the history of the trajectory and trace the factors that have affected the direction of undergraduate courses in "General English" or what was often called "Compulsory English". Within the departments of English in most Indian universities, "General English" is usually not considered a worthy subject to be discussed, though through it we affect the lives of many more students as well as, possibly, the teaching practices of many more teachers who teach other languages.

The chapter is divided into five sections. It begins with an anecdotal account of Dr Promodini Varma, who has been a consistent strong voice for change and has played a pioneering role within it. Then, it moves to a more detailed account of how spaces for meaningful language teaching practices were created through strategies of resistance and co-option. It concludes by tracing the trajectory of ELT in undergraduate courses in Indian universities as a movement from attention to content and large humanistic goals towards pedagogically serving learner needs while accommodating teacher attitudes.

Recollecting the experiences of teaching English at the University of Delhi, Dr Promodini Varma felt "the story of my life is also the story of what has happened in English studies over the last 30–40 years at Delhi University". Dr Varma started teaching English to what was then called BA Pass. The language paper in the course was based on the assumption that students have achieved a certain level of proficiency in English after 11–12 years of schooling. The course had prescribed readings from "high literature", with plays like "Shakespeare's *Julius Caesar*, Shaw's *Arms and the Man* and anthologies with selected pieces from Edward Gibbon, Walter Scott, Charles Dickens, Thomas Hardy, and GK Chesterton amongst others" (Varma 2014). Within two months of teaching *Julius Caesar* to the third-year students, Dr Varma realised the disconnection between the text and her students when one of her students was not sure if "Brutus was a man or a woman". At this point, Dr Varma was sceptical of the role of teaching language through literature. However, teaching William Golding's *Lord of the Flies*, a novel about a handful of British boys marooned on an island and their struggles for survival, was more successful with all her students passing the exams and a few even scoring first divisions. Even though not much had changed in terms of her teaching, the students perhaps identified better with the novel and in general students' English proficiency had also improved. Therefore, Dr Varma felt her faith restored in the role of literature to teach language but she was also questioning the same. When Dr Varma raised the problems of teaching Shakespeare to students who struggled with basic knowledge of the English language, Professor Brij Raj Singh from the Department of English, University of Delhi retorted, "How can we give an undergraduate degree from Delhi University to a student who has not heard of Shakespeare?"

History of General English

The story of ELT in India goes back to 1854, when university education began, and English was a compulsory and possibly the most important part of the college curriculum. It was believed that those who desire to obtain a liberal education must "begin with the mastery of the English language as a key to the literature of Europe" (Richey 367). It was naturally the only medium of instruction, and it was assumed that the language would be learnt in the process of reading and appreciating its literature. Therefore, beyond school years, it was not thought necessary to make any provision for ELT in colleges except to have a paper on "Composition and Grammar or Precis writing" and another on literature. By the early twentieth century, however, the situation on the ground had changed considerably. This can be seen by the fact that the Calcutta University Commission (1916–1917) recommended "better teaching methods and that teachers should be employed in the *intermediate classes* since *regional languages* were increasingly becoming the medium of instruction in secondary schools" (227, italics mine). With the freedom struggle, the impetus for regional languages as the medium of instruction gathered momentum and there was simultaneously an acknowledgement of falling standards in English. Post-Independence, the Indian University Education Commission (1948–1949) was the first commission to make a "complete and comprehensive enquiry into all aspects of university education and advanced research in India" ("Higher Education Inquiry in India" 176). It observed that:

> one of the evils of the present method of instruction is that it is focused too much on text-books. This evil is most pronounced in the study of languages and therefore it has become almost a racket. A text-book is prepared with very little effort as it consists of a number of pieces selected from different authors. Once the book is prescribed, the publisher and author are assured of a good return on their investment, but the poor student does not have a fair deal.
> (104)

The Commission also noted that:

> the practice of having *text-books* has become an ingrained part of the system which has in turn *vitiated the teaching-learning process*. The content and style of the pieces is often so beyond the grasp or interest of students that teachers feel compelled to lecture, reading through the text line by line, explaining or even translating into the local language taking pains to wring the sense out of every line and word leaving no sweetness in the best literary works.
> (104, italics mine)

In subsequent years, several measures were taken to retain, strengthen, and promote English as "our natural advantage", English as India's "window to the world"—its role as "link language" and "library language" to enrich Indian languages with Western thought and new learning. Therefore, adding to the existing resources of two regional Institutes of English and five ELT Institutes which primarily dealt with school English, the Central Institute of English, Hyderabad was started in 1958 to look into the needs of College English. Several studies were undertaken in the newly started institute to investigate into various aspects of an average college entrant's proficiency in English. In 1960–1961, for instance, Helen Barnard conducted a vocabulary test on 750 pre-university students in Ranchi University; in 1962, W.W.S. Bhaskar[1] made an analysis of common errors in pre-university English; and Lakshmi Ramaswamy taught reference skills on an experimental basis. The findings of these and similar researches elsewhere surfaced in the public domain through recommendations made by many subsequent English Review Committees of the University Grants Commission (UGC).[2]

The key features that were repeatedly proposed were "that special methods be adopted to secure an adequate knowledge of English as a second language; and that courses in Linguistics should be introduced in universities and teacher training colleges" (UGC 38).

The courses for College English that came out of these experimentations were popularly known as "Language through Literature" courses. Cognisance was being taken of the fact that most students did not have the competence or proficiency in the language to read canonical texts. Instead, courses began to provide practice in reading and comprehension through short stories, poems, and essays written by Indian writers on themes that were accessible to young learners. Attention on language was synonymous with remediation, that is, re-learning of those items that had been learnt wrongly at school, and on consolidation or strengthening of newly learnt items.

At the University of Delhi, the starting point of concern for ELT was the year 1969. The initiating role was played by summer schools and advanced summer schools run by the UGC with academic support from the British Council centres in India which concentrated on the teaching of English as a set of skills. Courses, running up to six weeks, would be advertised in the papers and would be offered at different universities across the country. The resource persons were British English Language experts and professors from the Central Institute of English and Foreign Languages (CIEFL) and from Departments of Linguistics and Literature. The first ever summer institute was conducted at Kurukshetra University in 1969, and Sudesh Sawhney (Shyam Lal College)[3] was among the participants. Dr A.L. Khanna (Rajdhani College) remembers having been taught by Dr Raj Kumar Khanna (Zakir Hussain College) in the first such summer institute in Delhi in 1970; Tara Chaddha, Kusum Virmani, and Madhu Gurtu (all from Shyama Prasad Mukherjee College for Women) attended the subsequent one in Kurukshetra in 1971. The summer institutes would reward the best participants by giving them a scholarship for a master's degree, or a postgraduate diploma in Language Teaching in the United Kingdom or at CIEFL, now EFLU (The English and Foreign Languages University), Hyderabad. In 1979, Harish Pant, who had taught at the Regional Institute of English, Shillong and Chandigarh, was appointed Education Officer at the British Council, Delhi. After him came Dr Prem Mathur, and both concentrated on supporting teacher training by bringing in scholars like Edmundson, A.L. Hill, Alan Maley, and Alan Duff who ran workshops on materials production and other related pedagogic issues. From the accounts of these initial years, the trend that unmistakably emerges is that ELT had some devotees and proponents who popularised it vigorously in and around the universities of north India like Professor R.P. Bhatnagar and Professor A.L. Shah from Jaipur, and Professor A.K. Kalia from Kurukshetra, while there were many in positions of power who were indifferent or hostile to its concerns.

The teachers who had grouped themselves around language teaching and voicing concerns of the learners they faced daily in their classes began to have some say in syllabus making from around 1969 when Professor Sarup Singh, then Head of the Department of English, called a meeting of English teachers. The introduction of new criteria for language teaching at school had been mooted, according to the proposed 10+2 system, allowing students to drop English as a subject, at or before the Class X examination. These teachers, therefore, made a strong plea that students who studied English only till Class VIII or IX could not be taught the same course as those who had studied it till Class XII or had English as the medium of instruction through school. Thus, the concept of "streaming" was born. However, nothing much came of this for some time. A few years later, when Professor Chaman Nahal was Head of Department, a group of teachers presented a memorandum to him asking for changes in the General English syllabus taught at the undergraduate level and a role for themselves within it. This group of teachers also designed a diagnostic test which empirically showed that there were distinctly two streams of students coming to the university.

In the University of Delhi, the initiative and momentum for change also came from teachers who had experienced the frustration and futility of teaching Shakespeare to those who knew little or no English. Among those who worked relentlessly for change were Dr Promodini Varma (former Principal, Bharati College), Dr Naresh Jain (Correspondence Department, now School of Open Learning), the Late Dr Raj Kumar Khanna (Zakir Hussain College), Vasant Sharma (now retired from Delhi College of Arts and Commerce), Sudesh Sawhney (now retired from Shyam Lal College), A.L. Khanna (now retired from Rajdhani College and formerly President of Teachers' Association, FORTELL), and Tara Chaddha, the Late Madhu Gurtu, Dr Kusum Virmani (all from Shyama Prasad Mukherjee College), and Dr Mukti Sanyal (Bharati College).

The first wave of reforms

In April 1985, when Professor Rupin Desai became Head of the Department of English, University of Delhi, he called a meeting of college teachers for a discussion of the General English syllabus. Usha Nagpal (Janaki Devi Mahavidyalaya), Promodini Varma, C.D. Siddhu (Hansraj College), Mita Bose (Indraprastha College for Women), and Tara Chaddha, among others, attended that meeting. Usha Nagpal followed this up with organising workshops in her college for which she invited N.S. Prabhu,[4] who had, by then, become famous for having engineered the Communicational syllabus. Information about experiments underway in Loyola College, Madras, and the Bombay University First Year Course in Communication Skills was disseminated widely, and more and more teachers began voicing their discontent with the existing courses and wanting to experiment with alternatives.

Dr S.C. Sood (Dayal Singh College), who had then just returned from the University of London having done an MA in Language and Literature in Education under H.G. Widdowson, was invited by Professor Desai to join the group.

From 1978 in Delhi, streams A and B had become necessary because under the newly implemented 10+2+3 policy with its emphasis on the Three Language Policy, students could drop English mid-way through school. However, the concept of Stream C came much later. Stream A was for those who had studied English till Class XII and B for those who had studied English up to Class X. Those who had not studied English even up to Class X were thus left at a loose end. In 1981–1982, the University of Delhi floated a Remedial English course for these students which had a syllabus but did not have course books. Furthermore, Remedial English was an extra subject that the student had to study, but the marks s/he obtained in it would not be counted towards the aggregate. Since they had not passed English at the Class X level, they could not study English as a subject but had to study Remedial English for two years and had only to "clear" the subject. This situation, as Dr A.L. Khanna realised (and took great pains to explain to the Department), led to an anomaly. There was a provision in the University of Delhi Statutes that those who had not studied English as a subject at Bachelors-level could not be conferred a degree. Therefore, he argued that "Remedial English" be upgraded and formalised to English C, which it was eventually. From its inception till the end of their working lives in the University, Dr A.L. Khanna, Tara Chaddha, Dr Madhu Gurtu, and Usha Nagpal remained the proponents of English C at Delhi University. Tara Chaddha recounts how, in the days of Remedial English, since there was an absence of course books, each teacher taught what caught his/her fancy and as examination script evaluators they would often be served blank scripts for students who had not been able to answer even a single question.

The first set of University of Delhi undergraduate texts that broke away from the set pattern of teaching language through canonical texts was produced through the summer workshops organised by the Department under the headship of Professor Malashri Lal in 1987. The workshops were held in the university where the teachers worked through the day and submitted materials in the evening. There was no external expert; teachers shared ideas and insights and evolved materials from studying ELT reference books that were made available by the British Council. Dr S.C. Sood submitted a syllabus designed for Stream B which worked as a blueprint for syllabus construction for other groups. Seven groups were formed: one each for English A, B, and C of the BA Pass and one each for the Honours students of Commerce, the Sciences, the Arts, and Social Sciences and one for the Honours students at the lower level or one for those who had had a regional language as the medium of instruction for school education. These texts took approximately more than five years to be published and implemented, perhaps because the Department was uncomfortable with the idea of teachers writing course books. They remained in manuscript form for many years and were vetted by several visiting British scholars. In 1991, the first set were published and used in classrooms. They worked well where both teachers and students were conscientious; many teachers took to these course books and were happy with the classroom interaction these texts generated. However, some teachers were outraged at "new-fangledness" of some of these texts. Besides, they assumed that special provision of extra tutorial time and small classes would be made which were often not possible administratively.

There were seven different course books: three of these were three-year courses with a text for each year: (Stream A) *Contemporary English: An Anthology for Undergraduates I & II* (for the third year these students studied *Othello*); (Stream B) *Developing Language Skills I, II & III*; (Stream C) *A Foundation Course for Undergraduates I, II & III*. There were also three A level courses for Humanities, Sciences, and Commerce which were all one-year courses and one B level course for students of Humanities. The courses were implemented in 1991.

The most innovative of all the course books from the language teaching point of view were the course books for English B/Stream B, called *Developing Language Skills- Books I, II* and *III*. They painstakingly used a functional syllabus for teaching conversational English. They also built in teacher training material so that teachers, who had little or no exposure to language teaching pedagogy and came from a literature background, would be able to do justice to it. The tasks were built around themes, conventions, and transactions that were a part of students' existing social and educational needs. These course books were meant for students who would have had only five years of English instruction in mother tongue medium schools and the course aimed to fill in the language inputs such students would need to get through college both in terms of their social life and study requirements.

Reviewing the new courses, Professor Jacob Tharu, former Professor at CIEFL, Hyderabad had noted that "there seems to be an attitude of welcoming rather than merely tolerating the heterogeneity in the population of college entrants' widely differing levels of preparedness in 'English' and varied expectation from its further study" (Tharu 1992). He further noted that the curricular response of providing a variety of courses seemed to be founded on the premise that the value and validity of the course depended on the extent to which it served the learner characteristics rather than a body of authoritative linguistic knowledge/theory functioning much like a literary canon. "General English was not merely the undifferentiated residue of 'grammar & comp.' that remained when 'literature' is creamed off" (Tharu 4). The variety of shapes also emerged from the fact that several teams of teachers who served as course book writers did not have any formal training in ELT/ESL/Applied Linguistics. Therefore, imagination gained over procedure.

Rajeshwari Sunder Rajan, P.K. Pabby and others who worked on *Contemporary English Vol. I & II* meant for English A responded to the then current discussions of opening up the canon in the mid-1980s with an alternative that was thought appropriate for the beginner literature students. The anthologies had selections of texts in translation from India as well as from the United Kingdom, the United States of America, Canada, and Australia; the guiding principle was more thematic (topics that would interest and be relevant to 19-year-olds) than representative of the best that is written in these countries. More importantly, the thrust of the language exercises accompanying each piece was developing close and critical reading leading to analysis of "writing strategy", "vocabulary", "analogic exercises" ending with "questions for discussion". Painstakingly and carefully worked on, each of the 28 pieces had on an average two to three pages of notes, glossary, and exercises. The "analogic exercise", which was an innovative exercise in these coursebooks, drew students' and teachers' attention to model writing; that writing style or strategy used in reading texts would be replicated or adapted to a slightly different context.

Having been used for over 14 years, these course books were finally replaced because of changes in the amount of curricular space that was given to English. The logistic problems that seven different courses created for the examination branch in terms of finding paper setters, evaluators, moderators, and so forth were also highlighted. The popularity and fondness of some of the course books were such that they continued to be taught, often in truncated forms. For example, *Contemporary English I* for Credit English and *A Foundation Course in English II* for Qualifying Lower.

The first wave of reforms can best be described as pioneering in many ways. To begin with, college teachers created spaces for dialogue among themselves and those engineering innovations elsewhere in the country; they negotiated and worked in collaboration with the English Faculty to create the curriculum and course content. In terms of content, they moved away from "highbrow" variety of English taught in the spirit of Arnold and Macaulay to experience the greatness of the language to serving learner needs. Very importantly, they acknowledged the diverse potential of the learners that come to the English course and attempted to serve those.

The second wave of reforms

The next set of reforms took place in 2005 in the context of further reduced space for compulsory language papers because other subject areas clamoured for better representation and space in the undergraduate curriculum. Thus, in the BA Programme, Credit Language courses were reduced to two years and a new concept of "Application Courses" was introduced which could be studied through either English or Hindi medium—for example, subjects like Environment Studies, Legal Rights, Media Studies, and Reading Gandhi. In view of the reduction of course time by a whole year, it became necessary to reformulate goals and reorganise content for English. Primarily, courses were reduced and rationalised to six from the earlier seven. Secondly, in order to accommodate the suggestion from the Faculty/Department to find course books from those available in the market, the once popular BBC course *Tiger's Eye* was introduced for Qualifying Higher. The course book was found suitable because it taught two key areas: Spoken English (through dialogues that allowed role play) and Remedial Grammar. However, for all other courses, the teachers wanted to write course books to suit diverse proficiency levels and learner needs.

In all the BA Programme Credit Language courses, explicit emphasis was placed on having goals formulated in a cline from basic/near-basic to intermediate and advanced in all four skill areas (listening, speaking, reading, and writing). Thirdly, grammar that had not been explicitly taught earlier, though tested in the end-of-year examination, was made a compulsory part of the curriculum by prescribing a grammar book with each course: *Advanced English Grammar, Intermediate English Grammar*, and *Elementary English Grammar*, all Cambridge University Publications. Most importantly, the course books for the three courses—*Fluency in English I & II, English at the Workplace I & II*, and *Everyday English I & II*—catered to three different proficiency levels at BA Programme and used three distinctly different methodologies. Finally, the scheme of evaluation and weightage given to each part was synchronised with the course objectives and teaching method to ensure proficiency development. In fact, a face-to-face 15 marks test of speaking was approved by the Department but unfortunately was never implemented.

While *Fluency in English I* and *II* continued to work with literary texts, the anthology almost exclusively used texts written by Indians. The number of pieces came down from 28 of *Contemporary English I* to 18 in *Fluency in English I*. This reduction of numbers was in acknowledgement of the fact that within the limited time available in formal instruction, classroom practices that language development entails can best be achieved if the texts are shorter, simpler yet within the reading ability of an average student to wean her/him away from relying on guide books and to encourage individual reading of authentic texts. The emphasis in this set of texts was more directly aimed at enhancing language proficiency while directing attention on different literary forms. Unit titles like "Reading Poetry", "Understanding Irony", and "Understanding Drama" state the teaching objectives clearly. Most importantly, the "teaching exercises" after each unit guided both teachers and learners through the intricacies and nuances of the working of the form. The intention was to get at the processes as directly and as clearly as possible. For instance, after having taken students through reading and understanding different forms in *Fluency in English I, Fluency in English II* took students through different stages of writing: "Free writing",

"Learning to Write", "Editing", and "Writing for Examination". Speaking and listening was ensured through discussions generated by the "Warm up" tasks. The content and methodology of these course books had been broadly well-received.

In *English at the Workplace I* and *II* that replaced the earlier course books for Stream B, the emphasis changed from substitution table and explicit information giving to an approach that was more cognitively demanding. This was a relatively new, dynamic, and challenging approach to language teaching. Traditionally, language proficiency is sought to be achieved by providing practice in the key skill areas of listening, speaking, reading, and writing. The approach in this set of course books was to unfold the very process of language learning itself. Therefore, the units were built around issues of language learning for a second language learner. It recognised and built upon the fact that these learners were adults, know their first language and have some understanding of how languages function. Units were built around issues like what a good language learner does to maximise learning and how different languages mark intimacy or show respect. Features of speech typical of bilingual and multilingual speakers such as code switching and code mixing and issues like word stress and stressed-timed and syllable-timed languages were also addressed. Insight formation and awareness-raising were key to the approach. Since the time at hand was less, young learners were being encouraged to introspect, speculate, substantiate, elaborate, and discuss: processes that they should find more challenging and satisfying than learning by rote or repeating.

Everyday English I and *II*, the course books written for Stream C students, continued with the approach followed in the earlier texts *A Foundation Course for Undergraduates I*, *II*, and *III*. Aimed at the beginner or near-beginner level, they used a simple, straightforward, traditional approach that is linguistically simple but appropriate for young students. Direct instructions, substitution tables, and extensive language exercises gave students opportunities to upgrade their skills.

The second wave of reform was distinct from the first wave of reforms in that it focused on a keener understanding of needs of students at different level of proficiency acquisition. By and large, the pedagogic principle was directing the students' attention directly to the micro and macro skills and strategies required for acquiring the different skill areas.

The third wave of reform

The third wave of reform was started in 2008 by the English Language Proficiency Course (ELPC) formulated and moved by Professor Rama Mathew, Dean and Head, Central Institute of Education, University of Delhi. Responding to the demand that undergraduates were unemployable because they did not have adequate English language communication skills, her proposal was accepted and trialled in five centres in 2008. Run as a short-term add-on course from 2008, it reached out to over 5,000 students in 33 centres till 2014–2015. ELPC had several aspects of well-run language courses which could be compared to professionally run language schools: it ran courses at the Basic, Intermediate, and Advanced level with objectives that were compatible with proficiency levels of the learners and their language needs. It required applicants to take an entry test for its Intermediate and Advanced levels. Like the Test of English for Speakers of Other Languages (TESOL) or University of Cambridge Language Examination Syndicate (UCLES) suite of examinations, a proficiency test focusing on all four skills area was administered at the end of the course indicating scores in each of the skill areas. This entailed preparing, standardising, administering, and scoring separate tests for all four skill areas. Teachers who taught on the course underwent a six-day intensive Orientation Programme (OP). Over 200 teachers underwent the OP; many of them were practicing or retired English teachers and said that the ELPC teaching experience had beneficial effect on their classroom teaching. ELPC encouraged researchers and school teachers too to teach on the course and the number of colleges interested in setting up centres progressively increased. The course successfully managed to break out of the prescribed book and used loose-leaf task-based materials which were put together by the materials team. These were revised every year: while the Basic-level materials had eight runs and five revisions, the Intermediate- and Advanced-level materials had six and four respectively. Students did not have a textbook but received photocopied handouts every day, which they filed in a folder given to them as part of the course. What was possibly being grudgingly accepted was that ELT at the University of Delhi had been taken over by the Institute of Life Long Learning (ILLL) and the Central Institute of Education (CIE), and that the Department of English was possibly unwilling to reclaim lost ground.

In 2014, the positive and encouraging feedback received from the ELPC experience in the now-defunct FYUP (Four-Year Undergraduate Programme), the one semester course called *Language, Literature and Culture*, indicated that General English was more directed towards methodology rather than to content. FYUP acknowledged parity between all languages and the need to develop proficiency in each. Therefore, courses in Hindi, English, Urdu, and Sanskrit were all named similarly and all of them were organised around similar content and methodology. The good thing was that the focus had finally moved from materials (what you teach) to methodology (how you teach). What had been first articulated in 1950 by the Indian University Commission report that attention be brought to the methods of teaching had been finally implemented. Instead of restricting the teaching of communication skills to the English Language class, it opened up the area to the entire gamut of the students' study by making group work in the form of projects and presentations a compulsory part of their class work.

This naturally provided spoken communication, which had been given no space at all in the teaching and evaluation process so far, the kind of space and visibility it deserved. Furthermore, since the major chunk of evaluation was done by the teachers in the college, theoretically speaking, there was a greater opportunity to match materials to students' proficiency levels. The onus had squarely been put at the door of teachers and students—should both of them be willing, great strides could be achieved! Secondly, English, which at one point of time had been compulsory and the most important part of the college curriculum, has been brought at par with all other languages. This was viewed as a democratising process.

In the FYUP restructuring of the English (Honours) syllabus, two Application Courses on Academic Writing and Composition and on ELT were passed. However, in spite of the roll-back of the FYUP, the English courses under the present CBCS (Choice-Based Credit System) continue to offer several papers that focus on language proficiency building in their AECC (Ability Enhancement Course Compulsory), SEC (Skill Enhancement Course), and GE (Generic Elective) courses.

In the meantime, the encouraging signs are the kind of strength language teaching concerns are gaining in terms of proliferation and growth of teachers' associations and their conferences, seminars, and workshops that University of Delhi teachers are active in; and online and print journal that teachers write in or subscribe to. Different colleges of the University of Delhi too have played a role in keeping ELT concerns alive: Dyal Singh College, Shyama Prasad Mukherjee College, Rajdhani College, and Bharati College, among others. From 2005, Bharati College has been organising language-related seminars with the support of the Regional English Language Office and the United States Embassy, New Delhi which supports discussion by bringing in experts. So far, we have been able to hold seminars on assessment and evaluation, streaming, teaching academic writing, and composition; and we have been able to run short add-on courses on Intensive Reading and Writing and Persuasive Writing for our students.

Conclusion

In retrospect, the activism of teachers committed to ELT has allowed them to make tangible progress in the evolution of the field in many ways. The number of teachers and researchers involved in language teaching, paper setting, and materials production has grown sizeably. A better understanding of assessment, evaluation, and proficiency testing has also led to greater transparency and rationality in allotment of weightages for unseen reading comprehension, vocabulary, grammar, writing, and testing speaking through oral presentations, which have become the norm in the University of Delhi. There is a greater awareness of, and improvement in, the teaching and testing of spoken English skills. Furthermore, there is a more realistic expectation of outcomes from courses: earlier, unfair demands would be made which were demoralising for both the learners and the teachers. The positive backwash effect of the activism and the sustained engagement with pedagogic issues has been on other language courses taught at the University of Delhi. For instance, Hindi, Punjabi, and Sanskrit departments have followed the pattern of formulating different courses for different proficiency groups.

Notes

1. To know more see, Bhasker, William Wanlace Sumaut, and N. S. Prabhu. *English through Reading*. Macmillan, 1974.
2. The UGC was formally established in November 1956 as a statutory body of the Government of India through an Act of Parliament for the coordination, determination and maintenance of standards of university education in India.
3. All colleges mentioned here are constituent colleges of the University of Delhi
4. N.S. Prabhu popularised task-based language teaching (TBLT). TBLT is also known as task-based instruction (TBI) and focuses on the use of authentic language and asking students to do meaningful tasks using the target language. Such tasks can include visiting a doctor, conducting an interview, or calling customer service for help. TBLT can be considered a branch of communicative language teaching (CLT).

Works cited

Barnard, Helen. "A Test of PUC Students Vocabulary in Chotanagpur: First Findings and a View of their Implications." *CIEFL Bulletin*, No. 1 (1962).

Bhaskar, W.W.S. "An Analysis of Common Errors in PUC English." *CIEFL Bulletin*, No. 2 (1962).

"Higher Education Inquiry in India." *Higher Education: Semimonthly Publication of the Higher Education Division of Education, Federal Security Agency*, 5(15) (1 April 1949): 176. <https://books.google.co.in/books?id=Pk_kH36izmMC>.

Ramaswamy, L., et al. "Reference Class for PUC Students: An Experiment in English Teaching with a Non- Linguistic Bias." *CIEFL Bulletin*, No. 2 (1962).

Report of the Calcutta University Commission: Analysis of Present Conditions Vol II, Part I. Calcutta: Superintendent Government Printing India, 1919. 227.

Report of University Education Commission. New Delhi: Ministry of Education, 1950. 104.

Richey, J.A. "Despatch from the Court of Directors of the East India Company to the Governor-General of India, No. 49, 19th July 1854." *Selections from Educational Records-II (1840–1859)*. New Delhi: National Archives of India, 1959. 369.

"Summary of Recommendation of the Kunzru Committee Report." *Report of English Committee*. New Delhi: University Grants Commission, 1957. 38.

Tharu, Jacob. "Book Review: The New Delhi University BA Pass English Textbooks." *Folio* (Newsletter of the English Association, University of Delhi) Ed. Vinod Sena, Promodini Varma, and Gulshan Taneja (Winter 1992): 2–4.

Varma, Promodini. Personal Interview. Delhi, 2014.

11
THEATRE, FEMINISM, AND SOCIETY
Notes from a practitioner

Anuradha Marwah in conversation with Anubhav Pradhan and Sonali Jain

Among the many abiding oddities of the English academia in India is a strange inability or aversion to practice. Though many of us teach—and love—drama, only very few are able to transition from the happy amateurism of collegiate theatre into the more demanding realms of theatre performed in city auditoriums or community spaces for the general public. Anuradha Marwah is one of those increasingly rare English professors who have been able to do so. As much a novelist as a theatre practitioner, Marwah's brand of socially committed, left-feminist theatre poses many challenging questions for the nature and direction of theatre pedagogy and practice in and outside the English literary academia in India. Anubhav Pradhan and Sonali Jain discuss theatre, feminism, and society with Marwah in a wide-ranging conversation.

1   Let us start with some of the political, social, and psychological implications of contemporary Indian theatre. How do you view the construction of gender in theatre within a variety of discourses: desire, power, language, sexuality, family?

The construction of gender takes place differently with different kinds of theatre. There is the classical format where myths from ancient texts might be reinterpreted in the classical medium posing a challenge to hidebound tradition. A good example would be Mallika Sarabhai's dance drama *Sita's Daughters* (1990). Then there's professedly activist work of someone like Jyoti Mhapsekar, the founder of the Stree Mukti Sangathana. Her well-known play *A Girl is Born!* (1994) may be mentioned along with Jan Natya Manch's *Aurat* (1970) to represent work that was being done to raise consciousness about women's issues. Jan Natya Manch doesn't declare itself as "feminist", but I don't think it matters in this case. In the mainstream/proscenium sphere it is significant that there are so many women playwrights—Poile Sengupta (English), Gitanjali Shree (Hindi), Irpinder Bhatia (Hindi), Neelam Mansingh Chaudhury (Punjabi), Binodini (Telegu), B. Jyashree (Kannada), Shanoli Mitra (Bengali), Usha Ganguli (Hindi), Sushma Deshpande (Marathi), Qudsia Zadie (Urdu), and Manjula Padmanabhan (English). It needs to be said that merely being a woman doesn't make one a feminist. But women directors like Anuradha Kapur, Kirti Jain, Anamika Haksar, Amal Allana, and Tripurari Sharma are more likely to reinterpret and re-conceptualise a mainstream text, be it the story of a family or interpersonal relationships, in liberative ways.

Many critics have written insightfully about women and theatre and performance in India—Shanta Gokhale, Nandi Bhatia, Anita Singh, and Rimli Bhattacharya, to name just a few. In an interview in *The Hindu* (21 August 2015), Mangai describes her book *Acting Up: Gender and Theatre in India 1979 Onwards* (2015) as "a dialogue between theatre practitioners and women's groups, between activists and artistes". I would say this works well as a definition of feminist theatre. It is always in conversation with feminist activism.

A heartening instance of the success of feminist work in India is the enthusiasm with which so many college theatres in Delhi have been performing Eve Ensler's *Vagina Monologues*. In the backdrop of conversations that have been going on in the public sphere about women's sexuality and the need to claim space, this is a significant assertion. But I would add that, on the whole, what we need to work towards by way of activist theatre in India, and even globally, is less political correctness and more artistic finesse. We should not fight shy of attempting complex subjects and forms. The intelligence of audiences can never be underestimated. The effect of theatre comes about due to the enmeshing of form and content and is at both conscious and subconscious levels. Sometimes, the oblique and the indirect mode may have a deeper and more abiding impact psychologically.

2   In your opinion, what has been the role of women in post-independence Indian theatre? For example, how do you react to a complete minority of women characters in an iconic play like Vijay Tendulkar's *Ghashiram Kotwal*?

The importance of women as subjects of social change, especially in post-Independence India, can hardly be contested. *Ghashiram Kotwal* works wonderfully well as description of a patriarchal, casteist society. Women are oppressed and exploited in it and the play lays bare the reasons of their plight. I think Tendulkar's greatest contribution is to bring sexuality in all its rawness and ugliness centre stage. He is indeed the maestro of stage craft to pull it off so successfully. A playwright with a consciously feminist-activist point of view would attempt to inscribe women/the powerless sections of society as agents of social change. Tendulkar doesn't do that in *Ghashiram*. But I think the two—descriptive evaluation and activism—can work in tandem with each other. The immense sympathy that is generated for the woman who is at the receiving end of oppression can make people realise the need for change. *Ghashiram Kotwal* could be positioned in a way to set the stage for feminist activism.

3   On a related theme, how do you respond to the fact that Beckett not only wrote the play *Waiting for Godot* with an all-male cast but went to some pains to defend it?

Several women have been and continue to be interested in playing *Waiting for Godot*. The play is a powerful critique of phallocentric power. The absent Godot pushes Vladimir and Gogo into the eternal passivity of waiting. Some critics have discussed *Waiting for Godot* as a feminist play due to its critique of power dynamics. To my mind, Beckett's objections to a female cast for *Waiting for Godot* arose out of an inordinate desire for creative control. An example of the creator's hubris! His infamous quotes "Replacing women for men was like replacing violins for trumpets" and "Women don't have prostates"—the reasons he furnished for an all-male cast—sound like tantrums rather than arguments. He deserved to be disregarded, and by appropriating his script women have done just that. *Waiting for Godot* is a liberative text, and there is no reason for playing it otherwise.

4   In a recent article, you yoke together *Waiting for Godot* and triple talaq. Can you please elaborate?

It was a slightly mischievous connection that I was making in the Opinion column of *The Hindu* ("The Wait for Another Day" (4 Nov 2016)). It seems to me that Beckett's unreasonable demand that the play *Waiting for Godot* be performed exactly as he had imagined it has affinities with the idealistic view given by some progressive opinion-makers: that triple talaq should be challenged only when the community is ready for it and only via a government that has the confidence of the minorities. This kind of view prioritises the intentions of the author over the effect of the work. Some of those who hold this view about triple talaq—like Faizan Mustafa whose article I mention—are people I respect, just as I respect and admire Beckett. But they had gone to the extent of mounting a defence for polygamy to argue against the proposed law. They were on the brink of condoning even the reactionary submissions of AIMPLB (All India Muslim Personal Law Board) in the case. I completely agree with them that the mainstream/liberal critique of triple talaq ties it up with the alleged "backwardness" of the Muslim community and that it is misplaced and myopic. But in countering it, the progressives cannot and should not end up holding a brief for a patently anti-women law. Let me give you another example of a similar debate that took place in 1987 at the time of the Deorala incident of sati. Lata Mani theorised it comprehensively in her article "Multiple Mediations" (1990). She agrees that the horror of the educated and urbanised elite at this "barbaric" and "backward" practice is essentially elitist and misplaced and creates a binary of "us" versus "them". But she goes on to argue that sati cannot be defended or condoned on the grounds that it is an indigenous cultural practice either. My rejoinder was making a similar point. I referred to *Waiting for Godot* also to suggest that to wait for an ideal political dispensation to repeal medieval marriage and divorce laws would be like asking women to wait for Godot.

5   You have been quoted as saying "Writing is often androgyny". Would you like to elaborate? How does it square with your position as a feminist?

There is no contradiction for me between conception of gender roles as fluid and a lifelong commitment to feminist goals. Feminism began with women trying to throw off the straitjacket of femininity. Women have experienced biological definitions as limiting and many women continue to find them restrictive. Feminists who conceptualise conflict in terms of power equations and posit clearly defined liberative goals for the entire community—black feminists, for instance—resonate most with me. When I write, even when I am expressing a man, I try to get under the skin of the character. Didn't Flaubert, the realist, say "Madame Bovary c'estmoi?" The language of performativity expresses this anti-essentialism even better. Judith Butler famously discussed gender as performance. So, in a sense, I too perform various characters on the pages of my novel or play. This is what I mean by androgyny in writing. Writing is something with which I seek to expand my world beyond my stated identity.

6   You have written the play *A Pipe Dream in Delhi* with an intense social commitment. How do you deal with the incidents psychologically? Have you worked through the tragedy by writing in all its bare bones?

A Pipe Dream in Delhi (2012) takes off from a real-life incident in Delhi–NCR. In December 2006, eight human skeletons were accidentally unearthed from clogged drains behind a rich industrialist's palatial home in Noida. They were the remains of some of the poor children who had gone missing from the adjoining urban village, Nithari. We were working with a community school there at the time. Authorities were cautioning the siblings and friends of the murdered children by explaining that these children had met with this fate because of greed. They had accepted food and money from a stranger. The survivors were dumbstruck with grief and guilt. It seemed to me like the continuation of the crime. The play asserts all children's right to have a childhood. It also attempts to show how that right is compromised on a daily basis in a society like ours. It is not only the callousness of the authorities but also the middle-class mind-set. The media in the play is hungry for sound-bites and spoofs; the privileged sections of society do not want to trouble themselves beyond a point. Even the young idealistic NGO worker has only potential funders on her mind. In such a set-up desires of poor children become danger zones and veritable death traps for them. My aim was not to build towards catharsis but to hold up a magnifying mirror to the everyday distortions we overlook: our treatment of domestic help and street children, for instance. The play advocates egalitarian state policies and responsible social activism, and, above all, interrogates middle-class notions of social responsibility. It was a difficult play to write as it made me critique myself as a member of the privileged and intensely selfish middle-class. There can be no working through the tragic results of our selfishness, only a reaffirmation of the need to try and bring about a more equal world.

7   The plot of your novel *Idol Love* works at two distinct levels. What do you wish to encompass by calling both the characters Rajni, despite the differences in time and space? Do you universalise the pain of unrequited love or do you propagate a larger political ideology for women?

Uppinder Mehan in a review of *Idol Love* in the *South Asian Review* writes that the Hindu Right in the turbulent period of the 1980–1990s was offering a "monolithic India" as the only solution to the country's problems. He goes on to conclude that multiple versions/identities of characters like Rajni and Riaz present a counterpoint by representing people who are wrestling valiantly (and sometimes "blindly") to keep their futures open in an increasingly "constrictive India". I don't think I can express my political purpose better than this. The pain of unrequited love is poignant in the book:

> I was not fortunate enough to meet my love,
>   Had I lived longer, I would only have waited longer.

In my novel, the secularist/lover is quoting Mirza Ghalib when he is tear-gassed and arrested at *The Last Mushairah of Delhi* that has been organised for love and against hatred. However, the book doesn't end there. Riaz reappears in the dystopian future as does Rajni. Love cannot be arrested and killed off when there are people ready to die for it. They will keep coming back to find the perfect Love and redeem humankind.

8   You have written primarily in English. What is your target audience? Does globalisation pose a challenge to your work, or does it provide opportunities?

Globalisation is both a challenge and an opportunity for writers/practitioners like me who seek to define the popular in terms of class and not through the market. I attempt to address ordinary people—the every-person—in my work. But my fictions, which are often set in small towns or very middle-class environs and written in an accessible and, at times, humorous style, have "serious" concerns at the core. For years I have been told that I am writing against the market. It is an unwritten rule that serious concerns can only be expressed in literary fiction; popular fiction needs to be commercial: simplistic or/and empty entertainment. The good news for me is that the market for popular fiction that was mainly confined to the trendy or aspirational is broadening now. I have hopes that my fourth novel, which is funny and very local, *Aunties of Vasant Kunj*, would have a reach beyond the normative literary novel-reader. The market that is being created for "popular fiction" in the country may now be mature enough for intelligent "hen-lit" that offers an alternate world view of and for ordinary women—a counterpoint to *Sex and the City* kind of narratives!

9 Let's talk a little about pandies' theatre now. Describing itself as staunchly "Left, Feminist, and Atheistic", it's almost three decades since the group first began performing. What has your association with pandies' been like over this period? And what is your assessment of the group's evolution?

Let me begin with my association with the group and my own evolution within it. Sanjay Kumar started pandies' in 1993 and I became an active member of pandies' in 2001. I started out by scripting plays, graduated doing a collaborative international theatre project with a Swedish producer and the American Center, and am now directing plays under a project, Samtal, which I started in 2018. I am fascinated by the way pandies' has progressed as a group. I wrote a play about us called *Sarkari Feminism* in 2010, a self-reflexive comedy. It is about the conflict between a progressive male theatre-director and a power-hungry chairperson of a women's commission. She recites plagiarised poetry in office. I had such fun with that! The theatre-director is committed to giving voice to underserved minorities—including sexual minorities. He falls in love with a fellow activist and wants to divorce his wife. The chairperson accuses him of duplicity, and most of the women in the commission turn against him. Scandalised by the transgender subject of his play, she cancels the theatre project sanctioned to him on the grounds that it has nothing to do with women's issues. Predictably, he finds no official support and must look for funds elsewhere. The Hindi-English play, directed by Sanjay Kumar, turned out to be quite a rip-roaring comedy. But it was also an attempt to describe our journey. What we are doing is complex and our evolution is in terms of negotiating the complexity of being Left-inclined and Feminist in an increasingly theistic and conservative environment. We clash with the establishment at many levels—even with what passes for "official" feminism. But this is how it should be. Praxis must challenge, stretch, and rewrite theory. We discuss and debate more and more as the group evolves. Some members have matured into independent theatre practitioners and artists; many are pursuing demanding careers, but they return to pandies' to perform, to touch base, to discuss, and to debate.

10   We understand pandies' is a volunteer-based organisation, that is, there is no membership fee or conditions and you work primarily with amateurs and not trained theatre professionals. What are the challenges involved in sustaining pandies' as an activist theatre group with such a flexible and open pool of members?

The training of actors in pandies' is not only a matter of picking up skills and techniques. More than that, it is about learning to critique social and political issues from a Left and Feminist standpoint. Performance is always related to life-performances here. There are more than a hundred flexible members. Sanjay and, now, I too are the leaders who hold the fort at Studio 81, Vasant Kunj—the performance and rehearsal space that we have built and keep running—on a completely voluntary basis. Like any other social intervention, pandies' demands commitment in terms of time, energy, and money. We are both college teachers and artists and look upon this as an extension of our work. Besides creative satisfaction, we derive immense satisfaction from the development we see taking place in the members. At any given point there is usually a core group of about seven or eight actors who can be counted upon to take a theatre project forward. It is a working model. It can be difficult and stressful at times. But then anything that is innovative and experimental is tough!

11   How does the *mauhaul* or *hawa* influence your output as a writer? Since you are as much a creative writer as a government servant, how do these identities inform and/or contradict each other when conceptualising and writing your plays?

You ask about plays and not novels, and I think there's a point to be made here. The theatre practitioner experiences oppression and censorship more immediately than the novelist. The subject-matter of the play *Sarkari Feminism* that I discuss here is an instance. A government functionary's disapproval of the practitioner's personal life led to complete censorship. Theatre is dependent on funding for its inception, and that makes it more vulnerable. It is not as though novelists or other artists are immune to censorship, but film and theatre have always been in the eye of the storm. This is also because as performance arts they are seen to have a more immediate effect on the minds and hearts of the people. What is happening around us—the hatred, the threats, the open persecution of like-minded individuals and institutions—places a big responsibility on cultural practitioners. As a theatre person I have started to feel keenly the need to communicate with the "every person". Yes, the hostile *mauhaul* has affected me deeply. It has served to unloosen some restraints and hesitations within me. I feel it is now or never. I am working more at theatre than I have for many years. I took charge of my college theatre society from 2017 to 2019 and worked hard to provide a bigger forum to the excellent Urdu plays the college has been putting up for many years; I have also started to work in Hindustani/Hindi. I am trying to broaden our audience-base and build relationships with Hindi-speaking communities who are not regular theatre-goers. We need to reach out to those who get left out from the reach of culture. It is imperative that violence and hatred be answered by the broad compassion of art.

12 Speaking of *mauhaul*, you have said that theatre helps improve the self-esteem of children in *bastis*. How? What has been your experience of bringing theatre to children in *bastis*?

I have done workshop theatre with pandies' in several places. These days, I find myself thinking so much about a workshop we did in 2006 with 25 adolescents from Jammu and Delhi refugee camps and 25 adolescents from the Kashmir Valley. Fifty adolescents belonging to the so-called warring communities and we, the six facilitators, stayed together in a camp in Gulmarg for five days. We workshopped all day and it was exhilarating. The stories started out in conflict situations, but in the workshops they grew into plays about togetherness, forgiveness, peace, and friendship. The play—four short plays strung together actually—was performed to a packed auditorium in Srinagar, and there was also a live telecast. We got a highly emotional response from the audience. The participants weren't from *bastis*. They were from refugee camps and orphanages, but all of them had been deeply affected by the ongoing conflict in the state. We saw personality transformations taking place in front of us. In five days these kids developed deep friendships with each other. They became visibly more confident, calmer, and less angry. Most of all, they acquired dreams and a proactive sense of purpose. The play represented this journey. This is what taking theatre to the *bastis* has meant for us also in Rajasthan and Delhi: resolutions of life-situations via performance and young people assuming leadership in their communities. Time and again young people have "acted" wiser than blundering adults. If only we would let them show us the way forward.

13 We've noticed pandies' recent performances reflect intensely on gender issues. *Crooked Kala(a)m*, *Ismat's Love Stories*, *Pagaleyan Da Sardar*, *Medea*, all of these dramatise violence and questions of choice in love

and relationships. How has your scholarship and pedagogy informed your writing in creating these stories?

I scripted *Crooked Kala(a)m* (2015) along with Sanjay Kumar and Anand Prakash and then went on to write *Ismat's Love Stories* (2017) and, of course, I directed *Medea* (2019). *Pagaleyan Da Sardar* (2018) is written and directed by Sanjay Kumar. What I did in *Crooked Kala(a)m* was to make Saadat Hasan Manto and Ismat Chughtai talk to each other. The play was on the works of Premchand, Manto, and Chughtai, and I scripted the section on Chughtai. I didn't want the "feminist" writer's work to come as a postscript to those of the two "big" male Progressive writers, so I wrote about both Ismat and Manto, their friendship and disagreements. pandies' has been dealing with feminist texts right from the beginning. What was new in *Crooked Kala(a)m* was the idea of knitting the writers' lives and works together. In the beginning there was some unease in the group about representing Chughtai and Manto as characters. But, then, as we carried on everybody began to feel that having the writers as characters was working to deepen the impact of the stories. It is perspicacious of you to connect play writing with pedagogy. We contextualise so much in our literature classes. I felt that it was important to do the same with Ismat and Manto—mainly to prevent fetishising of a work like "Lihaaf". It is important to remind students—and audiences as well—that "feminist" texts are not just about women; they have a historical context and are equally about humanity and humanness. Later on as director, I positioned the proto-feminist text, *Medea*, at the intersection of gender and racialisation. All women do not experience discrimination in the same way and to the same degree. Women from marginalised and underserved sections experience it more poignantly.

14 *Medea* is the first production under Project Samtal, your venture to bring world classics to Indian audiences across economic barriers. Why did you choose *Medea* to be the project's flagship, and how did you adapt it for performance? How are such classics of world literature able to speak to audiences today?

I started work on *Medea* with a very tentative plan; the conceptualising of Project Samtal followed later and very organically. The idea of taking quality theatre across economic barriers had come to me via the work of a Minneapolis-based American director, Michelle Hensley. At a workshop in Minneapolis in December 2017, which was basically for American theatre groups that are using her Ten Thousand Things (TTT) model of theatre, what struck me most was how this format—performance-in-the-round resulting in an immersive experience for the audiences—can set the imagination and the intellect free. I was enchanted by the high aesthetic standards and how Michelle was able to make the pursuit of excellence an activist goal rather than an exclusivist enterprise. I felt pandies' theatre could use her input. So, I invited her to pandies' theatre under the Fulbright Specialist Programme. Accompanied by Kira Obolensky, a prize-winning playwright, she conducted five workshops with our creative team from 17 February to 6 March 2019. The workshops focused on the technical aspects of performing in the round: movement, music, and costumes.

pandies' chose Euripides' tragedy *Medea* to take to diverse audiences due to many reasons. The play tells the story of a woman who wreaks terrible vengeance, but Euripedes' rendering of the age-old myth can lead us to pose questions about why this happened. *Medea* has a long history of performances all over the world and has led to several feminist and postcolonial renderings. It has raised pertinent questions in various societies, opening up spaces for activist and therapeutic intervention. Why do such betrayals happen? How does a woman negotiate heartache after such an incident? What are the options open to her? What is the role of the society in such situations? Above all, why are fairness and justice such important values?

Euripides highlights Medea's outsider status, and for me as the scriptwriter and director, Medea became the archetypal refugee woman. After exploring the obvious gendered issue, our *Medea* moved into the extremely important area of the treatment of the margins by the mainstream. The plight of Medea had resonances not only for women but also for minorities and Dalits.

Our *Medea* premiered in the Shaktishalini Shelter Home on 21 April 2019 and was followed by a show in the Nithari Baratghar on the same day. On 28 April we had two shows attended by about hundred middle-class theatregoing audiences in Studio 81, Vasant Kunj.

Our initial audiences were from a cross-section of society and included migrant labour, domestic workers, professors, and MNC employees, among others. The effect of the play was cathartic, but the discussions also made the audiences relate the situation to the here and the now. The most heartwarming and insightful responses to this ancient Greek play came from the two community shows in Shaktishalini and Nithari. We had tears there for the murdered children, but also for Medea, the classical killing mother. We were amazed by the ease with which Medea was familiarised as the woman next door in both these spaces. Her predicament was understood by all even if her actions could not be justified. The Greek names and Indo-western costumes had set everyone free to enter her world.

A tour of *Medea* in Rajasthan where we did five shows—two of them in remote rural areas—was the next stage in the development of Project Samtal. Again, the response was overwhelming, especially for the actors most of who were visiting a Rajasthan village for the first time. Every show was followed by long discussions, and it was not ancient Greece that we discussed but the audiences' daily lives. The reach of classical art amazed each one of us. I have just finished writing a long essay titled "Raging in Delhi and Rajasthan: Post-show Audience Discussions after Performances of Euripides' *Medea*" on the incredible audience responses we got.

In all we did 15 shows of *Medea*. It was selected as the concluding play for the Shadipur Natak Utsav, India's first community-curated theatre festival, organised by Studio Safdar. Project Samtal is conceptualised with this valuable experience in mind. It is a way of bringing our diverse practices—proscenium plays and activist community performances—together. It may be said that it is our effort to evolve a form of theatre that brings "big" themes and "aesthetics" associated with high art in service of activist goals.

15 Though *Medea* has been touted as your directorial debut, you've also been involved in the direction of other plays. What kind of work goes into orienting your cast towards the rigorously feminist standpoint of your work? What are the challenges, given specially that very few of your members are trained theatre professionals?

At pandies' we work as a team with defined roles for every member. *Medea* is my first directorial venture. For other plays—when I am the playwright—I attend rehearsals to give feedback in a purely consultative capacity. I want to touch upon the politics of being a woman theatre practitioner here. The fact that pandies' was started by my partner, Sanjay Kumar, eight years before I joined the group works mainly in my favour, but it also brings some challenges. I think it is important to speak about them as there are more men than women holding powerful positions in the field of theatre. I started out by helping with rehearsals (feeding the cast and crew and giving feedback) and by writing plays for pandies'. It is important for me to still do both of these. At the 2012 Women Playwrights International Conference in Stockholm, I discovered two things: one, that to be taken seriously as a theatre-person I would need to know much more about the technical aspects of performance; and two, that the biggest challenge for women practitioners is to find ways to produce their work. So, I am directing now, and alongside creative work I have also started to do a lot of technical and logistical planning for pandies'. The woman practitioner needs to be the Jill of all trades to master the stage. At the moment, I am working only with trained actors. My entire *Medea* cast is trained—in physical theatre, in Urdu/Hindi theatre, and of course in-house in pandies'. Then there was further training in performance in the round for all of them conducted by Michelle Hensley, who is a professional theatre-director. A classical play demands a high level of expertise. During *Medea* rehearsals we evolved a feminist standpoint through detailed discussions of character. We conceptualised the worldview of each character and how it intersects with the universe of the protagonist Medea, who is marginalised because she is a woman and an outsider—a refugee—in Corinth.

16 What is the footprint of such writing on your life outside theatre? As a scholar, a lecturer, an individual, how has your work with pandies' transformed you? Specifically, how does your work as a theatre-activist change you as a lecturer? What synergises the classroom with the stage, and vice versa?

I think my theatre work has made me realise the potential of everyday performances. I look at life acts as performances. The enthusiasm to try and outperform one's roles in life is what I try and communicate to students in class. I would say theatre really comes in handy in opening up the world and in conceptualising possibilities for the future. I think I have become more positive and assertive over the years and, also, better at teamwork.

Theatre has had a direct effect on my writing. My fiction has become consciously performative. In my latest book, *Aunties of Vasant Kunj*, I use the form of a seven-act play. It is an autobiographical novel with three protagonists who could also be three characters played by the same person at different times. These three "Aunties" rise to combat different kinds of oppressions with their Buddhism, feminist activism, and romantic love, but in doing so they improvise their acts. While I detail the dailyness of women's lives, I touch lightly on the universal dilemmas of identity and conflicting social roles. I have enjoyed writing it. In a sense, writing this novel has given me insights into my own very diverse life-performances as a mother, a teacher, a writer, and an activist.

17 Along with you, both Sanjay Kumar and Anand Prakash—pandies' other mainstays—are part of the English academic fraternity. How do you think our community's relationship with theatre has changed over the years? On the one hand, we do have theatre as a more visible part of syllabi and of colleges' co-curricular activities. On the other, much of this—like colleges' *nukkad nataks*—is sanitised by administrative limitations and the pressures lecturers work under to simply survive in their workspaces. Isn't it instructive that a group similar to pandies' has not emerged from our community in recent times?

I was taken aback to hear that in the English department syllabus revision meetings last year there was a discussion on whether modern drama should continue to be part of the syllabus. Apparently, there are some academics who feel it should be taught as part of Arts and Performance or Theatre Studies syllabi. This would effectively mean not teaching it at the undergraduate level in Delhi University. Drama classes are something all students invariably enjoy. Not only is drama an integral part of literature, studying it in class provides an entry point into literary theory and social criticism for a lot of students. I feel there should be more, and not less, drama prescribed in the course. You are right about the administrative pressures being overwhelming in the semester mode. There is so little time for the valuable extracurricular activities that connect teaching of literature with everyday life. But I do feel that introduction of courses like Creative Writing and Text and Performance are a good development. They are, in a sense, active learning courses. Students not only learn techniques of creative writing but also a whole lot about literature as well in the creative writing course. Similarly, creating a play in class as part of Text and Performance is a big learning about drama.

Yes, there aren't any college theatre groups that have gone on to become independent theatre groups like pandies'. But I would say that the general standard of theatre—especially of *nukkad nataks*—put up by college groups in Delhi University is excellent. This is in spite of the pressures of the semester mode. Collegiate theatre is also getting quite well established in the city. I think young people have the capacity to overcome challenges, but one wishes that our administration were more encouraging and supportive.

18 Finally, it's been a few years since your last novel came out. Do you see yourself more as a playwright now? How do you compare novelistic fiction with theatre as conduits of the left-feminist activism you espouse in your work?

I am hoping *Aunties of Vasant Kunj* will come out soon. I started out writing novels and I see myself as primarily a writer of performative prose—be it a novel or a play. As I write my novels in English and my theatre work has shifted to Hindustani, my target audiences for the two are different in spite of the overlaps. My novels, for instance, would not be read in places like Mangliawas in Rajasthan where we performed *Medea*. Similarly English fiction readers from the south of the country are also not likely to come for the shows of *Medea*. Both the English and Hindustani worlds are extremely important to me not only as sites where I develop liberative ideas but also as places where with each new work I learn to be a better artist and a more effective communicator.

12

NOSTALGIC POSSIBILITIES

Planning and heritage in Shahjahanabad

Anubhav Pradhan

An element of nostalgia is inevitable when thinking and writing about cities. Even as cities are crucibles of change and engines of growth, they are also products of their past. A city's image or character, its so-called spirit, is a carefully calibrated discourse constituted as much by its aspirations for the future as its awareness of its history across multiple indices of the local, regional, and global. There is, almost always, some claim to be made to glory gone by in the construction of urban civic identity and some historical epoch to be appropriated and reinvented in the projection of greater grandeur to come. Former triumphs and tribulations, resilient memories of times good and bad, these particularise the collective sense of urbanity with which cities gradually come to be associated.

If looking back is an integral part of looking forward in this constitution of urban selfhood, then it is imperative to examine the nature of this retrospective glance. Who are the agents and agencies controlling this process? What is chosen as representative and seminal? Which ends are serviced and achieved thereby? Taking Delhi as its case and Shahjahanabad as its site, this chapter examines the affective linkages girding literary and planning imaginaries of this area. Closely reading a cross-section of novels, memoirs, and tour guides and juxtaposing these against key policy documents and project reports on the redevelopment of Shahjahanabad, this chapter argues that nostalgia is a significant qualitative component of planning visions for the future of this precinct. Mediated by and large by this literary corpus on Mughal grandeur, this nostalgia forges socio-cultural continuities out of sync with Shahjahanabad's recent history of deeply unsettling political and communal ruptures. In seeking to selectively restore the area's lost glory as the cultural centre of Mughal India, the redevelopment of Shahjahanabad prioritises heritage tourism and trade over the civic and infrastructural requirements of the area's residences and its many commercial establishments. Evaluating the discursive prevalence of nostalgia as an affective determinant of public planning and policy in the case of Shahjahanabad, this chapter advocates therefore more grounded critiques of planning, heritage, and affect in South Asian cities.

Lost glory, remembered splendours: perpetuating Shahjahanabad

Shahjahanabad has many monikers: the Walled City, Old Delhi, and, most common of all, Chandni Chowk. Inaugurated in 1648 AD by Shahjahan as the principal seat of his empire, Shahjahanabad is the second Mughal city and the penultimate imperial capital to be built in the Delhi region. It was built upon the vestiges of Ferozabad and Dinpanah, former imperial capitals from the fourteenth and sixteenth centuries respectively, and was designed in keeping with Persian and Indian precepts of town planning to be a monumental reflection of Mughal notions of kingship. With the Qila Mubarak and the Jama Masjid as its twin foci and Chandni Chowk and Faiz Bazaar as the primary east-west and north-south axes, the material form of the city[1] evokes a "nested hierarchy ... [of] city, empire, and universe" which lay at the conceptual core of the patrimonial-bureaucratic apparatus of the Mughal Empire (Blake xiv). Such conceptualisation of the body politic of the empire as an extension of the body and will of the emperor meant that Mughal capitals were intended more to be mobile hubs of activity inextricably tied to the emperor's presence than materially rooted cities (Sinopoli 294), but reverses in imperial fortunes soon after Aurangzeb's death meant that Shahjahanabad came to acquire a de facto significance as the home of the imperial household and the representative hub of high Mughal culture.

Unsurprisingly, Shahjahanabad has also come to enjoy a standing academic reputation as "the crown jewel, the climax of the premodern urban process in the Indian subcontinent" (Blake 1). Numerous historians have written on the history and architecture of the city and its palace-fortress, and almost all the major events—intrigues, riots, invasions—have been commented upon in detail. Scholarly works on such historical figures as Zaka Ullah are as much on their individual personalities as on the foundational role of the city in shaping them, and the city of the last Mughals appears as a "fragrant recollection of ... the graciousness and dignity of the Moghul Age, with its culture and refinement" (Andrews 21). A substantial corpus of this writing is devoted to the Mutiny of 1857 and its far-reaching effects on the morphology and culture of Delhi in the wake of Bahadur Shah Zafar's banishment, conversion of the palace-fortress into a British barrack, and demolition of a substantial portion of the city. Many others have also written on the transformations occurring after the Partition of 1947: drastic demographic change, rampant commercialisation, and irreparable loss of the city's cosmopolitan culture (Gupta 44). Nonetheless, "the feeling one has been transported to the Islamic Orient" (Krafft 93) lingers on in much of the literature even when discussing contemporary Shahjahanabad. The pervasive sense of loss, mingling deeply with appreciation, has consistently strengthened the city's appeal as home to a unique urbanity:

> [I]t has an identity that is distinct. Popularly known as Chandni Chowk, or Old Delhi, its name conjures up romantic narrow streets, a variety of street food and exotic markets. And increasingly, not only tourists but residents of other parts of Delhi want to experience this city and its culture in all its richness.
>
> (Liddle xiv)

Such discursive association of a tarnished eminence with Shahjahanabad is amply apparent in literary works on Delhi as well, for the city's "long twilight" has been "an endless source of delight to Delhi's chroniclers" (Sengupta 12). *Twilight in Delhi* (1940), Ahmed Ali's exquisite lament for that "phase of our national life and the decay of a whole culture, a particular mode of thought and living" (Ali xxi) as symbolised in the speech, customs, and traditions of Shahjahanabad, was instrumental in corelate a dogged nostalgia with the city, repackaging the established precedent of *Shahr Ashob* for the emergent genre of Indian Writing in English. Ali's narrator insists that the city is still "the jewel of the eye of the world, still it is the centre of attraction" (Ali 4) even though "gone are the poets" and "gone is its culture" (Ali 5). As Mahmood Farooqui notes wryly in his Preface to *Besieged: Voices from Delhi 1857* (2010):

> The people who appear in these stories have long vanished, their descendants have cleared out to Pakistan or Hyderabad or Lucknow or appear in magazine pages, consistently for the last hundred years, as the poor, lost, condemned descendants of the Mughals. The bylanes of Old Delhi . . . Ah, the galis, ah, the Mir couplet, *Dilli ki na hain galiyan, awraq-e musavvir hain.* . . . But there were few takers. The Hindus who lived in Old Delhi have long moved out to Civil Lines, Mukherji Nagar and Rohini. The Punjabis who came to take their place in 1947 have also by now moved out to south Delhi, to Karol Bagh and elsewhere. The Muslims who now live there all seem to have descended from western Uttar Pradesh in the last thirty years. In sooth, there are no Dilliwallas.
>
> (Farooqui x)

Nonetheless, the "authenticity of its cultural milieu" (Varma 247) is what makes Shahjahanabad immortal for many writers. There may be no true Dilliwalla, but "purani Dilli" manages to still live on "like an ageing courtesan abandoned by her new suitors, waiting to die" (Varma 252).[2] Writing about the "paroxysm of nostalgia" (Dasgupta 153) which engulfed the city in the nineteenth century, both before and after the bloody events of 1857, Rana Dasgupta observes that

> ... Delhi's writers have consistently seen it as a city of ruins and they have directed their creativity to expressing that particular spiritual emaciation that comes from being cut off from one's own past ... the city is always already destroyed ... maybe the present book ... merely reproduces this ancient literary mood, for my ultimate experience of this city where nothing endures is also that of being bereft.
> (Dasgupta 154)

India's uneven encounter with modernity was particularly disruptive for traditional power centres such as Delhi, where transition to the industrial-bureaucratic apparatus of empire and thereafter to nationhood was repeatedly ushered in the wake of cataclysmic war and fury. Nostalgia, in the case of Delhi, appears to "entail an uncertain contestation between a "perfect" past that is represented as an object of memory or phantasy and a "tense" present figured in relation to the anxiety-producing developments of the age" (Clewell 3).[3] Hence, the pronounced sentiment that nothing of value endures in Delhi yet Delhi in itself is of value finds ready substantiation in the material conditions of the old city, Shahjahanabad, which "even in its ruins ... glowed like a splintered, uncut jewel" (Rumi 271).[4] This insistent nostalgia has the effect of valorising the supposed cultural splendours of Mughal Delhi despite the steep declines in the city's political and commercial fortunes in that epoch. The so-called English Peace, the five decades preceding the Mutiny during which Delhi witnessed a literary renaissance of sorts, is a particularly potent period for such retrospective glances at the city's past: it serves to provide a genteel and sophisticated benchmark to measure the alleged degradations of the present day and age. In her Translator's Note to *City of My Heart: Accounts of Love, Loss and Betrayal in Nineteenth Century Delhi* (2018), Rana Safvi cannot help look back at that era as deeply symbolic of "a multicultural, pluralistic way of life" which had "an élan of its own" and wherein "every day was a celebration" (Safvi xv). Similarly, for Abdul Rahman Siddiqi in his memoir *Smoke Without Fire: Portraits of Pre-Partition Delhi* (2011), true denizens of Delhi belonged

> ... much more to the world of dreams and vision than one in brick and mortar. They would look at the city not as it was but the city that Emperor Shahjehan had built and one of his great grandsons—the last Light and Lamp of the Mughal Dynasty (*Khandan-i-Mughalia ki Akhri Chasm-o-Chiragh*) Bahadur Shah Zafer portrayed in his poetry as *Ujra Diyar*—the city in ruins, the requiem for the Lost Empire.
> (Siddiqi 159)

Repeatedly articulating a yearning for the irrecoverable yet invaluable cultural ethos of Delhi of the late Mughals, such writings seem to have laid the groundwork for the complementary discourse of "nostalgic authenticity" (Clewell 10) in travel guides to the city. Writing for the Delhi Administration in *Delhi: History and Places of Interest* (1970), Prabha Chopra notes that "Chandni Chowk is justly famous as the commercial centre of Delhi . . . for its embroideries in gold and silver, ivories on which cunning carvers have spent years of toil, and jewels cut and uncut worth a king's ransom" (Chopra 125). In *Delhi and Its Monuments* (1987), Promodini Varma astutely observes on one hand that "the grandeur of the Mughals has been lost without British order and design being acquired" but cannot help feel on the other that the "old city" still has "a vitality and resilience difficult to find elsewhere, and a pride even more difficult to ignore" (Varma 112). Likewise, the *Commonwealth Games Guide to Delhi* (2010) asserts that "Old Delhi is full of unexpected sights and surprises" and "the energy of the vibrant markets and bustling streets is ever fresh" (Times Group Books 27). While such entrenched nostalgia bears ready witness to a "profound and understandable sense of unrecoverable loss" (Outka 260), it also generates a deep affective yearning for authenticity and recovery which manifests itself in the commodification of lived experiences and spaces as heritage assets to be showcased and savoured.

Planning heritage, thinking tourism: redeveloping Shahjahanabad

From the commencement of direct British rule, planning for the region has tended to ignore Shahjahanabad for other, more privileged enclaves. Before the transfer of the imperial capital, the largely English precincts of Civil Lines and of the Fort received greater attention and inputs in budgetary and infrastructural terms than Shahjahanabad (Legg 152). After the establishment of New Delhi, the local and central arms of governance sought to vigorously insulate—safeguard—the new city from the old one, which continued to be posited as more or less opaque and impervious to change. Delhi's population continued to increase throughout the first half of the twentieth century without any major civic amenities being introduced and residential extensions added for the benefit of the people: this was in keeping with the extreme biases of colonial government, which—for the most—saw substantial commitment to public welfare as financially undesirable (Legg 168). As a result, growing congestion and attendant illnesses in Shahjahanabad inflated the city's mortality rate,[5] which in turn worsened its standing reputation of irredeemable intractability in matters of hygiene and quality of life. Yet, simultaneously, aesthetic impulses to maintain the historical grandeur of the old city as well as to transform it, thus, into a fitting and worthy neighbour to the new one led to demolition and gentrification of such areas of Shahjahanabad as abutted New Delhi so as to achieve an "aesthetic landscaping of the boundary between the two cities" (Legg 200).

In comparison, the *Master Plan for Delhi, 1962* the city's first comprehensive plan, saw Shahjahanabad primarily in commercial—and not aesthetic or heritage[6]—terms as a Central Business District interspersed with and surrounded by residential communities and industries. It explicitly acknowledged that "redevelopment of the Old City by way of large scale clearance and reconstruction was not immediately practicable" (DDA 1962, ii) due to the magnitude of the problems at hand—"extreme overcrowding, congestion and insanitary conditions" (DDA 1962, 5).[7] Instead, it prescribed only ad hoc and temporary measures at reduced standards of space—such as 0.30 acres per thousand persons for local parks and playgrounds as compared to a minimum of 0.81 acres for the rest of Delhi—for improving the quality of life in the precinct. On the other hand, the *Master Plan for Delhi, 2001* noted Shahjahanabad to be of considerable historical and aesthetic value for Delhi—"an area of important urban heritage" (DDA 1990, 16)—even as it identified unchecked commercialisation and congestion as the key issues ailing the precinct. As part of its strategy for "Revitalisation of Residential Areas", the plan also distinguishes between neighbourhoods which are "of organic growth" and those which were "redeveloped during the Colonial Rule" or which have been "invaded by uses other than residential" (DDA 1990, 17) and suggests that only the former be given attention so as to maintain "the traditional character" and "create a unique environment of the urban heritage to be left for the successive generations" (DDA 1990, 17–18).

Hence, the association of a sense of loss and threatened authenticity with Shahjahanabad is not limited to literature alone. Even as multiple plans and policy-makers have articulated an exasperated inability to intervene successfully in Shahjahanabad so as to improve access to basic civic amenities, they have largely done so by framing the city as a repository of a rich local culture and heritage which is always on the verge of being lost—and which, therefore, has to be protected and revitalised. The *Master Plan for Delhi, 2021* is categorical in this regard, observing that "traditional areas in the Walled City need special treatment to conserve its heritage value while retaining the residential character" (DDA 2007, 27). The "glory of the Walled City" is evoked at multiple instances in the plan (DDA 2007, 52, 104, 105) and the city is upheld as a model of "traditional Urban Design" (DDA 2007, 104). The plan identifies Shahjahanabad as a Heritage Zone,[8] emphasises the need to revitalise its glory in view of the region's "economic & tourism potential" (DDA 2007, 52), and suggests that conservation approaches should "retain the overall traditional character of the Walled City" (DDA 2007, 104). To this end, it recommends that an area-specific redevelopment scheme be prepared on the basis of differential "development control parameters for the heritage areas keeping in view archaeological norms/architectural character and general parameters for the non-heritage segment of the traditional area" (DDA 2007, 211).

Therefore, with the notable exception of *MPD 1962*, planners and policy-makers seem to have conceived Shahjahanabad in dualistic terms as aesthetic yet opaque, a site of considerable heritage value but a place simultaneously immune to improvement. Similar to novelists, historians, and authors of tour guides, planners too seem to value in this case "the artifice of nostalgia" as an affective device to "shape the future by recalling the past in terms of nativist pastoral or romance" (Walder 16). The glories of Shahjahanabad which are constantly evoked pertain largely to the beauty of its built form or to the vestiges of its composite, syncretic culture anchored by sophisticated Urdu poetry—or a mixture of these two, the built informing the cultural and vice versa. But if nostalgia as we feel and understand it today is a product of modernity with a deep "sense of time that includes linearity, secularity, and inadequacy" (Walder 10), then such insistent juxtaposition of the congestion and commercialisation of the present against the imagined ease and contentment of the past directly facilitates valorisation of abstracted, idealised notions of architecture and culture in sharp contrast to—and some neglect of—lived realities, needs, and experiences. It also elides stringent interrogation of the inability of planning and governance through multiple regimes over more than a century to provide universal access to basic civic amenities and healthcare to residents and comprehensively balance the often divergent requirements of wholesale commerce with heritage tourism.

In many ways, therefore, plans to redevelop Shahjahanabad are outcomes of these interconnected planning visions for the rejuvenation of the city which have looked forward to a better, more beautiful, more bountiful future by looking back to what is imagined in terms like the English Peace, the Mughal Twilight, and so on as at just such a time. The Shahjahanabad Redevelopment Corporation (SRDC), a public-sector company constituted in 2008 "to promote conservation of built and natural heritage in the National Capital Territory of Delhi" (SRDC 3), prepared in 2015 a Project Concept Proposal (PCP) titled *Revitalization of Shahjahanabad (Walled City of Delhi)*. The PCP frames the importance of Shahjahanabad for Delhi in terms of both its built form and its cultural heritage: "a distinct identity and character as derived from its building public spaces and its long standing tradition as a cultural melting point" (SRDC 3). It reproduces large sections of *MPD 2021* verbatim, lists the usual range of commercial and industrial excesses in the area and the resultant problems of extreme congestion, insanitary living conditions, and pollution but then suddenly argues:

> Shahjahanabad's future will largely depend on its economic revival wherein sustainable economic development of the area must also include employment creation. **Considering historical evolution and present economic activity of Shahjahanabad, its natural comparative**

> advantage lies in becoming a centre of cultural tourism, creative industry, entertainment, and tourism.
>
> (SRDC 35, original emphasis)

The rationale informing this discursive leap from the manifold economic activity currently providing livelihood to thousands of formal and informal workers to a radically gentrified tourist economy seems rooted in nostalgic imaginaries of what Shahjahanabad was—and not what it has evolved to become. The PCP extensively enumerates the kinds of commercial activities and industries which have to be phased out and relocated, on grounds of both pollution and undesirability. Asserting that it is "necessary to re-organise and revitalise the whole commercial space and activity in the Walled City" (SRDC 39), the PCP seeks to inscribe a magisterial modernity upon the insistently pre-modern chaos of the city. It proposes that "incompatible wholesale trade" and "negative trade" such as paper, chemicals, and food grains be shifted out (SRDC 39) and the entire cloth trade be reorganised. It also recommends that the trade in "junk and second hand goods items" be shifted out and replaced with "compatible trade like handicrafts, artefacts and heritage and cultural tourism activities" (SRDC 40), underlining the gentrification and structural reorganisation often concomitant with nostalgic planning of how urban history and heritage should be framed and accessed in the public sphere. Framing itself as restorative, such nostalgia acts to strengthen the aspirational tendencies within urban planning and governance in Delhi to re-make it as an ostensibly more aesthetic, more clean version of itself regardless of the loss of livelihood and shelter which the resultant transformations often entail.

Likewise, a detailed City Level Project (CLP) report titled *Rejuvenation of Shahjahanabad* prepared by the Delhi Urban Art Commission in 2017 foregrounds the heritage tourism potential of the precinct as the primary motivation for extensive and meticulous intervention and reorientation of its built fabric and infrastructure. Observing that despite "years of plunder and neglect" the city still "showcases an array of traditional art, craft, beliefs and practices" which imbue it with the potential to become "a global tourist destination" (DUAC 8), the CLP identifies "increase in wholesale trade" (DUAC 53) as one of the primary threats to the area and suggests a development strategy which would tap into the "existing intangible heritage and develop an urban form to support this heritage" (DUAC 54). Shahjahanabad must become a "memorable experience for visitors", and so an "Interesting, Informative and Interactive ambience" must be created for them (DUAC 55). This will involve delineating and developing heritage corridors and routes within Shahjahanabad and promoting traditional activities such as pottery, jewellery-making, cooking, stitching, and theme-based painting for the benefit of tourists traversing these routes (DUAC 57). Additionally, the CLP recommends that the entire streetscape along these tourist routes be redesigned so that they become homogeneous in keeping with the pre-selected themes like market, *haveli*, and food: this, the CLP asserts, will "re-instil the overall late-Mughal character of the space and accentuate the frame of the building form" (DUAC 71).

Considered in tandem, the approaches which key state stakeholders like DDA, SRDC, and DUAC advocate towards the redevelopment of Shahjahanabad seem informed by a restorative nostalgia seeking to forcefully insert the city into the circuitry of gentrified heritage tourism. Taking rejuvenation as an operative principle, the plans and reports considered here foreground a development strategy premised explicitly on the transformation of dynamic, lived urban spaces into tightly aestheticised spheres of carefully crafted authenticity. As Nezar AlSayyad comments in "Global Norms and Urban Forms in the Age of Tourism: Manufacturing Heritage, Consuming Tradition", the authenticity most tourists seek is "primarily visual" and their "encounter with 'real' history remains marked by distance" (AlSayyad 10). The history of Shahjahanabad is a complex palimpsest, compound of various strains of local, regional, and transcontinental politics and ambitions. Likewise, the history of modern planning for Shahjahanabad is of systematic neglect of local needs and issues as against a larger, modernist impulse to preserve its built and intangible heritage from the depredations of its inhabitants. In this context, the obsessive promotion of rejuvenation as the key principle of planning and policy reinvents the city's heritage as "the deliberate embrace of a single choice as a means of defining the past in relationship to the future" (AlSayyad 14): it engenders a wilful distance between history as it was and is and as it is fervently imagined to be, obfuscating the shortcomings of a planning gaze geared primarily towards aestheticisation of history as tourism heritage. If nostalgia for a Common Place, a place of collective memory and identity, is symptomatic of a time of crisis (Boym 285), then such insistent nostalgia for the lost glory of Shahjahanabad— for an epoch of gentility and sophistication—may be read as reflective of Delhi's protracted, continuing tussle with the nature and condition of its modernity—utopian and ironic in equal measure.

Mediated nostalgia, contested futures: manufacturing Shahjahanabad

In many ways, this tussle is acutely apparent in public responses to the redevelopment of Shahjahanabad being currently executed by SRDC. After a lengthy incubation of more than 15 years, the project finally gathered approval from key state agencies and was inaugurated in December 2018. Its two primary components are the pedestrianisation of Chandni Chowk and the redevelopment of the Jama Masjid precinct. The Chandni Chowk segment was taken up first with a budgetary outlay of Rs 65 crore, involving the complete overhauling of the street from Red Fort to Fatehpuri Masjid by closing it to all motorised vehicular traffic, laying electricity and utility cables in underground trenches, and installing street infrastructure and facilities like water kiosks and public toilets in a wide central median running through the entire 1.3 km stretch of the project area (PSDA 41). Immediately upon the project's commencement, though, local businesses found cause to object to the plan's vision of complete pedestrianisation for its clear prioritisation of heritage tourism over wholesale trade:

> Sri Bhagwan Bansal, vice-president of Delhi Hindustani Mercantile Association, argued that over the past two decades many such schemes have been framed but were found to be impossible to implement because the planners conceived of Chandni Chowk as a tourism centre whereas it has been and will remain a trade centre, where thousands of citizens live and where lakhs come daily to buy and sell . . . Bansal noted that the proposed scheme made no mention of handcarts, which are the mainstay of business in this historical quarter. No e-rickshaws will be allowed either, and only registered cycle rickshaws will be permitted to run. The plan also seeks to turn Chandni Chowk into a no-parking zone for private vehicles.
> (Bhattacharya 5 Dec 2018)

However, speaking at the inauguration of the project, Delhi's Deputy Chief Minister Manish Sisodia struck a largely nostalgic note as he attempted to reconcile governmental aspirations for heritage tourism with the concerns of local businesses:

> We want to ensure that when tourists come to Chandni Chowk, they do not get stuck in traffic . . . traders too want redevelopment. The project will increase the number of tourists in the area. . . . Every student knows of Nai Sarak for books, every household preparing for marriage keeps shopping here a priority, and the fame of Paranthe Waali Gali and Giani's ice cream needs no introduction. The major re-construction and decongestion work will increase tourism and trade manifold.
> (Express News Service 8 Dec 2018)

Notwithstanding this evocation of the glory of Chandni Chowk, the project's design also drew criticism from historians and conservationists for not being in keeping with the ethos of the pathway as it had been originally planned in the seventeenth century under Shahjahan's daughter Jahanara. Even as key state agents such as SRDC's then director Alka Lamba and architect Pradeep Sachdeva, the approved consultant for the project, defended the project's design by couching it in terms of prioritising "today's needs", the "wide central verge that will hold utility ducts, transformers, sub-stations, police stands, even toilet blocks" became cause for alarm for its potential to irrevocably alter the built fabric and heritage of Chandni Chowk (Verma 9 Dec 2018). Observing that Chandni Chowk is "a ceremonial path from Red Fort to Fatehpuri Masjid", conservationist Navin Piplani recommended that it "should not be altered or destroyed" (Verma 9 Dec 2018). Historian Swapna Liddle contended that "many would want to see the original footprints of Chandni Chowk", while historian Sohail Hashmi noted that "this is only being done keeping in mind the tourist experience" (Lalwani 6 Jan 2019). A.G.K. Menon, a renowned planner, averred that "it is our job to preserve what is left of the legacy of Chandni Chowk" (Verma 9 Dec 2018). A group of four prominent architects, planners, and conservationists—Smita Datta Makhija, A.G.K. Menon, Sujata Kohli, and Ashok B. Lall—went on to file an objection petition in the Delhi High Court to protect "the historical and sacrosanct visual and physical axis of the promenade" (Ganesan 14 Aug 2019).

Significantly, these tripartite tensions among traders, project managers, and academic-practitioners on the aims and ends of the redevelopment project seem to be mediating the nostalgia which in large measure informs the discursive aura and appeal of Shahjahanabad/Chandni Chowk/the Walled City. State agents and stakeholders operate within a networked framework of aspirational urbanity with heritage tourism as one of its principle nodes, tapping into the increasing perception of "tradition as a cultural demand" and manufacturing a compatible heritage "as a field of commercial supply" (AlSayyad 15). Academic-practitioners, scholars invested as much in research as in the nitty-gritty of conservation, often formulate their praxis on the bedrock of authenticity, attempting to allay the deep anxiety that by its nature modern life is counterfeit or spurious by seeking to resuscitate the architecturally and culturally authentic as a "testable and desirable quality of tradition" (Upton 300). Working as much in tandem as in opposition to each other, these sets of stakeholders mediate the exigencies of everyday, lived reality with the entrenched nostalgia with which they view the city. Yet, traders most of all seem to be acutely aware of the subtle disapproval cast upon the nature of their livelihood by this multifaceted nostalgia in operation: both as a ceremonial pathway or a pedestrianised walkway, Chandni Chowk as imagined by these powerful determinants of public policy and opinion seems to present little space or scope for the kind of wholesale trade which it currently supports. Traders' interventions, resonant and impactful, contribute substantially to the inflection of such nostalgic imaginaries with functionalist concerns for the everyday, underlining the need for holistic stakeholder consultation in the constitution of development strategies.[9]

As Helaine Silverman points out in "Heritage and Authenticity", the careful creation of "inauthenticity in the living environment" (Silverman 72) to enhance the authenticity of iconic sites and monuments has been embedded in the practice of institutionalised heritage conservation from its inception in the early twentieth century. Given the transformative force exercised by heritage tourism upon its destinations and the impulse for greater authenticity in conservation practices, it is important to critically examine and qualify the political and economic subtexts of the nostalgias which inform the developmental strategies being formulated and executed in our cities. In the particular instance of Shahajahanabad considered in this chapter, insistent evocation of the cultural and architectural heritage of the city by a cross-section of academics and writers for well over a century seems to have complemented planning and policy discourse in its dualistic conceptualisation of the area as vibrant yet decayed, thriving yet threatened. It is imperative that we stop viewing "historic cities as static, timeless or 'traditional,' or preserving their monuments as cultural icons": we should, instead, closely read their socio-cultural landscapes to better understand "local engagements with modernity" (Hosagrahar 291). The possibility which Delhi's current planning regime sees in Shahjahanabad is geared more towards manufacturing an authentic cultural–historical ensemble for the benefit of domestic and international tourists over and above evolving a contextually rooted paradigm of development. The gradual commercialisation of the city must be seen not simplistically as a malaise but as a complex response to the quality of governance and civic utilities and the conditions of trade and work over the course of our recent history. Nostalgia, after all, is a "politically mobile emotion" (Bonnett 3) which can be as radical as it can be regressive: evaluating it analytically will facilitate more intersectional—and introspective—modes of understanding how perceptions of the past continue to inescapably shape the present and the future.

Notes

1 References to "the city" in this chapter are all, for the sake of convenience alone, to Shahjahanabad.
2 The trope of the courtesan has been rendered readily familiar, thanks to Khushwant Singh's *Delhi: A Novel* (1990). Delhi is like Bhagmati, the narrator's mistress in the text: "Having been long misused by rough people they have learnt to conceal their seductive charms under a mask of repulsive ugliness. It is only to their lovers, among whom I count myself, that they reveal their true selves" (Singh 1).
3 A pertinent recent example of this is Mayank Austen Soofi's *Nobody Can Love You More: Life in Delhi's Red Light District* (2012), in which the slow and steady decline in the quality of sex work in its traditional hub at G.B. Road appears all the more unfortunate with comparison to the sophisticated heyday of the tawaif culture in late-Mughal Chawri Bazaar. Looking at the mid-nineteenth century Randi ki Masjid in Lal Kuan, Soofi feels that "the disagreeable aesthetics of the modern world dampens the mosque's delicate beauty. It is looking at something—perhaps a way of life—that seems to have already disappeared" (Soofi 210).
4 In the words of R.V. Smith, one of the foremost contemporary chroniclers of Delhi, "Old Delhi developed a heart of its own, one that breathed in unison with its inhabitants" (Smith 101). Such is the appeal and charm of Shahjahanabad for Smith that even the younger generation of refugees who settled in the Walled City

after the Partition merged inevitably with the "mainstream" and "picked up the mannerisms and nuances of their new place of abode" (Smith 99).
5 Writing about his childhood in the 1930s, Siddiqi recounts the untimely death of his father due to tuberculosis—"the long, languishing disease without a cure" (Siddiqi 71). Importantly, this was the decade when Delhi witnessed a "40 per cent population increase in a decade and an alleged 255 per cent rise in tuberculosis in just 6 years" (Legg 161).
6 Section 9, "Community Facilities and Services", Sub-Section F, "Social and Cultural Institutes", acknowledges the "rich tradition of social and cultural life" in the Old City, but quickly adds that this "may die a slow death if the necessary impetus is not forthcoming" (DDA 1960, 38).
7 It is important to note that by this stage the term "Old City" encompassed not just the walled city of Shahjahanabad but also many of the pre-existing Mughal and British suburbs and extensions, that is, Paharganj, Motia Khan, Qadam Sharif, Sadar Bazaar, Subzi Mandi, Patel Nagar, and Karol Bagh. This contiguous area later came to be termed as a "Special Area" in the second plan. The third plan retained this nomenclature but specified that it consists of the "Walled City, Walled City and Extension, and Karol Bagh" (DDA 2007, 26).
8 Heritage Zones are defined as areas which have "significant concentration, linkage or continuity of buildings, structures, groups or complexes united historically or aesthetically by plan or physical development" (DDA 2007, 102).
9 For example, in opposition to DUAC's contention that "the proposed utilities on the central verge will create a continuous trail of visual as well as physical obstruction", Sanjay Bhargava, president of the Chandni Chowk Sarv Vyapar Mandal, reiterated that "There can't be any encroachment or hurdle on pavements. We will strongly oppose any attempt to install the transformers on either side of the road" (*Hindustan Times*, 17 July 2019). Eventually, the traders' viewpoint was supported by the Lieutenant-Governor of Delhi and the design remained unchanged.

Works cited

Ali, Ahmed. *Twilight in Delhi*. 1940. New Delhi: Rupa Publications India Pvt. Ltd., 2011.
AlSayyad, Nezar. "Global Norms and Urban Forms in the Age of Tourism: Manufacturing Heritage, Consuming Tradition." *Consuming Tradition, Manufacturing Heritage: Global Norms and Urban Forms in the Age of Tourism*. Ed. Nezar AlSayyad. London: Routledge, 2001. 1–33.
Andrews, C.F. *Zaka Ullah of Delhi*. 1929. Intro. Mushirul Hasan and Margit Pernau. New Delhi: Oxford UP, 2003.
Bhattacharya, Somreet. "They Can't Trade Business for Tourism: Chandni Chowk Traders." *The Times of India*, 5 December 2018. <https://timesofindia.indiatimes.com/city/delhi/they-cant-trade-business-for-tourism/articleshow/66945130.cms>. Accessed 10 February 2020.
Blake, Stephen P. *Shahjahanabad: The Sovereign City in Mughal India, 1639–1739*. Cambridge: Cambridge UP, 1991.
Bonnett, Alastair. "Introduction." *Left in the Past: Radicalism and the Politics of Nostalgia*. New York: The Continuum International Publishing Group, 2010. 1–18.
Boym, Svetlana. "Conclusion: Nostalgia for the Common Place." *Common Places: Mythologies of Everyday Life in Russia*. Cambridge, MA: Harvard UP, 1994. 283–92.

Chopra, Prabha. *Delhi: History and Places of Interest*. Delhi: Delhi Gazetteer, 1970.

Clewell, Tammy. "Introduction: Past 'Perfect' and Present 'Tense': The Abuses and Uses of Modernist Nostalgia." *Modernism and Nostalgia*. Ed. Tammy Clewell. Basingstoke: Palgrave Macmillan, 2013. 1–22.

Dasgupta, Rana. *Capital: A Portrait of Twenty-First Century Delhi*. Noida: Fourth Estate, 2014.

Delhi Development Authority. *Master Plan for Delhi, 1962*. Delhi: Delhi Development Authority, 1962.

———. *Master Plan for Delhi, 2001*. Delhi: Delhi Development Authority, 1990.

———. *Master Plan for Delhi, 2021*. Delhi: Delhi Development Authority, 2007.

Delhi Urban Art Commission. *City Level Projects: Rejuvenation of Shahjahanabad*. Delhi: Delhi Urban Art Commission, 2017. <https://www.duac.org/site_content/attachments/05%20Final%20Shahjahanabad%20November%202017%20156pp_L.pdf>. Accessed 17 January 2020.

Express News Service. "Delhi Govt's Ambitious Chandni Chowk Plan Talks of Trams, Fountains and Less Traffic." *The Indian Express*, 8 December 2018. <https://indianexpress.com/article/cities/delhi/government-ambitious-chandni-chowk-plan-talks-of-trams-fountains-and-less-traffic-5483865/>. Accessed 10 February 2020.

Farooqui, Mahmood. "Preface." *Besieged: Voices from Delhi 1857*. New Delhi: Viking, 2010. ix–xvi.

Ganesan, Rajeshwari. "Redeveloping Chandni Chowk: Is It Necessary to Axe Our Rich Past to Pave Way for Development?" *DailyO*, 14 August 2019. <www.dailyo.in/variety/chandni-chowk-redevelopment-red-fort-fatehpuri-masjid-delhi-government-rgo/story/1/31890.html>. Accessed 10 February 2020.

Gupta, Narayani. "The Indomitable City." *Shahjahanabad/Old Delhi: Tradition and Colonial Change*. 1993. Ed. Eckart Ehlers and Thomas Krafft. Delhi: Manohar Publishers & Distributors, 2003. 29–44.

Hosagrahar, Jyoti. "Heritage and Modernity in India." *Routledge Handbook of Heritage in Asia*. Ed. Patrick Daly and Tim Winter. Abingdon: Routledge, 2012. 283–94.

HT Correspondent. "Delhi's Chandni Chowk Redevelopment: Arts Body, Traders Fail to Reach Consensus on Transformers." *Hindustan Times*, 17 July 2019. <www.hindustantimes.com/cities/chandni-chowk-redevelopment-arts-body-traders-fail-to-reach-consensus-on-transformers/story-YDQXbKWGp1k5GBjeTEiTSL.html>. Accessed 10 February 2020.

Krafft, Thomas. "Contemporary Old Delhi: Transformation of an Historical Place." *Shahjahanabad/Old Delhi: Tradition and Colonial Change*. 1993. Ed. Eckart Ehlers and Thomas Krafft. Delhi: Manohar Publishers & Distributors, 2003. 93–119.

Lalwani, Vijayata. "'State-Sponsored Vandalism': Heritage Experts are Unhappy with Chandni Chowk Redevelopment Plan." *Scroll.in*, 6 January 2019. <https://scroll.in/article/907426/state-sponsored-vandalism-why-heritage-experts-are-unhappy-with-chandni-chowk-redevelopment-plan>. Accessed 10 February 2020.

Legg, Stephen. "Biopolitics and the Urban Environment." *Spaces of Colonialism: Delhi's Urban Governmentalities*. Malden: Blackwell Publishing, 2007. 149–209.

Liddle, Swapna. *Chandni Chowk: The Mughal City of Old Delhi*. New Delhi: Speaking Tiger Publishing Pvt. Ltd, 2017.

Outka, Elizabeth. "Afterword: Nostalgia and Modernist Anxiety." *Modernism and Nostalgia*. Ed. Tammy Clewell. Basingstoke: Palgrave Macmillan, 2013. 252–61.

Pradeep Sachdeva Design Associates. *Redevelopment of Jama Masjid Precinct and Chandni Chowk: Detailed Project Report*. New Delhi: Pradeep Sachdeva Design Associates, 2017. <https://drive.google.com/drive/folders/1ooZHtS-dhGYmKiXaf DlEBrbv_C_g0noJ>. Accessed 17 January 2020.

Rumi, Raza. *Delhi by Heart: Impressions of a Pakistani Traveller*. Noida: Harper Collins Publishers India, 2013.

Safvi, Rana. "Translator's Note." *City of My Heart: Accounts of Love, Loss and Betrayal in Nineteenth Century Delhi*. Gurugram: Hachette Book Publishing India Pvt. Ltd, 2018. xiii—xviii.

Sengupta, Ranjana. *Delhi Metropolitan: The Making of An Unlikely City*. New Delhi: Penguin Books, 2007.

Shahjahanabad Redevelopment Corporation. *Revitalization of Shahjahanabad (Walled City of Delhi): Project Concept Proposal*. New Delhi: Shahjahanabad Redevelopment Corporation, 2015. <http://srdc.delhigovt.nic.in/wps/wcm/connect/c11455 8047f23b7791c5fbbbd1c31d3c/Preliminary+Project+Report+03.12.2018+.pdf? MOD=AJPERES&lmod=2096182182&CACHEID=c114558047f23b7791c5fbb bd1c31d3c>. Accessed 17 January 2020.

Siddiqi, Abdul Rahman. *Smoke Without Fire: Portraits of Pre-Partition Delhi*. Delhi: Aakar Books, 2011.

Silverman, Helaine. "Heritage and Authenticity." *The Palgrave Handbook of Contemporary Heritage Research*. Ed. Emma Waterton and Steve Watson. Basingstoke: Palgrave Macmillan, 2015. 69–88.

Singh, Khushwant. *Delhi: A Novel*. New Delhi: Penguin Books, 1990.

Sinopoli, Carla M. "Monumentality and Mobility in Mughal Capitals." *Asian Perspectives* 33.2 (1994): 293–308. <www.jstor.org/stable/42928323>.

Smith, R.V. *Delhi: Unknown Tales of a City*. New Delhi: The Lotus Collection, 2015.

Soofi, Mayank Austen. *Nobody Can Love You More: Life in Delhi's Red Light District*. Viking: New Delhi, 2012.

Times Group Books. *Commonwealth Games Guide to Delhi*. New Delhi: Bennett, Coleman & Co. Ltd., 2010.

Upton, Dell. "'Authentic' Anxieties." *Consuming Tradition, Manufacturing Heritage: Global Norms and Urban Forms in the Age of Tourism*. Ed. Nezar AlSayyad. London: Routledge, 2001. 298–306.

Varma, Pavan K. "Shahjahanabad: The City That Once Was." *City Improbable: Writings on Delhi*. Ed. Khushwant Singh. New Delhi: Penguin Books, 2010.

Varma, Promodini. "Shahjahanabad." *Delhi and Its Monuments*. New Delhi: Spantech Publishers Pvt Ltd, 1987. 79–112.

Verma, Richi. "Why Experts Feel Revamp Will Ruin Chandni Chowk's Historic Fabric." *The Times of India*, 9 December 2018. <https://timesofindia.indiatimes.com/ city/delhi/why-experts-feel-revamp-will-ruin-chandni-chowks-historic-fabric/ articleshow/67006527.cms>. Accessed 10 February 2020.

Walder, Dennis. "Introduction: The Persistence of Nostalgia." *Postcolonial Nostalgias: Writing, Representation, and Memory*. Abingdon: Routledge, 2011. 1–23.

INDEX

Note: Page numbers followed by "n" refer to notes.

academia 3–5
AECC (Ability Enhancement Course Compulsory) 132
Aesop's Fables 71
aesthetics of education 82
AIMPLB (All India Muslim Personal Law Board) 136
Allana, A. 135
American New Criticism 55
Application Courses 128–9
assessment for learning (AfL) 116
attachment, theory of 88
audio-visual stimulation 101

Bansal, B. 156
BA Pass 122
BA Programme Credit Language courses 129
Bharati College 1, 110–12, 125, 132
Bhargava, S. 159n9
Bhaskar, W.W.S. 123
Bhatnagar, R.P. 124
bhava bādhā 69, 70
Book of Genesis, The 29
Bose, M. 125

Calcutta University Commission 122
CBCS (Choice-Based Credit System) 132
Central Institute of Education (CIE) 131
Central Institute of English, Hyderabad 123
Central Institute of English and Foreign Languages (CIEFL) 124
Chaddha, T. 124–6
charismatic leader 87–8

City Level Project (CLP) 153–4
classroom teaching 3, 9, 94, 131
college English at University of Delhi, developments in teaching 121–33; first wave of reforms 125–8; General English, history of 122–5; second wave of reforms 128–30; third wave of reform 130–2
Commonwealth Games Guide to Delhi 151
communicative competence 99, 107
communicative language teaching (CLT) 99, 100, 133n4
"Composition and Grammar or Precis writing" 122
computer-assisted language learning (CALL) 104
connoisseurship 117–19
Container 96
corroboration 118–19
criticism 117–19
cultures, and identities 93–4

Delhi Urban Art Commission (DUAC) 159n9; *Rejuvenation of Shahjahanabad* 154
devaluation 88–9
Dyal Singh College 132

Education Act 1870 45
Elizabeth, sister of Yeats 14
Empson, W. 55
English and Foreign Languages University, The (EFLU) 124
English as a Second Language (ESL) 2, 104

INDEX

English Language Proficiency Course (ELPC) 130, 131
English literature courses 68
envy 89–90
evidence-based decision-making 110–20; assessment/evaluation 113–16; connoisseurship and criticism 117–19; macro issues 112–13; micro issues 113

feminism 137, 139
fight-flight syndrome 92
Finney, F.N. 46
FYUP (Four-Year Undergraduate Programme) 131, 132

Garnett, E. 81
GE (Generic Elective) courses 132
gender: as performance 137; in theatre, construction of 134–5; in translated literature, teaching 64–73 (Indian texts in translation 72–3; number of translated texts 71–2; opative voice 64–7; *rasa*, losing 68–71)
Gender and Sexuality in Twentieth-Century Fiction 68, 71
General English, history of 122–5
Ghost Club, The 12
gratitude 89–90
group processes 92–3
Gurtu, M. 124–6

Haksar, A. 135
Hashmi, S. 157
Heritage Zones, definition of 159n8
higher education system, in India 86
holding environment 91–2
Howards End 37, 83n10

Ibsenism 5, 36–9
idealisation 88–9
identities, cultures and 93–4
"Indian National Skills Qualification Framework" 108
Indian texts in translation 72–3
Indian University Commission 131
Indian University Education Commission 123
injustice 89
inner theatre 86–91; charismatic leader 87–8; devaluation 88–9; envy 89–90; gratitude 89–90; idealisation 88–9; loners 90–1; narcissism 87–8

Institute of Life Long Learning (ILLL) 131
Ismat's Love Stories 141–2

Jain, K. 135
Jain, N. 125

Kalia, A.K. 124
Kapur, A. 135
Kathopanishad 71
Khanna, A.L. 124–6
Khanna, R.K. 124, 125
Kohli, S. 157

Lal, M. 126
Lall, A.B. 157
Language, Literature and Culture 131
"Language through Literature" courses 124
Last Mushairah of Delhi, The 138
Lawrence, F. 41
liberalism 3
Liddle, S. 157
linguistic competence 99
loners 90–1

Makhija, S.D. 157
Maley, A. 124
Master Plan for Delhi 1962 (MPD 1962) 152, 153
Master Plan for Delhi 2001 (MPD 2021) 152
Mathur, P. 124
Menon, A.G.K. 157
Meredith, H.O. 41n8
money, as emotional currency 94–5
Morel, P. 80
Mother India 63n3
multiple intelligences 101
Murdoch, I. 74–5

Nagpal, U. 125, 126
Nahal, C. 125
narcissism 87–8
Norton, C.E. 46
nostalgia 147–58
nukkad nataks 146

optative voice 64–7

Panchatantra 71
Pant, H. 124
Paradise Lost 35

INDEX

pedagogy 5, 7, 8, 62, 86, 98, 111, 127, 134, 142; classroom 3; eclectic 100; experimental 100; language 104
Peer Gynt 39
personal agenda 115
Phillips, W.H. 46
Pilling, J. 11
Piplani, N. 157
Prabhu, N.S. 112, 116, 125, 133*n*4
Project Concept Proposal (PCP) 153–4
proletarian schooling, radical unlearnedness in 74–84
psychoanalysis 85, 87
psychodynamic counselling 91, 92

Rajdhani College 132
Ramaswamy, L. 123
rasa, losing 68–71
reading poetry through translation 53–63
Regional English Language Office 132
Reid, R. 77–8
Richards, I.A. 55
Riding, L. 55

Sachdeva, P. 156
Samuel, H. 78
Satsai 69
Sawhney, S. 124, 125
Schumann, J. 115
Schweig, G. 72
SEC (Skill Enhancement Course) 132
Seven Types of Ambiguity 55
Sex and the City 139
sexuality 93, 135; in translated literature, teaching 64–73 (Indian texts in translation 72–3; number of translated texts 71–2; opative voice 64–7; *rasa*, losing 68–71)
Shah, A.L. 124
Shahjahanabad 147–58; redevelopment of 151–5
Shahjahanabad Redevelopment Corporation (SRDC) 156; *Revitalization of Shahjahanabad (Walled City of Delhi)* 153–4
Sharma, T. 135
Sharma, V. 125
Shyama Prasad Mukherjee College 132
Siddhu, C.D. 125
Simon, R.K. 41*n*1
Singh, B.R. 122
Singh, S. 125

Sisodia, M. 156
Society for Psychical Research, The 12
Some Versions of Pastoral 55
Sood, S.C. 126
streaming 125, 126
sublimation 88
summative assessment 102, 103
Sunder Rajan, R. 128
super ego 88
SWOT (strength, weakness, opportunity, threat) analysis 108

task-based language teaching (TBLT) 133*n*4
teacher, as facilitator 99–100
teaching-learning process 8, 9, 123
Ten Thousand Things (TTT) model of theatre 142
Test of English for Speakers of Other Languages (TESOL) 131
Tharu, J. 127
Treaty of Utrecht (1713) 51*n*2
triangulation *see* corroboration
Trilochan 56

undergraduate English language learner, challenges of skilling 98–108; ability and aspirations and demands of the job market 106–7; assessment/evaluation 102–4; heterogeneity 99–101; teacher as facilitator 99–100; technology 104–6
United States Embassy, New Delhi 132
University Grants Commission (UGC) 133*n*2; English Review Committees 123
University of Cambridge Language Examination Syndicate (UCLES) 131
Ur, P. 102

Virmani, K. 124, 125

Ward, E.S.P. 46
Ward, H.D. 46
Widdowson, H.G. 126
Women in Love 74, 76
women in post-independence Indian theatre, role of 135–6
Women Playwrights International Conference (2012) Stockholm 144
world literature courses 68

Zadie, Q. 135

Printed in the United States
by Baker & Taylor Publisher Services